THE ENGLISH GARDENING SCHOOL

THE ENGLISH GARDENING SCHOOL

A COMPLETE COURSE IN GARDEN PLANNING AND DESIGN

Rosemary Alexander & Anthony du Gard Pasley

MICHAEL JOSEPH

LONDON

First published in Great Britain
by Michael Joseph Ltd
27 Wrights Lane,
London W8
1987

**British Library Cataloguing in Publication
Data**
Alexander, Rosemary.
 The English Gardening School: a complete
 course in garden planning and design.
 1. Gardening
 I. Title II. Du Gard Pasley, Anthony.
 635 SB450.97
 ISBN 0-7181-2773-0

**Conceived, designed and produced by
Robert Adkinson Limited, London**

Editorial Director:	Clare Howell
Editors:	John Gilbert
	Lucy Trench
Art Director:	Christine Simmonds
Designer:	Laurence Bradbury
Design Assistants:	Sarah Collins
	David Powell
Illustrators:	Rick Blakely
	Pat Gregory
	John Moreland

Phototypeset by Tradespools Ltd.,
Frome, Somerset
Illustrations originated by
La Cromolito, Milan
Printed and bound in Italy by
SAGDOS Spa, Milan

Contributors
Susan Macdonald
Garden preparation and maintenance

John Moreland
Garden design and construction

Frontispiece: The
gardens at Bramdean
House.

CONTENTS

INTRODUCTION

The English Gardening School was originally founded to provide a location in central London where garden enthusiasts could benefit from professional studies of a wide variety of horticultural subjects, with particular emphasis on garden design, both the theory and practice.

This book is the distillation of the courses given at the school. It aims quite simply to increase the reader's awareness and appreciation of the many different elements involved in designing a garden. Garden design is not simply a matter of placing and growing plants: it is the culmination of a process which begins with the soil and the seasons. It involves everything the garden designer may do from the construction of buildings on the site, to the way in which the garden will be used.

As professionals, the authors have frequently been called in to give advice on gardens where an owner has striven for years without quite achieving the desired level of excellence. By taking the reader through the design process step by step, from assessing what exists and what is required, through the costly but vital elements of hard landscape to the selection of plants, ornaments and furniture, they hope that this book will prove as useful to the amateur garden enthusiast as to the potential designer.

Two qualities are essential to the garden designer. Firstly, he or she should have the ability to see things clearly and understand their intrinsic nature. Secondly, there is the need to analyze what is seen, defining good and bad points and deciding how best they may be used or concealed. Most of us have these qualities, which are generally left to lie dormant, but for any serious student of design, their development is of primary importance and should be considered before anything else.

At the beginning of the courses at the English Gardening School, the student is asked to make a conscious effort to see and understand all the simple objects in and around the garden. A short spring tape measure, carried in pocket or handbag, is a useful aid, since it can be brought out at any moment to check the width of an opening, the height or depth of a step tread or seat and any other detail which may happen to catch the attention. In this way, not only is the eye trained to be ever more perceptive, but an instructive vocabulary of proportions and scale relationships can be built up for future use.

In most large towns and cities there are exhibitions of various kinds of art form from which much can be learned. It does not matter that they do not appear immediately to have any direct bearing on gardens or gardening. All art forms are related and each can offer lessons which can be applied in other fields. It should be possible, after a period of training, to be able to look at an object of unknown provenance or period and make a reasonable assessment of its quality. It is this instinctive ability to disregard the inessential and perceive the true quality of the piece which must be developed. As Sir Joshua Reynolds wrote: 'It is the proper study and labour of an artist to uncover and find out the latent cause of conspicuous beauty and from thence form principles for his own conduct. Such an examination is a continual exertion of the mind.'

Without the power to analyze clearly the good and bad points of any given site, the garden designer is powerless. It is important, therefore, to develop the ability to assess the essential qualities of a situation, and then decide how they can best be dealt with, in a short space of time. A clear summary of good and bad points, the problems involved and general strategy for improvement should always be the first consideration, leaving the finer points to follow at the stage of detailed design.

Opposite: A view of the lecture room building at the Chelsea Physic Garden, seen across a formal garden which has been designed to display a collection of historic plants.

7

This warm corner of the Physic Garden provides a sheltered microclimate in which quite tender plants will generally survive the English winter.

These order beds, which are only found in the older botanic gardens and teaching establishments, are an invaluable aid when explaining plant families and relationships to the students.

With experience, this analytical ability will become almost second nature and no opportunity to exercise it should be missed. Supposing that you are standing in the street waiting for a bus. Look around you and consider whether you find the view entirely pleasing: if not, what could be done to improve the situation? You may think that the street is too narrow, in which case you would like to double the width. At that point you must consider exactly what the result would be: people and traffic would appear more sparse, since they would be moving in twice the amount of space; there would be more light in the street because the shadows would be proportionately shorter; the relative balance between vertical and horizontal would be changed. But has this alteration cured the problem or simply changed it? Perhaps the real problem is the material from which the buildings are constructed, and the view would be improved if they were all painted white. Now the quality of light will be quite different, as it will be reflected from side to side and upward as well as falling in the normal way from above. Shadows will be less intense, the features of passers-by will be clarified, on a bright day the view will be hard and sparkling, on a dull one cold and curiously depressing. It is not, then, enough to prepare a garden plan, perhaps supported by enticing sketches of the finished result, if you yourself are not absolutely clear about the full implications of your proposals. You must be able to visualize the end results of your proposals throughout the year. Every aspect of the proposed design should be thoroughly examined before being implemented because without an accurate forecast of the way in which the garden will develop through the years, you can offer only a partial solution.

The definition of good design is very difficult but if, as a result of the chapters which follow, the reader can plan and plant a garden with confidence, be aware of why certain shapes and levels work and others do not, of why certain combinations of colour, texture and foliage are pleasing and harmonious, while others disturb and distract, the purpose of the school and this book will have been achieved. Naturally, the process of learning and understanding continues throughout one's active life, and with experience, one's style becomes more refined and discerning. All that is taught in the school, especially in studio design sessions, cannot possibly be included between the covers of one book, but the guidelines here laid down should provide a sound basis for the pursuit of good garden design, whether by the enthusiastic amateur or potential professional.

Authors' Acknowledgements
We are indebted to our many colleagues and fellow lecturers, whose particular experiences combine to provide such a wide range of knowledge for us and our students. We are especially grateful to Sue Macdonald for compiling the practical section on garden preparation and maintenance, to John Moreland for the section on garden construction, to Hazel le Rougetel for advice on shrub roses, to Eain Caws for his advice on legal requirements, to Heather Angel and Hugh Palmer for special photography and to Clare Howell for commissioning and overseeing the development of the book. We also thank the Trustees of the Chelsea Physic Garden for making available their unique and historic garden as our base and source of inspiration, in particular to the Curator, Duncan Donald, and the head gardener James Compton. Finally we thank our students, past, present and future, from whom we have learnt so much, and whose enthusiasm and constant search for knowledge has encouraged us to produce this book as a guide for amateurs and professionals alike.

THE PRINCIPLES

OF GARDEN DESIGN

ANALYZING YOUR GARDEN
THE STRUCTURE OF THE GARDEN
PRACTICAL APPLICATIONS

THE GARDEN AND ITS SETTING

A contoured map of the district will help establish the general position of the garden area and how it relates to the surrounding landscape. First draw a section line on the map through the site (A to B). Then, using the horizontal scale of the map, extend vertical lines on an enlarged scale. Join up the points made where the horizontal contours cut through the section. The resulting graph will indicate the relative levels and what can be seen between two points.

The garden cannot be looked at in isolation; it must be considered in the context of its surroundings. Every site, however small and confined, is in reality only a part of some larger whole with which it interacts, affecting and being affected by its environment. This close relationship, which makes the garden a single piece in a jigsaw of buildings and streets, fields and woods, mountains and estuaries, is a major element of design. It makes nonsense of those pattern books of 'ideal' plans which treat a site as having a form outlined by boundaries, but without a context. A first inspection, therefore, should reveal not only what lies within, but also outside the boundaries.

The zone of visual influence

Every garden has a zone of visual influence, which may extend no further than the backs of the houses in the next street, or may reach to a stretch of public footpath on a distant hillside. The extent of this zone—very similar in effect to the ripples on a pond into which a stone is dropped—must be defined before any consideration is given to design. Even before the preliminary visit to a country site, inspection of a contoured map of the district will suggest to the garden designer areas of high ground from which the garden may be visible. These maps are normally on a small scale, but it is quite simple to locate the general position of the ground in question and its approximate level in relation to the surrounding landscape.

Section lines can then be drawn on the map through the site to likely areas of high ground, and diagrammatic sections drawn up using the horizontal scale of the map and a much greater vertical scale to emphasize the difference in level. The result will not be in any way realistic, but it will clearly show whether the property can be seen from any given direction. This technique of drawing sections to two different scales—essential when dealing with long distances—provides a very useful check when information is needed about the relative levels and visibility between two points. With this knowledge the possible van-

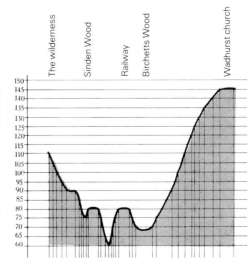

tage points can be visited, taking particular note of the view from the roads, footpaths, carparks and other public places.

Planting and the landscape

Naturally no details of the garden would be visible from this distance—the colour of the borders or the species of shrub planted would be of no consequence— but trees and the hard definition of boundary lines can be read with ease from afar. There was an instance when the owner of a thatched cottage overlooking a famous stretch of river valley wished to plant a blue cedar in the garden. The property ran along the natural boundary between arable fields on the lower slopes and what appeared to be mature woodland crowning the hill. The scene seemed to be rural and unspoiled, although in fact the trees concealed a fashionable village. A blue cedar, planted at the edge of a cornfield, would immediately have suggested the presence of a sophisticated garden and, by

implication, the probable presence of others. At once the traveller on the valley road would have sensed that he was in a slightly self-conscious suburbanized arcadia, and the rural illusion would have been lost.

On the other hand, tree planting can help to absorb an obtrusive feature into the general landscape pattern. The softly rounded shapes of trees, and the shadows which they cast, will break up hard outlines, reduce the effect of light reflected from cars, windows or pale surfaces and create a woodland impression from a distance, even when the individual trees are quite widely spaced on the ground. As in all forms of camouflage, it is essential to avoid plant material of striking shape or unnatural colour, since these will only draw attention to what is concealed.

All too often land boundaries cut across the natural flow of land form, and if these are emphasized unduly the results can be visually disturbing at a considerable distance. For example, a

In a town garden where the zone of visual influence is small, the rounded shapes of trees help conceal the windows of adjoining houses.

Space flows through the landscape where any hard boundary line across would be out of place.

It is easy to identify the furthest extent of the garden's zone of visual influence (in this case the distant hills) from the site. This can then be checked on a map of the locality.

rectangular plot of land on a hillside might be invisible if separated from its surroundings by a simple post and wire fence. Hedged or divided by low stone walls it could appear as part of the pattern of local hill farming, but edged by rows of Lombardy poplar or cupressus it would soon seem an intrusion totally out of context in the landscape. Similarly, divisions cutting across the floor of a valley, even if made of rounded trees native to the locality, can have a disturbing effect because they interrupt the space which flows like a river through the low ground. Such breaks in the continuity implied by the land formation are as disturbing when seen from above as from the lower levels. It is in cases of this kind that a preliminary study of the zone of visual influence is so important. And when there is doubt about the location of the garden from a distance, a still day and a bonfire piled with green branches on the site can generally solve the problem.

Planting in the city

In the suburb or city distances are less, but access can prove more difficult since the zone is generally bounded by private dwellings. Sometimes use can be made of the staircases and landings in blocks of flats, and the moving vantage point of the top deck of a bus or a train on an embankment can prove useful—the writer has made many strange return journeys by public transport for the sake of a quick glimpse of a site. Within the urban environment it is not only a question of avoiding errors, but of how much can be contributed to the general scene by planting within the garden.

Often the monotony of a long straight road can be improved by the placing of a single tree of suitable form, whose branches not only break the severe lines of the facade, but cast a patch of shadow onto the pavement, effectively dividing

Planting trees within the boundaries of a private garden can help obscure wires and poles which would otherwise stand out against the sky.

the street into two parts. Where there are gaps between buildings at a crossroad, an unpleasant view along the backs of houses can be screened by clever tree planting in the corner garden, while wires, clustered drainpipes, ugly chimneys and other urban clutter can be obscured by a maze of twigs. Sometimes a fine building or feature—as for instance a church spire—may lose its impact through a jumble of surrounding structures which can be hidden or softened by strategic tree planting. In the same way, a building which is too large and out of scale with its position, or has only one good element such as a central doorway, may be reduced in size and have its good points emphasized by the judicious use of trees and shadows.

These are just a few examples of the way in which private planting can contribute to public pleasure, but to be successful the tree positions will have to be carefully plotted from the outside and afterwards incorporated into the garden. It will be necessary to have one person on the site, placing and moving tall stakes with flags on top to represent the trees, while others are outside viewing the effect from various angles. Getting tree positions correct is difficult since a slight change in the location of the viewer —who will normally not see the scene from a fixed position—may require a completely different arrangement. Generally a compromise will have to be reached since it is seldom possible to achieve a perfect solution from every angle.

The casual view
Not all benefits are so generalized. The secret glimpse into other people's lives provided by lamp-lit rooms at dusk, before the curtains are drawn, extends to

Strategic planting can soften or enhance a feature beyond the garden boundary.

the quick glance over the gate or the more deliberate peer through a hedge or the keyhole of a garden door. Although looking through keyholes is not normally encouraged one should never neglect those in garden doors, as they often reveal an enchanting vignette. Perhaps the most famous is that of the villa of the Knights of Malta in Rome, through which the eye can follow a long straight walk at the end of which the dome of St Peter's appears to grow from the ground like some gigantic mushroom. It is an interesting thought that far more people will see the garden from the outside than will ever enter the charmed circle and understand the plan as a whole. The fabric of our days is woven much more from a mixture of small pleasures and disappointments than from great events, and surely one of the functions of a garden is to give pleasure not only to the owner but also to those who pass by.

Study the site from the outside, therefore, at close quarters as well as from a distance, and consider what small pictures, complete in themselves but suggestive of unseen mysteries, can be contrived for the casual viewer. The earliest spring bulbs and flowers may logically be grouped beside the front path to cheer guest and passer-by alike. A tall shrub rose framed in a patch of blue sky between the chimney pots, or a flaming autumn tree scattering a bright pattern over the paving below would all make memorable pictures apparently seen by chance. However, all need careful thought and planning from the outside to integrate them into the pattern of the garden within.

Sometimes, where a permanent view into the garden may threaten its privacy, it may be possible to provide a window in the surrounding wall—perhaps filled with a beautiful wrought-iron grille—which can be closed at will by an internal shutter. In this way the stranger not only has a chance to enjoy the garden, but also the excitement of never knowing whether the view will be there or not.

Above: Private planting can also enhance public places and a tree within a garden will become a valuable feature on the street corner.

Left: Passers-by will enjoy a quick glimpse through a doorway. A good design will reveal many vignettes to delight even the casual viewer.

17

WITHIN THE GARDEN

Sites are either introvert or extrovert and this quality, inward-looking and enclosed or outgoing and expansive, will have a major influence on the nature of any design which is subsequently developed. Where surroundings need to be obscured, because they are ugly, out of scale or inharmonious, attention and interest will have to be kept within the garden itself. The eye should be constantly drawn away from the boundaries, further and further inwards until it is held finally at some central point.

Of course, such gardens do not necessarily have a single focus. Major objects can be placed so that each forms the climax of a view within the garden, while at the same time it is related to the others by an unseen geometry overlaying the apparent design. Such schemes, although allowing movement of eye and mind within the boundaries, are by nature static in feeling.

The extrovert site, possibly featureless in itself but in sight of interesting features beyond its boundaries, has a very different character. Here the aim of the designer should be to include the more distant objects into the garden scheme, using flowing lines and shapes related to the wider landscape, in order to link them in a unified composition.

The borrowed view

Too little use is made of what the Japanese call the 'borrowed view', in which the design of the garden is extended beyond its natural boundaries. There are many ways in which this may be done. Even the smallest city garden may be planned to take advantage of a group of chimney pots, an interesting gable outlined against the sky, or trees clustered in gardens further down the street. In one particular large town garden a spire seen over the rear wall was emphasized by being reflected in a canal. This was framed by groups of trees which hid the backs of ugly buildings on either side.

In this introvert garden, the eye is led away from the dark foliage framing it and is drawn towards the lighter elements—in this case, the paving and the centrally-placed furniture.

Sometimes, where the view is over flat fields or rolling country with no particularly dominant features, much may be obscured, leaving only narrow openings which give tremendous drama to the impression of distance. This effect is lost if too much is revealed, exposing the intrinsically boring quality of the surrounding landscape. Even where the view is intricate and full of interest, it needs to be broken down into carefully composed pictures, so that the eye can appreciate a section at a time, the rest being lost in shadows and planting. As the observer moves about in the garden the pictures change, creating effects which surprise and excite, whereas if all were revealed at once the impact would be much reduced.

Left: In an extrovert garden the views which extend beyond the garden boundaries are as important as those within. Here, the eye is led to the church and its tower which provide a striking focal point.

Below: The successful composition of a design depends on the creation of a series of pictures within the garden. Here, the eye rests initially on the lead figure of a greyhound which in turn subtly directs attention to the view towards the lake.

Using the landscape

There are many significant lines in the landscape which need careful study if the garden is to become fully integrated and make the most of its surroundings. Firstly there is the shape of the skyline to which the eye is immediately drawn. The strong pattern of the skyline gives a powerful shape, which may well be repeated within the pattern of the garden, a method frequently used by the Brazilian designer Burle Marx, whose gardens seem to express the essential quality of their dramatic setting.

As the eye travels downward from the skyline it may be held by other landforms at lower elevations, by the edge of a wood, the line between hill grazing and valley arable, the winding of a road or river, or the slow geometric curves of a canal. All these are significant shapes which may be reflected in the pattern of the garden, relating it to its setting and giving the design an air of inevitability which no drawing-board exercise alone can ever achieve. Indeed, this quality of the inevitable, the impression that the garden came about naturally and could not exist in any other form, is one of the tests of good design.

If the immediate reaction is 'How clever', then there is often something meretricious about the scheme. True brilliance is revealed only gradually and may not occur to the observer until long afterwards, when thoughtful analysis uncovers subtle relationships which are not apparent at first sight.

Garden boundaries

Consideration of the world beyond the garden leads inevitably to the question of boundaries and whether they are to be defined or concealed. All too often they are seen as an arbitrary line drawn along the edge of the plot, using standardized materials which have no relationship to their surroundings, whereas they should make a positive contribution to the design of the garden as a whole. In

The distant view is framed and dramatized by the narrow opening in the curved stone wall; whereas, if the whole panorama were exposed, it would lose impact.

the most extreme case—that of the eighteenth-century ha-ha or sunk fence—the boundary can vanish entirely, allowing the garden to become a part of the landscape. Such a solution need not imply the presence of a grand landscape park of many acres: quite small country gardens can have short sections of ha-ha which allow controlled vistas to flow out across the countryside, while the boundaries on either side are concealed by planting. In such cases, post and rail, post and wire, or black (not the harsh green too often used) plastic-coated wire mesh can merge unobtrusively into the shadows of adjacent shrubberies and plantations.

A variation on the open view, which can be applied to town or suburban gardens, is to use trellis or panels of screen-block walling as part of the boundary to give an impression of space beyond. Neighbours would have to be consulted and the panels so arranged that they did not reduce the privacy of the adjoining property, but with this proviso it is possible to improve the apparent size and proportion of several small gardens at once. Unfortunately, many of the screen blocks currently available are too strident and complicated in design to suit a garden setting, but there are a few simple shapes which would be appropriate. Plain forms and quiet colourings are best because they enhance rather than compete with the intricacy of flower and foliage. (Paving stones and fountains, furniture and urns, fabrics and summerhouses should be similarly unadorned.)

Sometimes it is desirable to expose parts of the boundary—those more closely related to roads and buildings—while the sections associated with open country views may be concealed or planted out. Whenever this technique is employed, or in cases where the boundary is treated as a major design feature, it is important to use the right materials rather than accept a stock solution. Walls of brick or stone, built in the same manner as the house,

are quite the best answer, and although they are initially expensive they need little subsequent maintenance if properly constructed. Over a period of time an interwoven wooden fence, which disintegrates and needs to be replaced every five years or so at ever increasing expense, is not as cheap as it appears at first sight, quite apart from the disruption caused to the surrounding planting by these constant renewals.

In the past garden walls were made of two or even three thicknesses of brick, but with careful design and good foun-

Above: This historic brick ha-ha, invisible from the house, allows uninterrupted views across open country.

Below: A ha-ha is a concealed wall and ditch below the garden level, which does not obstruct the outward view, yet prevents livestock from entering the garden.

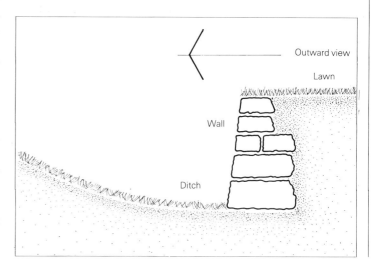

Outward view

Lawn

Wall

Ditch

dations this is not always necessary. A single-brick wall with frequent buttresses, whose rhythmic punctuation can form the basis of interesting garden designs, is perfectly satisfactory, and there are many variations on the old 'crinkle-crankle' or serpentine fruit wall whose form gives great stability to the thinnest structure. Fortunately there are now a number of very effective artificial stones which can be used for walling, so the cost of walling need not be prohibitive.

Even when full-size walls are too expensive, it is often possible to introduce the brick or stone of the house to a limited extent, providing the necessary visual link. A low plinth of brick might form the base for panels of close board fencing or hardwood trellis, which would last much longer within the hard framework and could be more easily replaced without major disruption. This can also be a useful technique where the material of the house is unsympathetic—perhaps that hard, bright red brick so beloved of the Victorians—and only a small quantity is necessary to relate to the building.

Brick and stone link the different elements of the garden to the house behind.

The house

Normally the house is the most dominant feature in any garden, from which and back towards which the design will flow, and it therefore deserves careful study before any major decisions are taken. Buildings of different periods suggest particular types of plan or ways of using hard and soft materials, but there is a danger in too great an enthusiasm for period details. Just because Blenheim Palace and an eighteenth-century farmhouse were built at the same time does not imply that the balustrades and fountains suitable to one would be appropriate for the other. All too often one sees a simple building overwhelmed by details which, although more or less in period, are far too elaborate for a house of that kind. It is better by far to create a period feeling by the correct manipulation of space and proportion than to overload a garden with complicated features.

The use of local materials is very important. Not only should the garden reflect the age and quality of the house, it should also fit naturally into its context. In the past, when poor roads made communication difficult between various parts of the country, people used materials which came easily to hand and each area developed its own methods of building. Within the same county there may be several methods of constructing walls or pavings from identical stone, and these should be studied carefully and used correctly for they add greatly to the pleasure of being in the countryside.

Subdividing a plot

Curiously enough a small plot can be made to appear larger by subdivision. Although the idea sounds strange it can be explained easily by analogy with the ground-plan of a house. When the foundations are first set out the whole building looks scarcely large enough to contain a single room. As the walls begin to rise the enclosures appear to be no more than cupboards, but once they get above head

By using a uniform light coloured material for the boundary of a long, narrow garden, it can be made to appear larger. The low changes of level also create a series of integrated spaces. The hard effect of the inert materials is here offset by the planting and the focal point of the mature tree.

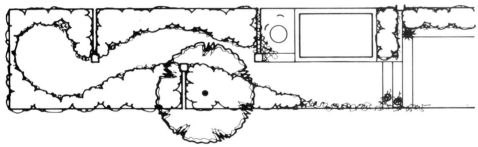

A long and narrow site can be made to appear larger by subdivision, creating a series of separate compartments within the garden.

height the situation changes and a series of spaces develops. Not only can the divided garden appear larger, but its proportions can be altered and improved. False 'boundaries' may be created in order to give a better shape, and remaining portions planted out, giving an illusion of a garden set in woodland.

Analyzing the site

Before proceeding further it is essential to gather up all the information discussed in this chapter and prepare a site analysis, showing inward and outward views, places where trees are needed or would be unsuitable, notes on hard materials and boundaries and so forth. For this purpose the camera is an important tool, but the eye is more selective than film and can pick out the essential lines and shapes which compose a view. Try to develop a kind of visual shorthand,

making quick sketches of the necessary information to act as a reminder when away from the site and looking at photographs. This can be practised at any spare moment, wherever you happen to be, until it becomes second nature. Facility is essential, since what may seem easy on a summer day becomes far more difficult on an icy winter afternoon with rapidly fading light.

Using a camera

In comparison with the site, the scale of the surrounding landscape is frequently so vast that many obvious lines and shapes may be overlooked with the naked eye, however well trained. Systematic photography has many purposes, both in the early stages of the project and in the long term. It can capture the appearance of the garden in the different seasons or can concentrate on particular aspects that will influence the design, perhaps views out of the house, or views from the garden back to the house showing such details as windows, drainpipes and altered brickwork. It can also serve as an 'aide-mémoire', recording the position of manholes and other functional details or the condition of existing trees or shrubs. In this way photography will form an essential part of the written report that the professional designer will prepare in the early stages of the project (see page 100), and it will save much time in making notes and sketches.

Later, regular photographic records will demonstrate how the garden has evolved and the planting integrated and matured. It will show what areas need adjusting, or in certain seasons brightened with bulbs or variegated foliage. It will record the effect of certain processes such as tree pruning, in which, if the work has been done skilfully, it is difficult to see which branches have been removed from the tree canopy. Photographs can also record a pleasing detail for future reference or be used as a basis for perspective drawings in books and magazines. Finally, a professional designer can build up a photographic folio

of successful projects to show prospective clients.

When photographing a garden use a simple automatic camera or a more complex 35mm SLR (single lens reflex) version with a 28mm wide-angle lens and a tripod, which is especially useful for panoramic views. Colour print is usually the most suitable, but black and white film can also be used. It is important to have a sufficient supply of film, with a range of suitable film speeds (ISO 100, 200 or 400) as light can be difficult if the sky is overcast, the garden in heavy shade or the light fading. All the developed film should be clearly labelled with the name of the garden, the place and date, and then be filed for future reference.

Different viewpoints

In a small town garden the best views from the house are often captured by photographing from an upstairs window, not forgetting to include the adjacent gardens, houses or other buildings. The scene will alter from summer to winter—that sycamore, when in leaf and casting heavy shade on the garden, may be hiding the view of either an unsightly factory or a handsome church spire, but

Panoramic views are a useful means of recording a complete view of a garden. This series of photographs was shot from left to right, taking in the foreground as well as the middle and far distance.

in winter when the tree is bare, the garden will appear sunny and light and have a different outlook. Note too the height of surrounding buildings and the angle of the sun. In summer it rises higher and may be above the neighbouring block, but in winter the same block can cause total shade. Go to the far end of the garden and photograph the house. This will give a visual record of the downpipes, windows, gutters and angle of roof which will be especially useful if a conservatory is to be built. Remember to include views of adjacent houses here too, with their general condition and any alterations as this may be necessary for a planning application. If a similar structure occurs on an adjacent site, the planning authorities will quickly see that there has been a precedent.

To photograph a larger garden, it is easier to divide it up into different areas. Begin at the entrance, be it the front door, gates, lodge or drive. (First impressions are very important so the 'sense of arrival' should be in keeping with what goes on inside. The front door may need repainting a different colour, for instance, or the gateway piers repointing or renewing.) Then take a series of panoramic views, either by standing in a central position and moving round in a circle, or by shooting a 90° angle.

Choose an angle or level to take in as much as possible and begin photographing at the far left-hand corner, moving round clockwise until arriving at the far right-hand corner or the starting point. If possible, maintain the same level all the way round (this is where the tripod helps) and overlap the shots slightly so the photographs can then be butted together, mounted on card, and used to give a complete record of the view. Occasionally it will be necessary to take both a far-distance and a middle-distance panorama to get trees, telegraph poles, buildings and boundaries in sufficient detail. After shooting the panoramas take a 'flat' view (or a series of 'flat' views) of the house, moving along in a straight line from end to end, and finally take close-up photographs of details such as trellis, paving, climbers or drainage that may be forgotten later.

Aerial photography can be very useful for a larger or undulating site. In addition to showing the layout or ground pattern in the same way as a plan, previous designs or earthworks are often revealed, particularly in historic landscapes.

THE SOIL

The interaction of soil and climate is a strong influence on both the proposed design and the plants that can be grown. The most successful gardens are created in response to this, rather than trying to force nature to accept a hostile scheme. Soil consists of, for the most part, mineral fragments or particles of eroded or weathered rock, and the ratio and size of these particles combine to make up the soil texture which dictates the behaviour of the soil.

Soil structure is the binding together of the various solid particles with clay or organic matter to form soil crumbs. Generally, the darker the soil the richer it is and the better the structure. But the structure can be improved—peat or compost, for example, will help break up heavy clay soil, or in sandy soil will hold the coarse particles together and retain moisture.

It must be stressed that soil is a 'living system' including—in addition to the particles—humus, water, air, bacteria and dissolved salts. The texture will remain fairly constant but the structure can easily be affected by cultivation. Working the soil when it is wet can disturb the balance of water and air by pressure, shattering the crumb structure, puddling the soil, and thus re-arranging the particles so they set to a solid mass.

The pH of the soil

The acidity or alkalinity of the soil is measured on the pH scale, and in Britain it varies from pH4, which is very acid, to pH8.5, which is alkaline; pH7 is neutral. Plants vary in their degree of tolerance of an extreme pH, but most will grow satisfactorily on soil that is close to neutral. Acid soil, which is good for rhododendrons, camellias, heathers and other ericaceous plants, usually lacks lime, nitrogen and phosphate, but minerals such as manganese are available and can be harmful in some cases. Alkaline soil is unable to provide iron, manganese and boron in a universally acceptable form, and plants that are unable to take up these minerals will become a very pale yellowish green.

Natural plant associations occurring in the woods or hedgerows will indicate the acidity or alkalinity of the soil. Scots pine, bracken, rhododendron and most ericaceous plants are to be found in acid conditions, while ash, Austrian pine, daphne, ox-eye daisy and cowslips grow on infertile chalk or limestone soils. The common stinging nettle and chickweed thrive on potentially fertile soil high in nitrogen, gorse on poor infertile soil, and the wild strawberry on dry, stony soil. Obviously each ecological area has its own vegetation, but to be more accurate a simple soil test is required.

Right: Ox-eye daisies and non-invasive grasses flourish on infertile chalk or limestone soils.

Below: The presence of heather and bracken indicates acid soil caused by an accumulation of decaying leaf material.

Several soil testing kits are now available, ranging from the soil pH meter which is simply stuck into the ground, the needle registering extremes from neutral, to the 'kit' form, with instructions, glass tubes and a colour chart. More elaborate kits are available for estimating the level of major nutrients, but do remember to use distilled water to obtain a correct reading.

The soil should be taken from 7–15cm (3–6in) below the surface—the lighter the soil the deeper the hole for testing, as plants will put their roots down further in lighter soil. Only a small amount, equivalent to two tablespoonfuls, is needed for testing. Remove the soil with a trowel, and put each sample into a separate polythene bag, marking clearly on the outside of the bag and on the plan where and at what level the sample came from. Do not take samples from frozen or waterlogged soil or from mole hills, and allow the samples to dry out naturally before testing.

It is also possible to have a complete soil test done at a professional laboratory, which is particularly useful if working abroad or under complicated conditions. Once the pH factor is established, you will know what range of plants will thrive, and what nutrients or soil improvers should be added before planting.

Various soil types

In addition to its alkalinity or acidity, soil is classified according to its texture and behaviour. This property of soil will also influence the choice of plants.

Light sandy soil has large particles with gaps between which the water runs quickly, removing nutrients, warming up early in spring and drying out quickly in summer. It is usually acidic and lacking in plant food, but is suitable for plants that like fast drainage. Silty soil, however, is made up of fine, closely packed particles; it is easily blown about, creating dust storms, and difficult to cultivate unless combined with organic matter.

Even smaller particles will be found in clay soil, which are so fine, that the water can only drain out slowly, so the soil tends to become waterlogged and hard to work. On the other hand, clay soil also retains nutrients. It warms up slowly in the spring and is liable to bake and crack in the summer.

Chalk is very alkaline and limey. It will soak up and hold large quantities of water, but is too hard to allow roots to penetrate through to the water. The roots then form a dense, shallow surface layer, using up the surface water supply and restricting other plant growth. Loam, though, is a gardener's delight, a well balanced mixture of sand, clay and humus that is easy to work and rich in plant food.

Other specific types of soil will be found in particular situations. In woodlands the soil is enriched by well rotted leaf mould; damp, peaty soil contains partially decomposed vegetable matter, and is acidic and low in nitrogen; in cities the soil may be old and sour, and will have to be revived by the addition of lime and organic matter, or even the importation of new soil.

This exposed soil profile shows the build-up of different layers of materials. In this case, the soil is too hard for the plant roots to penetrate, resulting in them forming a dense shallow mat on the surface.

27

CLIMATIC CONDITIONS

The climate, or weather, is a major factor in determining the selection of plants and the way in which the garden is used. In Britain, for example, we have a temperate maritime climate, with occasional extremes such as harsh winters and dry summers, so it is possible to grow plants introduced from many different parts of the world; in these cool, damp conditions grass grows especially well and lawns are an integral part of the traditional English landscape. In any particular garden the choice of plants will be largely influenced by the altitude and the length and harshness of the winters, so further consideration should be given to the regional and local climates. The regional climate within a country will vary considerably. In Britain the north is colder than the south, and the west warmer and wetter than the east; the coastal areas are cooler in summer and warmer in winter; and the rainfall lighter or heavier according to the locality.

At a local level the climate is dependent on topography, altitude, exposure and neighbouring landforms. Coastal areas, for instance, will be affected by the salt spray but will have a better quality of light, whereas industrial areas are liable to air pollution and fog. More specifically, certain areas of the garden will have their own micro-climate. Though strictly speaking this term refers to the thick layer of air within a few feet of the ground in a relatively small space and over a short period of time, it is commonly used in reference to the nature of the particular garden or of areas within it.

Analyzing the climate

Certain elements of the climate should be looked at individually and their effects on the garden in question analyzed. The choice of hardy or tender plants will be affected by the altitude and local air currents—cold air will flow downhill, get trapped at the bottom and cause a frost pocket until broken up by the wind or sun. One of the most damaging factors is wind and, on the coast particularly, the first priority is to plant a shelter belt against gales. Sometimes the wind direction is somewhat unpredictable, and although the direction of the prevailing wind may be obvious there may be variations in different parts of the garden. Wind can funnel through valleys or be channelled by buildings into eddies, breaking branches and flattening or scorching herbaceous plants. The north and east winds are usually the worst and, as well as affecting the seating areas, the cold, drying effect of the wind will slow down plant growth.

The aspect or orientation will also influence the layout of the garden and sunny or south-facing areas should be fully exploited. Here walls are valuable for they trap the sun's energy. Roses, herbaceous borders, silver-leaved plants, scented flowers, fruit, vegetables and most alpine plants benefit from the sun, as do pools in which reflections create much of the charm. But the shade is equally influential, especially in a town garden. Cast by buildings or trees, dense or dappled, deep in winter or reduced in summer, it will be both a beneficial and

Frost pockets
Cold air always flows downhill and into low ground but can be trapped in pockets by solid planting or buildings.

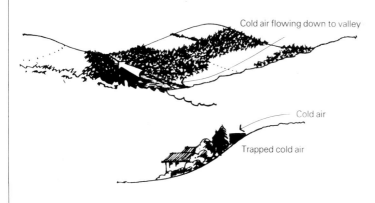

Cold air flowing down to valley

Cold air

Trapped cold air

negative element, perhaps restricting the choice of plants, but also providing variety and welcome relief from bright sunlight. If a conservatory or pergola is planned it should be positioned where there is not only enough light in the dull winter months, but also some means of screening the scorching summer sun.

Rainfall and drainage are other factors that should be taken into account, for abundant rain encourages lush growth, particularly in the west with the warm influence of the Gulf Stream. On sloping sites the rain drains naturally, whereas on a flat site the water will tend to lie for some days and a crossfall must be provided for any paths and paving.

General information on the regional climate can be gained from a climatological atlas or meteorologist, but usually the easiest way of collecting data on rainfall, temperature and sunshine is to contact the nearest weather station at a similar altitude. This information, and that specific to the site, should be shown diagrammatically on the plan as part of the site analysis. Coloured pens, blue for the wind direction, yellow for sunny areas, will bring the information to life and if this is very complex it can be done as a series of overlays on tracing paper leading up to the final plan.

Creating shelter

Once this has been established you can consider various ways to modify or exploit the climatic conditions. The most elaborate, and expensive, means of doing this is with buildings. A loggia or arbour facing south or south-west can, by trapping the sun from midday until sunset, provide a sheltered space near the house where the short hours of winter sunshine can be enjoyed. Alternatively a sunny, sheltered corner can be established at the far end of the garden, with a self-contained terrace and living area to provide escape from both the elements and other people.

Other ways of creating shelter involve

the use of walls, fences, trellis, hedges and groups of trees. Walls will give immediate long-lasting shelter and require almost no maintenance, but they are expensive. The area immediately to the leeward side will be sheltered, but there is always a danger of an 'eddy' effect when the wind turns back on itself. Fences serve the same function as walls. They take up less floor space and are cheaper to erect, but they need maintaining, particularly at the base where they are likely to rot. Trellis is really an open fence which allows wind and sun to filter through. It can be constructed in many different ways, the style depending on how solid or lightweight a screen is needed.

The living screen—hedges and trees —will obviously take longer to establish. In time, however, hedges are the strongest and most effective windbreaks, filtering the wind when severe gales might demolish walls or fences; a few leaves and twigs may be lost, but they will grow again. When planting hedges

Depending on the climatic conditions of your garden, a sheltered space can be made into an outdoor living area.

29

it is best to use smaller plants as they will be less shaken by the wind, so the root hairs will develop quicker and grip the soil. Conifer hedges, if likely to suffer from wind scorch, can be sprayed with S600, the chemical usually sold to prevent the needles dropping off Christmas trees, which will slow down transpiration. Groups of trees will not only deflect the wind, but they will also obscure unsightly views and protect the garden from being overlooked.

All these screens should, where possible, appear to be related to the house, perhaps even stemming directly from it to give the design unity. Even in hedging the design can echo the architecture. Whatever screen is chosen, its height should be related to the area to be sheltered: the nearer it is, the lower it should be for visual effect and human comfort.

Other improvements

Aspect, light and shade are interrelated. Since excessive sun is as unpleasant as heavy shade it may be advisable to create dappled shade with a pergola or series of arches, planted with suitable climbers, or with trees or shrubs that do not have a heavy canopy of branches. On the other hand a part of the garden that is in deep shadow may take on new life if surrounding trees are removed, but before taking such a drastic step do ensure that the trees are not acting as a windbreak.

Shelter belts
Cold air must either be allowed to flow downhill beneath the trees or through gaps left in the shelter planting.

A solid barrier which ends abruptly can create turbulence on the lea side.

It is better to allow 30% of the wind to pass through the shelter belt. A well chosen mixture of species will achieve the desired effect.

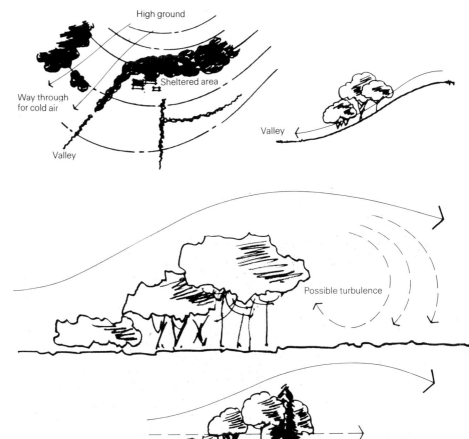

Rain can, to some extent, be deflected by planting since the area under a tree canopy will often remain perfectly dry after a heavy shower. But in winter many trees lose their leaves and if total protection is required, by the main entrance to the house for example, a roof or porch will be necessary.

Poor drainage and the likelihood of frost pockets can be reduced by inter-rupting the path of cold air as it flows downhill. But cold air does not flow away through gaps between buildings and trees; it accumulates instead around the base of any object in its path, making it colder, so some form of unbroken shelter should be devised. This shelter will also reduce heat loss, which results from the combinations of falling temperatures and the wind.

Climate plays a major role in determining the selection of plants. Tresco Abbey, in the Isles of Scilly, enjoys a temperate climate and has a unique collection of thriving sub-tropical plants protected from wind by shelter belts.

THE ENVIRONMENT

In any country that has been closely occupied by man for thousands of years there is no such thing as an entirely virgin site. Every plot has a history of previous human use and it is worth trying to discover something about this before commencing major alterations. Naturally an area which has been arable or grazing land for centuries holds few secrets, but even so there may be hidden problems. On one occasion an apparently virgin meadow on acid soil contained an area which showed a strong alkaline reaction when tested. This turned out to be the remains of a lime pit in which the bodies of cattle slaughtered during a nineteenth-century outbreak of foot-and-mouth disease had been buried.

The history of the site

The sites of old gardens and buildings can be more complex, because changing fashions and economic circumstances have made many alterations over the centuries, traces of which often lie below ground and may prove useful when contemplating new work. This is particularly the case when an old house has been demolished and the grounds redeveloped, as it is certain that some of the new garden will contain portions of foundations, old drives or forecourts and other hard elements over which the developer has brushed a minimum layer of topsoil.

A visit to the local public library, county record office or planning department will often reveal old photographs, prints or documents which shed light on the past history. Old Ordnance Survey maps at the scale of 25 inches to the mile prove useful too, as they were revised at long intervals and therefore show former layouts complete with trees and buildings as they were in the early years of this century. Memories are very short, and major features like hard tennis courts can vanish and be forgotten within twenty years or so, only to reappear and cause problems for the garden designer trying to alter levels or plant trees in that area.

The earlier layout of an established garden can often be traced through old survey plans. These will reveal certain facts which may not be visible at ground level.

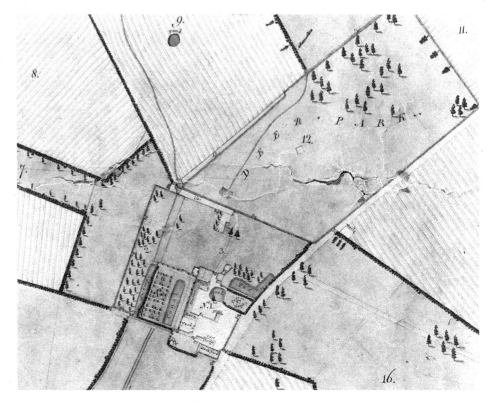

Traces of an old garden are clearly visible from the air. Sites like this are now often restored to the original design.

Sometimes, with evidence of the past, it is possible to reconstruct or adapt a complete period layout, but even where this is not the intention, historic relics can prove useful as well as inconvenient. On one occasion basement walls and flooring from a vanished mansion were uncovered and used as a terrace and retaining walls in a new garden. On another, the bases of nineteenth-century glasshouses, hidden beneath a scrub-covered mound and discovered with the aid of an old Ordnance Survey map, were used to conceal a new parking area in a way which would not otherwise have been economically possible.

Environmental factors

As gardens grow smaller, problems of privacy arise: design solutions will be suggested in other parts of this book, but the problems themselves have to be defined at the outset. One of the worst problems is that of noise, from cars, from planes, from industrial processes, from neighbours with wireless and television sets heard through open windows, from children and dogs. Some of these nuisances can be mitigated; some, like aircraft, must be endured. However, likely sources of trouble, such as a busy highway or a house obviously containing noisy dogs and children, should be noted in relation to the prevailing wind. Possible ways of baffling the sound or placing seating areas where they will be least affected should then be considered. In bad cases of noise pollution the whole pattern of the garden may be dictated by the need for peaceful locations in which to relax.

Since the Clean Air Act 1952, industrial pollution is far less of a problem than in the past, but cement works, gravel-crushing plants and similar activities create considerable dust which is carried

Below: Even in the sixteenth century, privacy was an important factor. The requirement for shelter and an unimpeded sunny outlook governed the selection of this site at Edzell Castle. It has now been restored to its original plan, although the house itself remains a ruin.

Opposite: Detail and interest within this garden manages to distract the eye from the busy railway line running along the boundary.

for a long distance by prevailing winds. In such cases thick screens of fast-growing deciduous trees may be needed to filter out as much material as possible before it reaches the house and surrounding garden. Not only industrial works produce polluted air: cooking smells from nearby gardens and houses can also be unpleasant. Where possible, potential problems in neighbouring gardens should be noted in relation to the prevailing wind, and ways formulated to place seating areas away from the direct air flow.

Visual privacy is another problem of over-development. Although, logically, it seems unlikely that neighbours will spend fine afternoons at their bedroom or bathroom windows, the feeling of being overlooked is always uncomfortable. Various solutions will be proposed later in the book, but the presence, position and

angle of these possible viewpoints must all be noted at this stage. There may also be overhead service wires and television aerials making ungainly patterns against the sky, or underground services creating equal problems below ground, and all must be noted.

Another less obvious but potentially annoying menace in city gardens is the domestic cat. They may well not be present during a site visit but evidence of their presence can generally be found if they are in the habit of visiting the garden, and one can be sure that they will be back more frequently and in greater numbers once alterations and replanting take place. Although cats are very determined, there are measures that can be taken to keep them at bay, but these must form an integral part of any new design.

EXISTING FEATURES

Apart from completely new sites on former agricultural land, every garden has some existing planting or features which must be considered with the greatest care before any alteration is made. It is all too easy to rush in to some neglected plot and 'tidy it up' by cutting down scrub, pulling out trees, knocking down old structures and tearing creepers from walls. It seems much simpler to make a clean sweep and begin again, but it is seldom wise and the first job is to consider how and why these things came to be where they are in the first place.

Wherever possible an established garden should be lightly tidied and maintained for a year before any drastic alteration is made. It is often impossible to tell what may appear in its due season and how it may have been already arranged to create beautiful effects. Those most beautiful gardens, with delicate and sensitively adjusted plant relationships, may be reduced to a barren desert by ignorant treatment in later years.

Trees and hedges are fairly obvious features, but if the garden has been long neglected, the new owner may be faced with an impenetrable mass of brambles, thistles, tree suckers and overgrown shrubs. Frequently, in the rush to achieve some form of order, heavy machinery is brought in and the vegetation on the site ripped up and burnt with little respect for any existing features. This method is often much easier and quicker for the contractor, but leaves the owner with a characterless site on which to create an entirely new garden. Part of the pleasure of gardening is regeneration and discovery, and so much more can often be gained by doing the clearing in stages. Fine and rare specimen shrubs such as magnolia or arbutus can often lurk in the brambles, and an established York stone path system may be completely obscured by overgrown grass which was once a lawn.

Most contractors will point out their discoveries, and often be able to save their client substantial sums of money by recycling the paving, or by restoring some of the original character to the garden by saving those Victorian tiles, now so scarce, of which the modern copies are so disappointing. An ornamental pool may have been filled in with rubbish or rubble by a less interested occupier, weeds may have seeded on the surface, or the water be stagnant, but the pool will still merit resuscitation.

Preserving existing plants

Old shrubs and roses can often be revived by being properly pruned and manured. Even if they are in the wrong place, they may prove to be of old and unobtainable varieties from which cuttings can be taken to provide a new supply. Preserving plants that require resiting can easily be done by clearing and preparing a temporary nursery bed or repository. Shrubs can be reshaped and root-pruned prior to this, and herbaceous plants split or divided up, so saving money and increasing the stock. The repository can also serve as a temporary home for plants acquired by the new owner on instinct or impulse—they will be more expensive, or unobtainable

The common elder, *Sambucus niger*, is a handsome shrub which is worth retaining from an old hedgerow to give maturity to a new garden.

when the new plan has evolved, and are growing larger in the interim period.

With a few exceptions the best time for regeneration or radical pruning is March or April, prior to the new growth appearing, and reshaping is best done in August or September, when the plant is about to go into the winter recess. As with most gardening operations, *how* it is done is more important than when, and this depends on experience. Another problem in the case of rhododendrons, or varieties of the same herbaceous plant, like tradescantia, is colour. If the flower shade is not known before replanting, unfortunate collisions can occur.

Hedges and trees

Although one should never retain anything on the site simply because it is there, much thought should be expended before it is removed. Any tree or hedge which is already established will, if suitably pruned and cultivated, always grow faster and produce a mature effect more quickly than something newly planted. Even an overgrown hedgerow, inconveniently placed for a division or boundary, will be found to contain a number of strong young trees which, released from the dead and malformed specimens around them, can form the basis of a grove beside a lawn or behind a shrub border. The fact that the available materials are 'common' is quite unimportant. Strong specimens of thorn, elder, holly or field maple are handsome in themselves and make an excellent background to more decorative subjects.

Other 'living' parts of the garden may need to be adapted rather than removed to bridge the difference between mature and new planting. This is really a question of reducing the scale or proportion of existing items so that they do not appear too old in the company of vigorous youth. Most mature specimens respond quite happily to fairly radical treatment, providing it is done at the right time and with a knowledge of the plant.

Regenerating hedges

Hedges, particularly, can benefit from being cut back. *X Cupressocyparis leylandii*, for example, planted several decades ago as a hedge or screen, may now look ragged and uneven both in height and width. By reducing the height by about one third and trimming the sides at a sloping angle so that the light reaches the lower branches, this eyesore can be transformed into a neat and healthy hedge. If fed and watered during its recovery period and trimmed annually, it can then be maintained at a reasonable size. Recently the National Trust have had to adopt this policy with some mature yew hedges in a well-known garden, for not only did the hedges look past their best but they also smothered the stone path and made access impossible for visitors. By reducing the height and cutting back the hedges drastically, first on one side and then a few years later on the other, the balance of the original scheme has been restored.

Deciduous hedges, which have developed into lanky young trees and are blocking views, can be cut back by about two thirds with no ill effects. It may be wise, though, to trim one third initially and then, if the hedge is doing well, cut it back further the following year.

Quite often there is a dense, overgrown band of trees and shrubs along the boundary of the garden which might look better thinned or removed entirely to give more light and air. However, this may well have been planted as a windbreak where loss, either through felling or too drastic thinning which results in subsequent failure of the remaining trees, could have a disastrous effect on the garden for many years to come. The fact that such a plantation is not on the south-west boundary of the garden is not necessarily significant, since the prevailing wind can be deflected by the configuration of the ground or buildings, to blow from an entirely different quarter. Even where an important view is ob-

When planning a new design, it is often better to establish which mature plants to retain before any drastic clearance. In this case, an old fruit tree gives an instant appearance of maturity to a recently established garden.

scured, advice from local experts should be sought before opening up a vista because the necessary cut may become a means of funnelling wind into the garden and creating destructive air turbulence. In some cases, though, it may be necessary to remove quick-growing intruders, such as sycamore or birch, to maintain the original design of the plantation. It should be remembered, too, that many deciduous woodlands used to be coppiced regularly, and sometimes still are,

to provide a crop of timber of suitable size for chestnut paling and other similar products.

Neglected orchards should also be examined with care. It is true that gnarled old fruit trees may not be productive and the crop is difficult to gather, but their shapes can be very picturesque and even poor specimens may support climbing roses or clematis, at least for a time. In an old, reconstructed garden such aged trees give a suggestion of

If the canopy of this tree were to be reduced by competent tree surgery, it could increase its lifespan as well as improving the visual balance.

continuity while in a new garden with buildings of modern design their twisted forms provide contrast to the smooth surfaces and sharp angles in a way which is faintly Japanese.

Caring for trees

In many established gardens the trees were all planted at the same time and, although their lifespans differ, there is a danger that they will all die simultaneously. Even if there is only one mature tree it will have an impact on the proportion and design of the garden, and it may need to be restored to good health by correct pruning and maintenance. Early in the preliminary planning stage a skilled tree surgeon should be consulted. Most local authorities have a list of recommended tree surgeons, or the Arboricultural Association will suggest someone local.

It is not only the outward appearance of the tree that is important, for as a tree grows there is continual change both above and below ground. Roots are vital to trees for food, water and support, and species such as ash, elm, willow and poplar consume at least 50,000 l (11,000 gall) of water a year, so they may endanger buildings by exhausting the ground water, especially on shrinkable clay soils. During drought trees seeking water can send out roots to a distance of 90 m (300 ft), often causing the water level in ponds and lakes to drop dramatically and therefore eroding the banks. If these thirsty trees are removed from the garden the ground will gradually absorb water again and may swell, causing buildings to lift and distort. The skilled tree surgeon will readily anticipate such problems.

Existing trees are not always treated with the respect they deserve by building contractors and it is wise to include in the contract a penalty clause for any damage caused. Prior to beginning work the tree should be protected to its full spread with fencing, and if the roots are to be exposed they must be covered in sacking and kept continually damp by

39

hosing down. Generally the spread of the roots equals the height of the tree, plus one third, and only 5% of the roots may be removed without injury to the tree.

Even car parking can damage the development of a tree. At one well known country house open to the public an area under some excellent specimen trees was designated as car park. But the trees soon began to show signs of stress with the frequent weight of the cars bearing down on their root systems, so the car park had to be relocated in order to save the trees.

Tree surgery

The tree surgeon should provide a report on the health of the tree and recommend any measures to improve it. Then, by regular observation and action, both the grief caused by the loss of a tree and the cost of repairing damage can be avoided. Often the useful life of a tree can be extended by the removal of top-heavy branches, by bracing or splicing old and brittle branches with cable, by removing diseased limbs and cleaning up cavities. Large, old trees are particularly susceptible to internal rot, which weakens the tree and causes parts to break off. If the internal condition of the tree is suspect the tree surgeon has an electrical device called a shigometer which detects decay in the roots, base and trunk. Visible signs of danger include large, open wounds or cracks; fungi; dead bark, branches or tops; holes made by insects, birds or other wildlife; injured roots, often due to previous construction work; and die-back within parts of the tree canopy.

Many people feel very strongly about the demise of a tree and there are now several associations, such as the Arboricultural Association, which protect trees and give advice to those concerned about them. The task of conserving trees, which take so long to grow to maturity, requires just as much thought and care as restoring old buildings. In theory, trees removed or destroyed must be replaced by the owner with those of an appropriate size and species, and owners or unscrupulous developers may be fined large sums for wilful destruction. But in practice it is impossible to replace in a lifetime what may have taken two hundred years to grow.

Buildings and other structures

In former days when costs were less and good materials were available locally, all kinds of ancillary buildings were put up to serve needs which may no longer exist: wash-houses, apple stores, cart lodges, bothies, engine-houses, well-houses, and many more, especially if the main house was a working farm. Often there is a temptation to remove these structures, which may not be in very good condition, but many can be adapted to serve new purposes more cheaply and decoratively than would be possible if one were starting from scratch.

Old farm or stable yards make ideal sites for swimming pools, which they shelter and conceal while the surround-

ing buildings become open loggias, changing-rooms, kitchens, chair stores, plant houses and games rooms. On the largest scale, a barn will make a wonderful party room, possibly with kitchen and toilet facilities all under the same roof. Conversely a game larder or apple store, suitably restored, can become a charming summerhouse. There is no need, of course, to slavishly preserve existing features—even if the garden does have a historic link with the past—unless they are compatible with the proposed plan.

Naturally the garden will have to be reconstructed to bring these structures into play, but that is up to the skill of the designer. Even if the building has lost its roof, this can be replaced by vines on a wooden trellis so the whole thing becomes a small walled room open to the sky. The possibilities of ruins, either partly restored or made more picturesquely ruinous, are endless—the camomile seat at Sissinghurst, for instance, appears to have been constructed with fallen or ruined columns.

Opposite above: The scale of this old archway has been cleverly altered to make a decorative garden feature.

Opposite below: The most unpromising building can be turned to a new use. Here, an old privy, retaining some of its original features, has been made into a useful garden building.

Farm and stable yards often make an excellent, sheltered site for a swimming pool. Here the loose boxes have been adapted to form a long loggia overlooking the pool.

BASIC DESIGN ELEMENTS AND TECHNIQUES

Above: The careful control of space in this woodland context suggests the movement of a fast-moving stream.

Below: The spatial void in this garden has been altered by the placing of the metal 'baskets' of roses which draws attention to their shape, giving a new dimension to the surrounding space.

Mass and void

When starting to consider the structure of the garden it is important to realize at the outset that gardens are essentially compositions of mass and void. Depending on the scale of the garden, the masses may consist of large shrub groups, building and walls, woodland or hills—anything, in fact, which rises above eye level and dominates the eye. Voids are grass, hard surfaces, low planting or water which the eye can pass over. It is the interaction between these two elements plus a third—objects in space—which make up the real structure of the garden. Just as one can walk into an empty house and feel that it would be possible to live there with no more than a bed and an orange box, because the proportion of the rooms is so satisfying, so a garden can be complete in itself, however dull the details. Conversely, an ill-arranged composition can never be put right with cosmetic planting.

The nature of space and light

Space is a positive rather than a negative element and it has a dynamic quality which rises far above a mere absence of mass. By means of good design space can be made to flow like water, moving slowly down the stately canal of an avenue, flooding round island shrub beds to fill some great inland sea of lawn, or rippling swiftly down a woodland path.

Once an object is placed in space several things occur. Firstly, the nature of the space is changed by this new addition; secondly, the shape and quality of the thing itself is emphasized by being placed within this particular void; and thirdly, new shapes are created in the air around the object. People get so obsessed with the nature of an object—a plant, a tree, a statue—that they forget that it is only part of an equation: object plus setting equals the total effect. To think only of one of these elements is to invite disaster, or at best arrive at good results by chance rather than design.

Light plays an important part in this, since the way in which things are seen in a particular context is vital to their appreciation. The actual quality of light—not merely its presence or absence—is an important factor. The further south one goes the more intense the light, so the proportion between mass and void can change. Small, brilliantly lit voids can be carved from dark, shady masses, and shadow patterns on walls or pavings can play an important and reliable part in the total picture. Anything which is seen in these bright spaces will appear clear cut and sharply defined, so that every undercut line on a piece of sculpture, every furrow of bark or shape of leaf will read as a strong statement, underlined by varying depth of shadow.

Left: Looking from dark to light adds drama and depth to a composition.

Below: Light plays an important part in the design of a garden. In a soft northern light, only the strongest shapes in the foreground stand out while the background forms become blurred and indistinct.

The further north one goes, the less intense the light. The proportion between mass and void must change as the voids have to get greater and greater to allow sufficient light into the composition. Masses gain in importance and individuality as they diminish in size and are seen as a counterpoise to the surrounding voids. Even at its brightest the light has a soft blue-tinged quality which tends to blur outlines and flatten shapes that now lack the strong definition of sharp lights and shadows.

It follows, then, that the whole method of designing and the pictures which are attempted will be quite different in the southern and northern hemispheres. On the one hand a backdrop of velvet shadow against which are displayed bright incidents of almost theatrical intensity, on the other wide spaces drifting off into a blue distance, within which it is the outline form of objects rather than their intimate detail which counts. This is the reason why attempts to copy styles from other countries are so seldom successful. The nineteenth-century 'Italian' gardens which were made so fashionable by Sir Charles Barry and his followers are seldom convincing even on the brightest day because their proportions are not correct. In order to admit sufficient light, the voids have to be so enlarged that the effect is of an English garden with Italian trimmings, rather than the real thing. English landscape parks imported to Italy are equally unsuccessful since their attempts at sweeping parkland and clumped trees simply result in a blazing savannah too lacking in shade for comfort.

Looking from dark to light—or even better, looking from light through darkness to light beyond—adds drama to even the simplest scene, while in reverse the effect has the flattened quality of a painted backdrop. Certain things such as trees with a striking branch structure, wrought ironwork and pillars are better seen in silhouette, while sculpture, rock-

The involved patterns of wrought-iron look best silhouetted against sky or water.

work and plants of sculptural form are best seen in full light. Even so, thought must be given as to whether the light should fall largely from above, at the front or from the side.

Scale and proportion

The next thing to consider is the question of scale and proportion. Within a building the architect is in complete charge of the environment and his task is to create spaces which relate to the scale of the human figure. Indeed, the whole structure of Palladian architecture uses man as its module and it is only when the architect departs from this relationship by creating spaces too mean or too vast and stairs too steep that we feel uncomfortable and out of place. Outside, however, the situation is different. Outside lies the immensity of nature and the designer's role changes to that of an intermediary, providing a link between the human figure and its superhuman setting. Even in a town garden surrounded by buildings the distant sky forms the roof, giving a strange proportion very different from that of a room.

If interior proportions are used exter-nally, the result is always poor because the relationship to nature is lacking. In the garden things need to be wider, shallower, more generous than they are within a building, and vertical ele-ments—of trees, walls or hedges—are needed to relate the human figure to its surroundings. Of course, once the gen-eral principle is understood, it is possible to play tricks and deviate from the rule in order to achieve special effects. One knows from the laws of perspective that things diminish in size proportionally as they are distanced from the observer and that this is a mathematical progression. If two objects—for instance, two urns—are of exactly the same design, one tends to assume that they are also the same size. Supposing one is smaller than the other and placed at a distance, both it and the area in which it stands will appear to be much further away than they really are. A small statue placed at a low level will enlarge its surroundings while one placed high will seem remote; a large sculpture near the observer will dominate and diminish its setting.

Quite apart from the question of per-spective in relation to scale, there is the

Opposite above: Light falling from above sharply emphasizes and defines the form of tree trunks and foliage.

Opposite below: A tall narrow opening emphasizes the length of this path and increases the sense of distance. Tension is created by the transition from shade to sunlight.

equally important question of perspective in relation to plan form. The designer works in a basically unreal way, since nothing in the garden can ever be read as a pure plan, even though it was first evolved in this form. Even from the top of a nearby high building the shapes of the garden below, as conceived on plan, will be slightly distorted by perspective, and this distortion will increase at intermediate levels until reaching normal eye level when it is at its greatest. Straight lines behave predictably, but curves can often appear much more extreme on the ground than they did on plan. It is possible to get some idea of the effect by bringing the drawing board up to eye level and looking along, rather than down on, the plan, but the inexperienced designer will do well to have a scheme set out with pegs and string on the ground before construction begins. The strings can be adjusted until the

desired effect is achieved, and with practice the exact relationship between a curve on plan and one on the ground will become apparent.

Creating new contours

One of the first things to consider in the garden is the shape of the ground itself. Few sites are absolutely flat, though many appear so, and far more become flat through inexpert design. Even slight changes of level can achieve interesting results and every effort should be made to emphasize the subtle gradations of the ground or create new ones using material already on site. Where building works are in progress, there is often spare soil available which is carried away at considerable expense instead of being used to enhance the quality of the garden. If this is the case, it must be made clear at the outset that top soil and subsoil must be stored separately, and that subsoil

Slight changes in level maintain visual interest in a garden. Here, new shapes have been created using retaining walls and banks.

must never be spread over top soil. If any ground shaping is proposed, the top soil must be stripped from the whole area to be treated, and set aside before the subsoil is reshaped. If available, subsoil from operations in other areas can be added before the top soil is respread over the new contours.

Quite slight level changes can produce excellent effects when allied to planting, and the two must be considered together from the outset. Supposing, for instance, that a broad shallow valley is desired, perhaps curving away to lead the eye to a tree or other existing feature. It may only be necessary to excavate to the depth of 50 cm (18 in), the displaced soil being used to create gently rolling mounds at the side which will at once increase the valley impression. Trees and shrubs which will gradually grow together can be grouped behind and on top of raised ground, directing the eye along the confines of the 'valley', which will appear much deeper than the small amount of excavation would imply.

The eye always exaggerates height in relation to breadth and in consequence anything placed on raised ground gains in importance, appearing larger and more distant than it is in reality. The circular domed temple on its hillock in Kew Gardens seems to be an imposing building on top of a steep hill and, now that one can no longer approach it, the illusion is maintained. Years ago, when there was public access to that point, it was disappointing to find how small the rise and how insignificant the building was when it was reached. This curious power of exaggeration may be used to advantage when creating new raised ground.

Although ground may rise or fall from the main faces of a building, it should never fall across the line of sight, since this creates the most uneasy feeling as though the structure were sliding downhill. If this does occur, it is essential to create an air of stability, either formally by terraces and levels, or informally by

Left: The uncomfortable slope of the ground, which could not be altered, was counter-balanced by the movement of a small stone figure in the foreground.

Below: Scale and proportion should always be taken into account. An object on raised ground appears larger and more remote than in reality. Both the circular-domed temple and the mount at Kew Gardens are in fact quite small.

In order to look rational, planting must flow with the contours rather than cut across them. This is particularly noticeable in undulating landscape.

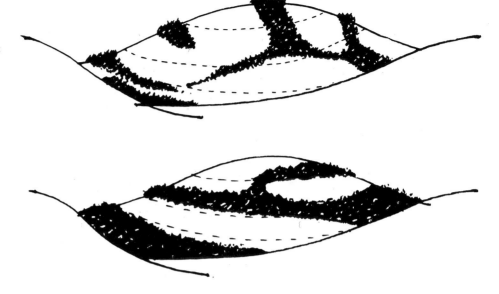

scooping back into the hillside and perhaps bolstering the lower part of the slope with heavy planting.

Natural land forms
Before attempting naturalistic ground shaping, it is essential to take careful note of the effects to be found in nature itself. There are general rules as, for instance, that all slopes must be smoothly flowing, merging imperceptibly into level ground with no intervening angle, and that a mound or hillock will not be even but will have one long shallow side with the opposing one rather steeper. A group of such mounds will have the long and short sides in the same relationship to one another since the formation is caused by weathering over millions of years.

However, due to the underlying geological formation, the general shapes of the ground in various areas is very different and it is important to study the particular area in which you are working to get the exact feel of the landscape. The general forms of hills, mountains and valleys can be reproduced on a much smaller scale within the garden to create a proper relationship. Using the contoured map which you have already obtained to define the zone of visual influence (see page 12), look at the various

A contour drawing
Although contour lines may look harmonious on plan, it is always necessary to make sections to check that the resulting ground formation will be satisfactory. In this case, the section reveals that the shapes are too extreme.

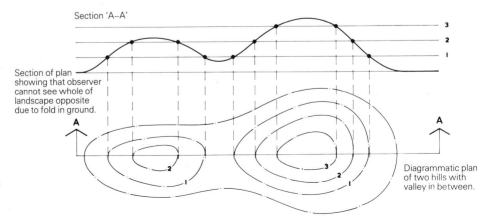

Section 'A–A'

Section of plan showing that observer cannot see whole of landscape opposite due to fold in ground.

Diagrammatic plan of two hills with valley in between.

ground formations which can be viewed from the garden and observe how the contour lines relate to the shapes before you.

Designing contours

Contour lines are a simple way of expressing the shape of the ground, and it is important to understand how they work as there is no other clear way of showing your proposed ground shaping in plan form. Essentially it is like building up a model using layers of cardboard of even thickness. Starting with the valley or plain at the foot of the hill as a base board, the high ground is built up. On a map these 'layers' may be cut at 15 or 30 m (50 or 100 ft) intervals and sometimes more, while in the garden they may appear at intervals of 1 m (3 ft) or less. The lines on the map show the exact point where the slope of the hill reaches that particular height. Consequently on a long shallow slope the lines will be far apart, but where the ground is steep they are close together.

When indicating contouring on plan it is always wise to make check sections through the proposed features before finalizing your work. Generally if something looks harmonious on plan it will appear so in reality, but contour lines are different. It is very easy to be beguiled by drawing beautiful flowing shapes only to discover that in three dimensions the results are clumsy, unnatural and not at all what you intended. Remember that, however great the changes of level which you plan within your site, they must merge imperceptibly into the natural landform. Nothing is less convincing than recontoured ground which stops abruptly at a boundary line. Even if the break is designed to be hidden in planting, it is still suspect.

Modern earth-moving machinery has taken much of the toil out of reshaping the land, but it does bring other problems in its wake. Depending on the nature of the soil, heavy machines running back and forth in a restricted area

can compact the subsoil to a considerable depth, destroying both the structure of the soil and the natural drainage. Clay is worst affected and gravel the least, since gravel is coarse and does not cohere so there is considerable air space between the stones. On any heavy soil it will certainly be necessary to have a subsoiler in after the ground shaping is complete, to break up thoroughly all the affected areas to the full depth of compaction. Additional artificial drainage may even be needed to hasten the return to a natural system.

To create the level area for the pool it is necessary to adapt the existing contours. In this case a retaining wall would be required to extend the pool area.

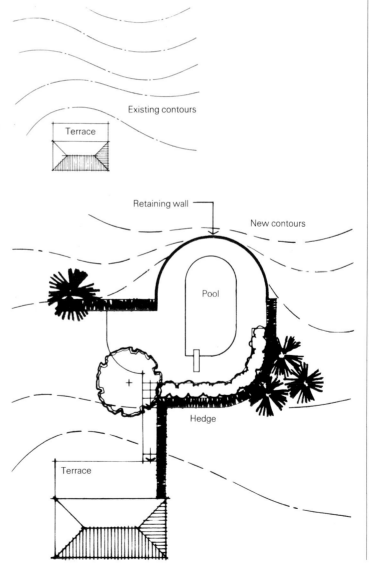

DESIGN FEATURES

Unless it is to be a mere formless jumble of interesting plants, a garden requires a firm underlying structure within which decorative elements can be grouped. The structure can be entirely formal—walls and hedges, terraces and stairs, canals and avenues—or it can be entirely informal and consist of asymmetrically-placed trees and contoured ground. The important thing is that it must be there, underlying everything else and holding the whole garden design together. How this structure is to be achieved very much depends on the nature of the garden and its existing buildings, and is conditioned by other factors such as the cost of construction and maintenance; but the component parts are the same, and are considered in detail in the following pages.

Ideally garden structures should be specially designed for their setting as with this garden pavilion festooned with golden hop. When this is not practical it is often possible to adapt ready-made structures to reflect the character and style of the garden.

GARDEN BUILDINGS

The opportunity to design a house and garden on a virgin site, unrestricted by what past and present owners have already done, seldom occurs. In reality the most ambitious schemes are modified by the existing and often awkward positioning of drains, manhole covers, oil storage tanks, sandpits, carports or the pump house for the swimming pool. These are rarely placed in the unobtrusive manner that the garden designer would prefer, for the garage must be near the house and the road, the greenhouse near the kitchen garden, and so on. But, with some forethought and imagination, they can be disguised or incorporated into the design—special manhole covers are available that can be filled with paving stones or gravel to blend with the paving, oil tanks can be veiled in trellis or rampant climbers.

Garages

The most dominant construction is likely to be the garage, or even garages since many families run more than one car and therefore the space required for parking and garaging has increased. Sometimes existing barns or other outbuildings can be successfully converted into garages but usually new garages have to be built as tastefully as possible, or existing ones disguised. If the new garage is at low level it is likely to be out of view and even a large complex will be quite hidden; or the garage can be covered with creepers and the glass roof over the hard standing similarly veiled.

Greenhouses

The greenhouse is frequently an unattractive garden building, and as it ought to face east-west to make the most of the sunlight, there is often little choice in where it is located. To make the best of it use local materials—brick, flint or stone—as a base, and follow the architectural lines of the adjacent walls or roofs of nearby buildings; or partially 'sink' the building so the slope of the roof may hardly be noticed. Timber structures are less obtrusive than metal and can be of cedar, which requires little maintenance, or of softwood, which requires regular painting. Any paintwork should not necessarily be white, for a subdued French green or matt black is much more in keeping with the garden. Metal frames allow more light as the bars are thinner, and obviously a greenhouse glazed to the floor will be lighter, while one supported by walling or half sunk into the ground is warmer. Specialist advice will be needed on ventilation, heating and watering. Most greenhouse suppliers will tell you what works best with their particular models, and it is worth asking several firms for their advice, weighing up the running costs as well as those of the construction before making the purchase. Solar panels, used mostly for heating swimming-pools, are not so easy on the eye, but can be very cost effective. In larger gardens a heated and a cold greenhouse may be required, but in fact cold frames are

Careful planting can be used to screen even a garage wall as well as to display attractive climbers to great advantage.

Right: The greenhouse need not have a purely utilitarian function, but can be made into an attractive feature for displaying potted plants.

always useful for raising and hardening off seedlings or establishing cuttings. Again they can be of metal and glass, or constructed on a solid base.

Storage Space

Storage space for wheelbarrows, fertilizers and weedkillers is also necessary. The old maxim 'You can tell a good gardener by the way he looks after his tools' is still true and an efficient storage system saves hours of frustration looking for the right implement or product. The tool shed should be set out with plenty of hanging and storage space, a work table or bench for potting and other jobs and a lock and key to keep children out and prevent accidents. Too often the garden shed looks like a 'privy' at the bottom of the garden and is not at all conducive to work. The compost heap should also be nearby, but remember that it can smell and attract flies.

And so to dustbins. They must be within easy reach of the kitchen and also accessible to the dustman. Some councils have rules about what the dustmen are allowed to do, so check before deciding where to put the bins. It may be a good idea to build a small, low store to accommodate them and embellish it with planting, for if the area looks neat there is less likelihood of litter being scattered around the access path.

Play equipment

Finally, children's play equipment should not be forgotten. Although a little more trouble to design and construct, a play-house built into the branches of a tree or a homemade swing or hammock to loll in are much original than the 'off-the-peg' aluminium equivalents that are so often given to children.

Right: Although this tree house is quite elaborate, it shows a number of ideas which could be adapted to make a simpler version. The very old tree needs considerable support to hold the weight of this structure.

Tennis courts

Because of their generally uncompromising size, shape and orientation, swimming pools and tennis courts can cause considerable difficulty for the garden designer. Of the two, the tennis court with its tall surround, strict north-south axis and large area of hard surface—the colour of which is never very satisfactory—is the worst. However, careful analysis of the problem will suggest some solutions.

Firstly, the court has to be a true level, which on many sites will mean that it has to be dug into the landform in some areas. The excavated material can then be used to raise surrounding contours, either formally or informally, to help hide the court surface from the remainder of the garden. Secondly, the best view of the play is from above, so a terrace looking down on the court may be built, crowned by a pergola with climbers which will completely hide both court and netting while providing a shady walk or sitting area. This is a particularly good solution where there is a large amount of spoil available on site which would otherwise have to be removed.

On flat ground or where only small improvements can be attempted, a low hedge of perhaps 1m (3ft) in height will hide the court surface from even a short distance away, while a pergola or line of pleached trees cut level with the top of the surround, will disguise the hard line of the netting against the sky. If the netting itself is black, and not the green more commonly used, it will tend to get lost in shadow. In this way it will still be possible to see the play and maintain a sense of space, without the court dominating the garden.

In this case, the surface is concealed by a formal hedge (above), while the top of the wire netting is obscured by the pleached lime trees (below).

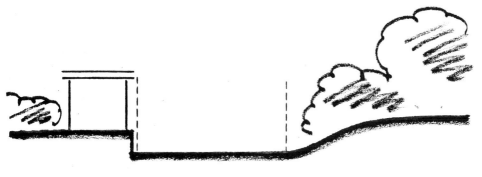

A hard tennis court can be completely concealed by lowering the level and using the excavated material to form a raised terrace crowned by a shady pergola, and banks planted with shrubs.

Swimming pools create an artificial element in an informal garden. Rather than use unconvincing carved shapes, this formal pool was created by raising it above the lawn level and clothing the retaining wall with *Vitis coignetiae*.

Swimming pools

Fortunately swimming-pools are often given an enclosure of their own, both for comfort and convenience, so they do not dominate the scene as much as the tennis court. Disused stable or farm yards and walled gardens are ideal, although it must be remembered that the excavating machinery has to get into the proposed site to dig the hole and remove the spoil, unless one is prepared to face the expense of hand work. If there are no suitable enclosures available, one can be created, either by building walls or planting hedges. Fences never seem very appropriate in such a position: they imply that the pool was an afterthought and that a temporary barrier has been erected to provide shelter.

The suppliers of swimming pools expect one to use a standard pre-cast coping and matching pre-cast paving, but this is not really necessary. It is perfectly possible to use brick or old York stone if these will form a more appropriate setting, especially if the pool has to be seen in relation to paths or terraces and is within view of the house. In this case it can be designed as a formal water basin, the interior being either grey or white so that the only colour comes from the mass of water itself. Indeed, these colours, or a dark holly-leaf green, always look better than the improbable sky blue which can appear garish in a soft light .

When preparing a scheme for a pool one must remember how many people are likely to be using the area, and allow sufficient space so that those who are sunbathing or sitting in chairs beneath an arbour are not splashed or disturbed by children running along the edge. And, of course, where small children are concerned, it is wiser to give them a separate shallow pool of their own so they are not tempted near the deep water.

Gates and doorways

First impressions are important, and the entrance to the garden—or to a garden within a garden—should always make a clear statement as to what is to be found within, even if the statement is itself a deception designed to create an unexpected revelation. An unpretentious entry might lead to an exciting view which would gain from the contrast, but a handsome gateway of striking design leading to nothing more than rough woodland or an empty field merely gives a sense of disappointment.

As soon as there is an opening, whether in wall or hedge, the immediate reaction seems to be to fill it with a wrought iron gate, but this is frequently not the best solution. Wrought or cast iron is always best seen against a plain background: sky or water, grass, gravel or paving are all good because the design of the ironwork is shown in clear silhouette against them. Anything of more intrinsically involved design, whether buildings, planting or even trees and shadows, immediately sets up a confusion between one image and the other, so that neither is seen to advantage. In such cases it is generally best to choose a design in metal, wood or a combination of the two, with simple verticals or an all-over geometric form, which gives an air of proportion and stability to the background detail in the same way that a sheet of graph paper, placed over a picture, enables one to understand it more clearly.

A solid wooden door which reveals nothing until it is opened is often better than one which shows too much. The pleasures of imagination and anticipation are very great and can often produce better pictures than those which are revealed to the eye. In the past the charms of reticence were well understood and it is only comparatively recently that complete exposure has become popular.

Even the proportions of the opening in which the gate is hung are important. A

tall, narrow opening is mysterious, almost sinister, while one which is much wider than it is high, with gates which are lower in the centre than at the sides, suggests a hospitable welcome. Gate piers crowned with finials, and gates which rise in the centre or have a central over-throw, suggest a screen designed to keep out rather than welcome the traveller, allowing only the favoured few to pass through.

Where low gates are needed to contain or exclude dogs or children, then they should make a simple statement of their purpose and be designed to that end. Trying to decorate an obviously utilitarian feature creates an air of distraction and fuss rather than visual pleasure, and the results are often unsatisfactory.

The entrance to a garden should always be in keeping with the style and scale of the house.

This neat entrance with carefully trained climbers gives a suggestion of the garden beyond, which can be partially glimpsed through the fretwork panel at the top.

STEPS.

Steps should be broad and shallow, suggesting effortless progress, with frequent landings from which to view the garden. Here the landings are of grass which links the lawns above and below.

Sometimes there seems to be a rather apologetic air about steps in gardens, as though they were merely a practical necessity, but in fact changes in level give some of the best opportunities for dramatic effect and the creation of sculptural form. In general, steps in gardens should be broad and shallow, giving the suggestion of an effortless progress from one level to another; if they must be steep then they should also be narrow, like an exciting stone ladder climbing up the hillside. The classic proportion for steps is twice the rise plus the depth of the tread and should equal 675 mm (27 ins), the most suitable rise being between 113 mm and 150 mm (4½ to 6 ins).

Very shallow steps are dangerous to the poorly sighted and if they are over 150 mm (6 in) deep they are uncomfortable to use.

Block steps have a crisp mathematical precision, but in the more Northern countries, where the light lacks definition, a separate tread which overhangs the riser by about 25 mm (1 in), gives a bar of shadow which emphasizes the horizontal quality of the composition. This is particularly the case where the steps are composed of fluid curves rather than straight lines, since the light will move over the surfaces in an irregular way giving an interesting rippling effect.

Where flights of steps separate grass levels, there is a temptation to make the

Left: Steps can be blended into their surroundings by training a small-leafed climber across the risers, to relate to the adjoining side walls. This does, however, lose the effect of light and shade created by the overhanging treads.

Below: A simple method of stepping the path in a wild garden is to use split logs for the risers with treads of consolidated gravel which drift off into the planting on either side.

steps also of grass, but this is seldom successful. Not only are they very tiresome to cut, but they get muddy and slippery if much used, and since the risers have to be formed from some hard material the effect is still not green from a distance. A better effect may well be achieved by training some close-growing plant, such as a small-leafed ivy, over the fronts of the steps to provide the green link.

In a woodland or wild garden steps with risers of split logs or railway sleepers and treads of consolidated gravel, are appropriate, either as a separate flight or as a stepped path where the ground is steep. Where a path is stepped in this way, the distance between each step should be an even number of paces to make walking easier, and the risers must all be of the same height.

Steps have other uses, too, since they can be used as a setting for pots, either placed in formal rows at the edges or grouped informally on landings for changing effects of seasonal colour. In fine weather steps can be scattered with cushions to add an extra element of seating, and space should be allowed for this in addition to that needed for normal passage.

PATHS AND PAVING

Paving

Grass grows almost too well in British gardens so it tends to get used in places for which it is unsuitable. In fact, it should only be considered a wearing surface at a very low level of use. Once the number of users becomes too great the grass turns to mud. Long before the mud-track situation arises, the composition needs to be changed from one of soft surface containing one or two hard elements to one of hard surface with soft additions. For instance, a courtyard with a central lawn edged by a narrow path and planting may need to be paved as people make short cuts across the grass. Once the concept of an entirely hard surface is accepted it will be realized that quite large areas of the paving can be omitted, to be replaced by planting without blocking any design line or risking damage by trampling. Frequently, the paving may be simply patterned with two materials to suggest directional flow. This can absorb trees, low-level planting and seats to give a three-dimensional effect in place of a single plane.

This path of random rectangular York paving links the lawn to the buildings on the upper level and provides a neat foreground for the adjoining flower colour.

Patterns

A clear-cut, all-over pattern has the effect of unifying a space, a technique which is particularly useful where surrounding buildings and objects are strangely positioned and have no apparent relationship to one another. If this is the intention, then it is important that the design can be quickly understood by an observer at ground level; there should be few—preferably only two—different materials and these should be clearly related to those of the adjoining structures. Once this principle is clearly understood, it will be found that quite large sections of the pattern can be left out—for instance, in areas of planting—without their loss being noticed, since the implication of the design is perfectly clear.

It is unwise to design wildly complicated paving patterns from numerous ill-assorted materials. These tend to disrupt rather than unite space, and serve no useful purpose. Simple materials, well laid and in scale with their surroundings, are always preferable to those that are self-consciously contrived.

Paving materials

All the hard materials used for paving have different characteristics, both from the point of view of wear and of appearance, as well as that of cost. Perhaps the simplest and least expensive are those which can be laid over a whole area without cutting and fitting individual elements. Of these gravel, used for garden paths and drives for several hundred years, is perhaps best known. Providing that it is correctly laid and cambered, and given suitably firm edgings to keep it in place, it provides an excellent surface, variable in colour and texture depending on the origin and size of the pebbles. Nowadays, with chemical weedkillers, it is perfectly practical from the point of view of maintenance also.

Between the disappearance of cheap labour and the arrival of weedkillers

gravel was banished in favour of tarmacadum. This has an unpleasant colour and texture, only made worse by the practice of rolling in a small number of white marble chips. It can, however, be sprayed with hot tar and have crushed gravel or limestone—depending on location—rolled into the surface. When this has set hard, it is best to repeat the operation once or twice to ensure a good coating, particularly if wear from vehicle wheels may be expected.

In-situ concrete

In-situ concrete, an intrinsically bland and boring material, is, however, one which is capable of considerable variation both through the use of different aggregates and from surface treatment. Either the aggregate can be exposed, or a texture can be superimposed on the surface by the application of different materials during the setting process. The board-marked concrete once popular with architects has become something of a cliché, but the same process can use sacking, rush or sisal matting and similar materials to relieve the normal smooth-floated finish. Where a good foothold and improved drainage are desirable—as for instance around a swimming pool—a strong ribbing effect can be produced by two men 'chopping' the damp surface with the edge of a wooden lath. Unless provided with wooden expansion joints, concrete will crack, but this is not a disadvantage since the lines created by necessity can become an important element of pattern, a technique well demonstrated in many modern American gardens.

Precast slabs

Consideration of concrete leads to the many kinds of precast slabs which are available to the garden designer, some imitating stone with varying degrees of success, others being frankly artificial in both colour and texture. Everything depends, of course, on the purpose for

Brick and stone can be combined to create interesting patterns in a formal setting. Although this example is very elaborate the same principles could be adapted to make simpler schemes.

A gravel path firmly edged with natural stone forms a simple setting for lawn and planting. It is best to use a local gravel whose colour tones in with the surroundings.

Smooth, water worn pebbles from a beach or river bed can be used to make interesting paths in a country garden. Here they are bordered by bands of slate, creating additional interest.

which the slabs are required, but there are certain guidelines which should govern choice. Any slab which represents stone should be made of a consistent material, not have a stone finish applied to the outside which can become worn by traffic or weather. It is also important that there should be a fairly large range of slab sizes available so they can be laid in a random rectangular fashion, since natural stone slabs are seldom supplied in only one or two sizes.

The frankly artificial versions may well be laid in a single size but it is important to check how their colours and textures will weather. Many quite strong and ugly colours weather to delightfully soft shades, but others do not; while some, which look pleasingly mellow to begin with, come to resemble plain concrete after a few years. One difficulty common to all precast slabs is that of cutting them neatly, especially on a curve, and this must be borne in mind at the design stage if their use is intended.

This traditional stone paving is used effectively as a simple foil for the planting and containers.

Natural stone

The natural stone most used for garden work is York, either new or, more frequently, secondhand. It wears, weathers and cuts well, and has a pleasing variation of colour which makes it ideal for large as well as small areas. Even more than other materials, its appearance is much affected by the pointing between the slabs once they have been laid. If they are flush pointed the individual quality of the stones is lost and from a distance the effect can be of in-situ concrete, while the hard precision of a struck joint makes them appear artificial. By far the best is a raked joint, which prevents the growth of weeds while exposing the slight irregularities of the edges to give an interesting texture.

Natural stone is best laid in a random rectangular formation, which gives a calm, large-scale effect quite lacking in 'crazy paving' with its jigsaw of fragmented shapes. Unfortunately, this was a very popular material in the 1920s and '30s, so one often has to make use of existing supplies. It can, however, become agreeable if used to infill a simple rectangular pattern made from bands of the same stone in an even width. In that case, it is even more effective if the bands are of a completely consistent colour, rather than repeating the probably varied tones of the crazy paving. Bands of brick or an entirely different stone are less successful since they add a strong contrast of colour to the already disruptive pattern of the infill.

Granite setts and cobbles

Granite setts or cobbles also provide a strong contrast of texture to smooth areas of stone or gravel. Both are expensive and labour-intensive to lay because the individual unit is small, but their roughness can add emphasis to the surroundings of an urn or sundial, or be used as a subtle barrier to imply a certain direction of movement. They can also be used around trees in paved areas to maintain a

hard surface while discouraging weeds. Bricks are another small-scale element, especially suitable in country gardens and as an infill to more ambitious formal patterns.

Terraces

The terrace—not patio—provides the major horizontal link between the house and its garden. This role is frequently misunderstood, resulting in errors of scale. Historically, the terrace provides the baseboard above which the house rises, and it should, at minimum, have a width of two thirds the height of the house to eaves level. Often, though, a width equal to the full height will produce a better proportion, since there should always be some plants at the foot of the walls to soften the hard right-angle, and these always tend to occupy more space than at first seems possible.

The material of the retaining wall and parapet—if the terrace is raised above surrounding ground level—should be closely related to that of the house; and the surface of the terrace, too, may well make some references to the house in the form of one pattern inlaid into another, garden-related, material. Where the terrace and adjoining lawn are on the same level any form of parapet or balustrade are pointless and make an irritating intrusion into the flow of space. If some kind of break is required, it is better to sink the lawn to allow a step down and then slope it imperceptibly up again, rather than introduce a vertical element between the two. This trick of lowering the ground level around a structure can make it appear far more important than the very slight soil movement involved would seem to imply, and is well worth considering even at the expense of some land drainage.

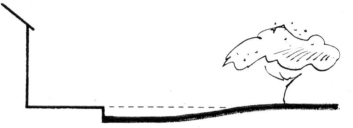

In a hillside garden, there are likely to be several terraces. The first would be purely architectural, decorated with a little planting which would be greatly increased on the second level. The third might still have a formal retaining wall, but a surface of grass and planting, while the fourth might be only of grass with a grass bank linking it to the natural ground levels below. In this way the rigidity of the building would be broken down gradually and invaded by the softening influence of the garden.

Far left: A restrained amount of planting in the paving can reduce the hard effect of a large terrace without reducing its practical value as a sitting area.

This series of terraces down the steep hillside links the house to its wider landscape setting. The lower terraces largely consist of lawn and planting, softening the effect as they meet the natural ground levels.

WATER

Right: The level of water is very important in relation to its visual effect. Here, the side of the pool is set too low making it the focal point, whereas the correct level on the left allows the effect to be softened by the reflection of the plants.

Below: The reflections in this dark water double the value of this beautifully composed planting (*Rodgersia* and *filipendula*), the colouring of which cleverly picks up the tones of the brick wall in the background.

Since water, whether still or moving, attracts the eye more than any other feature in the garden, its placing must be carefully considered. Used formally, it may be designed as a background to water lilies and other aquatic plants, as a still mirror to reflect surrounding planting and other features, or as an area of bright movement, alive with fountains. Whatever the purpose, it is important to get the level correct. All too often one sees the water level set too low, so that the first element reflected is the side of the pool itself. This has the effect of making the surface appear twice as far down as it really is, so reducing its apparent area. Instead, the level should be as close to the surrounding ground as possible so that the side reflection is minimal. Sometimes, indeed, the water can be raised above ground level to gain some special effect, like the former swimming pool at Hidcote which is raised to knee height and seems to fill its yew-hedged enclosure.

Reflection and light

When the aim of the pool is to act as a reflecting mirror the colour of the water is important—the average swimming pool scarcely reflects at all, since the light deflected up from the white or blue interior destroys the reflective quality of the surface. With increasing interest in energy conservation there is a growing use of black as a lining colour, and hopefully we will soon be able to have swimming pools which double as reflectors. Certainly a black background produces the best reflection and it has the added value—from the point of view of

the purely ornamental pool—of giving an appearance of limitless depth, while hiding such elements as plant containers and irregular levels. Even a really shallow pool, perhaps on a roof terrace, can be given apparent depth by this means. Plant groups, statues and even the façades of buildings can benefit greatly by being doubled in the reflected image. In some cases, even, where the position of the object in relation to the observer prevents a clear view, it may be the reflection rather than the reality which is important.

If the direct rays of the sun are excluded—as they may well be naturally, in a woodland clearing or surrounded by high buildings—the reflected sky above appears a much deeper blue and even on dull days the water has a silvery quality which lightens the surroundings. The ability of water to reflect light as well as objects can be extremely useful in town gardens, where it is necessary not only to keep attention firmly within the confines

of the site but also to reflect as much light as possible back into the building. The same occurs in the inner courtyards of large building complexes where conventional gardening is so difficult. A large pool, possibly raised almost to the level of the window ledges with just an access path for the window cleaner outside, will lighten all the rooms around while providing constant interest with fish, water lilies and marginal plants for minimal labour.

Fountains

Now that small electric submersible pumps are easily obtained and fitted, even the most modest garden can have a fountain. It is not only the play of light on the moving water but the sound it makes which is so attractive, and the two things should be considered together. As usual, the simplest solution is generally best and too many of the nozzles produce

irritating, complicated patterns of thin spray which give out a poor sound. Experiments should be made with a plain jet of water set at various heights—which must all fall within the pond even in a wind—since this will often give a

more satisfying result than the spray heads. Birds enjoy fountains, too, and if the water can fall first into a shallow basin before dropping into the pond, they will often use this as a birdbath.

Natural and artificial ponds

When attempting to create naturalistic ponds or streams it is important, first of all, to place them in a natural way in relation to the surrounding landform. Normally water occupies the lowest level, creating a datum to which everything else relates, and so it seldom appears convincing when placed high, especially if the ground is sloping. The surrounding contours, too, must be carefully considered since the edge of the water is in itself a contour line, and if this or the reflection of the adjoining landform look unnatural the whole feature will be exposed as a fraud. When trying for a natural effect there is no substitute for nature itself. Every opportunity should be taken to study, sketch and photograph ponds and streams, taking particular note of the shapes formed by the water, the way in which it flows around or over obstacles, and the exact condition at the edge.

With artificial ponds it is generally the point where land meets water which is the most difficult to handle. If this forms a hiatus, with a shoreline of concrete or lining material, it destroys any natural illusion. In general terms, the material from which the pond is made must be carried up well beyond the intended edge of the water. It should form a shallow angle which will permit a marshy zone merging into a gravel 'beach', exposed only when the water level sinks.

Playing water brings life into the garden not only through movement but also through the light reflected from the water surface.

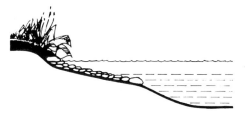

LAWNS

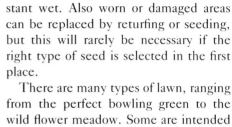

Grass

Grass, or lawn, plays a passive role in the structure of the garden, and the eye passes unconsciously over it to rest on the more dominant surrounding features, for which it acts as a foil. As the 'carpet' of the garden it is likely to take up the largest overall amount of space, so careful thought should be given to the finished shape and proportion. As a general rule the proportion of mass to void in a garden should be one to three, the lawn counting as a void. In small town gardens, however, it is often impossible to maintain this ratio and, along with the borders, walls and paving, the tiny patch of grass will look out of place. It interrupts the eye and makes the garden appear even smaller, as well as being a problem to mow. Here it is better to use gravel, or to continue the paving over the whole area.

Types of lawn

A lawn, whether seeded or turf, is inexpensive and quick to establish; it is easy to maintain and it can adapt to most

situations except heavy shade and constant wet. Also worn or damaged areas can be replaced by returfing or seeding, but this will rarely be necessary if the right type of seed is selected in the first place.

There are many types of lawn, ranging from the perfect bowling green to the wild flower meadow. Some are intended primarily for visual effect and will never receive much use, so they can be sown with a very fine seed. For normal family use, however, the lawn should be able to withstand walking, sitting and games, so a more robust mixture of decorative and utility grasses is recommended. Here the odd daisy or buttercup is quite acceptable.

It is not easy to establish grass under trees or in shade, as the roots of the tree use up the moisture and cast-off needles of cedar or pine create a 'thatch' through which the grass cannot breathe. However, special blends to cope with this are available from most seed merchants.

In less formal parts of the garden a 'rough-cut' lawn, underplanted with bulbs, looks very attractive and gives a rural effect, especially in orchards or under clumps of birch trees. As the bulb foliage dies down the grass grows to conceal it, and then in June, when the fragile display of Queen Anne's lace and other early wild flowers is over, the grass can be cut. For ease of walking a path can be mown in the long grass, and this will link the formal and informal parts of the garden.

Flowering meadows adrift with poppies and cornflowers can look wonderful but are much more difficult to establish than is generally supposed. It is not enough to scatter a few packets of wild flower seeds into existing grass, as the coarse grasses will quickly swamp the few that do manage to establish themselves. To be really effective the whole operation must be started from scratch. Weed-free, infertile soil, low in nitrogen, should be prepared and then sown with a

The broad expanse of this well-maintained lawn creates a calm introduction to the view of the distant landscape.

non-invasive mixture of grass seed. Wild flower seeds, carefully selected for the particular soil and degree of dampness, should form 15 to 20 per cent of this seed mixture. If the seed is mixed with fine sand it will spread more evenly, otherwise the grass seed, being heavier, will come out of the drills first and the flowers later, leaving a patchy effect. The meadow should only be mown in early spring and late summer and all the cuttings should be removed.

Planning the shape of a lawn

The shape of the lawn can be rectangular, curving, circular, geometric or totally informal. But whatever form is chosen it should always be bold and simple to offset the more intricate nature of the planting, or to enhance specimen trees. Any curves should be smooth and generous, making allowances for the foreshortening that occurs when the lawn is seen from the ground rather than on plan. To create curves that are as satisfactory on the ground as they are on plan, it is advisable to mark out the lawn with a long length of hose or coloured string. The design can then be viewed from various angles and levels and, when finalized, be marked by sprinkling sand along the outlines.

If a circle under a tree is to be kept clear for paving or a seat, peg a piece of string in the centre, attach a cane or skewer to the end of the string at the required distance and plot the circle on the ground. An established tree is a valuable feature in a new lawn, providing a feeling of age as well as attractive shade and shadows, and if the ground beneath it is kept clear it will not suffer by being damaged by the mower.

Mowing considerations

The mower should be taken into account, too, when planning the shape of the lawn. A small mower can negotiate tight corners, but for more generous sweeps a bigger machine is better. Any narrow strips of lawn, behind a border for instance, should be the same width as the mower. The stripes left by a cylinder mower can also be incorporated into the design. These may be straight up or down, cut on the diagonal or curved to form flowing lines. In a formal garden the chequer-board pattern, created by moving first up and down and then across, is very dramatic. Slopes in the lawn should be natural and not too steep, or they will have to be cut with a rotary mower which is a slow and hazardous business.

Left: Neat mown grass strips bordered by rough-cut grass offset the curve of the path, separating the formal from the informal elements.

Below: The bold stripes left by the mowing emphasize the length of the lawn and lead the eye to the enclosures beyond.

HEDGES

The junction between the lawn and the path can be kept neat with narrow timber strips to prevent the 'shrinking' of the lawn that occurs after several years of trimming with an edging tool.

Hedges

From the very earliest times, walls and hedges have been used by man to define the boundaries of his property and for protection against intruders and the elements. Present day man, a less patient creature than his forbears, is inclined to erect a wall or fence in preference to a hedge, an instant, maintenance-free barrier being considered more suitable for his needs. A hedge, however, can provide effective shelter from wind, screening from neighbours or unsightly buildings, a barrier against livestock, and a background to borders, as well as delineating boundaries. It also provides a valuable habitat for wildlife, allowing birds and hedgehogs to live undisturbed.

Contrary to popular belief, a hedge can be established quite quickly, provided the species chosen and the soil type are suitable and that the ground has been very thoroughly prepared. As the hedge will be a permanent feature within the garden, the first thing to establish is the function that it must fulfil, which will determine the height and width.

Boundaries and screening

For boundary or screening purposes the tallest plants are beech (*Fagus sylvatica*) which prefers a lighter soil, or hornbeam (*Carpinus betulus*) which can cope with heavier moist conditions. In both cases, the brown leaves persist during winter months until very strong winds or the new season's growth pushes them off. The coniferous evergreen, Western red cedar (*Thuya plicata*), which grows to approximately 3m (10ft), is fast growing and useful on the perimeter of a property, or to hide adjacent buildings, and can

Although hedges are normally planted in straight lines, the sinuous curves of these beech hedges create an exciting effect of motion.

be more easily controlled than the ubiquitous *Cupressocyparis* x *leylandii* (4.5 metres—15 ft—or more), seen everywhere, but effective if kept carefully trimmed. Both are gross feeders, depleting the soil of moisture and nutrients, making it difficult to establish any other growth in the immediate vicinity and tending to become bare or brown at the base due to lack of light; as with all hedges, this can be overcome by clipping with a slight batter which allows snow to slide off without the hedge breaking in the middle.

Both these conifers are prone to permanent damage from wind, the brown scorched foliage being frequently seen in the colder, more exposed areas of Britain. Yew (*Taxus baccata*) the aristocrat of hedging and thought of as a low-growing conifer, can reach 3m (10ft) quite quickly if really well fed with Vitax Q4 or a mixture of dried blood, hoof and horn, but it requires good drainage and must be kept irrigated and protected from scorching winds until established. It is also poisonous to animals so needs to be carefully sited.

Internal hedges

For internal hedging, or demarcation within the garden, and a height requirement of 1.5–3 m (5–10ft), there is a wide choice which can be divided into formal or informal. Yew and the common holly (*Ilex aquifolium*) are most useful for architectural effects, the latter having vandalproof prickles, the dark sombre green foliage of both providing a useful backcloth for more colourful planting. Privet, used for so long in suburban gardens in its common dark green form, can, by utilizing the golden form *Ligustrum ovalifolium* 'Aureum', 2.5m (8ft), give the impression of a shaft of sunlight into the darkest area. The Chinese honeysuckle (*Lonicera nitida*), 1.5m (5ft), also has golden relatives, but tends to become leggy and brittle when mature, and therefore although inexpensive, is

unsuitable for long term planning. The common laurel (*Prunus laurocerasus*) is a glossy alternative, ideal for shady or polluted atmospheric conditions, but it must be cut with secateurs, not shears, which cut straight across the leaf, leaving a nasty scar. An unusual marbled effect can be achieved by planting a mixture of common and copper beech, holly and hawthorn, known as a tapestry hedge.

Above: Golden yew buttresses create dramatic effect against a dark yew backcloth.

Below: Purple-leaved beech is an unusual alternative to green hedges and provides an excellent dark foil for planting.

67

Informal hedges

Informal hedging is frequently over-looked and under-used, particularly considering the possible advantages of flowers and berries. The many varieties of barberry (*Berberis*) and firethorn (*Pyracantha*) also have discouraging thorns, as do many of the old-fashioned species roses suitable for hedging. *Griselinia littoralis* and escallonia thrive in coastal areas, but are liable to frost damage when grown inland, whereas the sea buckthorn (*Hippophae rhamnoides*) is wind resistant and salt tolerant, surviving on arid soils and inland, and producing translucent orange red berries from September till February.

Low-growing hedges

For compact low-growing hedges, or those under 2m (6ft), box, a native British evergreen, can be an effective outline, either in bush form (*Buxus sempervirens*) or the lower growing form (*Buxus suffruticosa*). Lavender provides a scented hedge, particularly successful in conjunction with roses, and to provide a relaxed but formal edge to a mixed or herbaceous border.

Planting

Most deciduous stock should be planted between mid-October and April, while conifers are planted in late September–October, or between March and early April. The distance between individual plants will depend on the species, but if planted too close together, some may die through being choked, leaving an awkward gap. As the hedge grows wider, there will be less food and moisture for each plant, which makes single row planting healthier and more successful than a staggered double row. Plant preferably in straight lines, these being the best foil to the natural curves of foliage and flower and easier to pursue with shears or secateurs, and trim as often as necessary, either once a year (usually in autumn) or twice (July/August and October) or as often as necessary to retain a formal shape.

Pleaching

Pleaching really means the interweaving or training of branches to create a framework, often seen as a hedge on stilts. In this case only subjects which can be trained to provide a single clear stem up to a height of 2m (6ft) or more can be used, the most usual species being our native lime (*Tilia cordata* or *T. platyphyllos*), less likely to produce unsightly suckers than the common lime, and hornbeam (*Carpinus*), but it is quite possible to use a number of other species, provided their early growth is fairly pliable.

By planting a line of trees to be pleached at the rear of a hedge, a two-tier hedge effect can be achieved, which, if there is sufficient space, looks softer and more interesting than a single tall screen. A simple framework of verticals and wires is needed to establish the framework, the selected laterals then being tied across them and clipped or pruned often enough to retain the shape.

Pleaching can be used to create tun-

Rows of pleached hornbeams are clipped into shape to form a hedge on stilts.

nels or arbours, or is a very effective and amusing method of making a garden room, the contortions and writhings of the bare winter branches making a fascinating design, distracting the eye from the view beyond.

Topiary

Topiary is the use of shears or secateurs to train trees and shrubs into architectural form, but usually without any visible framework. In Henry VIII's time at Hampton Court this shaping was done by a 'toparius'—a gardener particularly skilled in this craft, and much sought after, a box hedge sometimes being clipped into emblems or the owner's crest.

Topiary continues to be an important feature in the sculpture of the garden, not just on large estates but also in small cottage gardens, where the amusing, fanciful shapes are often the creation of the owner. This formal treatment is also most appropriate in an urban setting, outside town houses, where hawthorn, pyracantha or any other reasonably stiff plant material may be trained to echo the shape of the front door.

The most frequently seen topiary is carried out on yew, the matt dark green foliage standing out well against the more fluid shapes and varied colours of other foliage and flowers. Either an existing shrub can be clipped into the required shape by using a template or string to ensure an accurate line, or, if the required effect is to be on top of a hedge, a main leader with several subsidiary leaders should be encouraged at regular intervals.

When these are large enough, two or three should be selected and tied to a framework of canes or wood, which will eventually encourage the leaders to branch out so that they can then be cut to the desired shape. The shoots should be tied loosely with thick tarred string.

Informal Structure

Besides the more obvious structural elements of hedges, avenues and pleached screens, there are others which are equally important but far more subtle. The informal garden, too, must have an underlying structure if it is not to degenerate into an aimless mass of wandering beds, and it is this planting to define space, frame a view or provide a counterbalance to landform that must be considered here.

Even the smallest garden needs a tree to give a sense of vertical scale; the placing of this tree in relation to the ground plan is of vital importance. Very often the single tree will have to fulfil several functions—of shade, shelter from prying eyes and concealment of neighbouring buildings—which may well mean that it has to be positioned first and the rest of the plan evolved around it. In larger gardens groups or single trees may be arranged to lead the eye to a view or even to frame that view. A bold vertical clump can be poised against a cross fall, while rounded tree forms may crown new ground shaping to emphasize an effect of height.

On a smaller scale, shrubs—planted in large clumps of a single variety rather than as beds of garden-centre collections—can fulfil similar functions, or provide a horizontal counter-point to the trees, helping to create those arrangements of mass and void which are discussed on page 42.

Above: Clipped yew hounds running along the top of the hedge provide a witty touch to this formal garden.

DESIGNING WITH PLANTS

Form

To create their effect plants rely on the three attributes of form, texture and colour, but it is form that we appreciate first in the wider context of landscape or garden. All trees and shrubs, and even some herbaceous plants, have a significant outline which is clearly defined and unique to themselves. How else can we tell an oak, an ash or a beech at a distance too great to observe details of bark or foliage?

When studying plants in relation to garden design it is therefore important to take careful note of the specific form of a well-grown specimen at the outset, and to realize that several specimens of the same plant, closely grouped, will retain the outline of a single member but on a larger scale. The eighteenth-century clump of beech in the park and the twentieth-century bed of one variety of rhododendron on the lawn read as a single massive beech or an outsize rhododendron. This knowledge is useful in larger-scale work where a single plant would take too long to achieve the desired effect, or would appear too small in its context. When Le Nôtre needed a pair of Lombardy poplars to flank the end of the main canal at Versailles, he had to plant a clump of several trees in order to achieve a sufficiently bold outline when seen from a distance.

Texture

To begin with, therefore, planting design is a question of making arrangements of abstract objects to achieve a satisfactory balance of shapes, having a certain height and width, to occupy the space available. This can be drawn up as an elevation, or a series of elevations, and altered until the composition when seen in the imagination from all angles is entirely pleasing. Once this has been achieved it is time to consider the next attribute, that of texture. Just as plants have individual shapes, so each has a particular texture. They may be fine or coarse, absorb or reflect light, hold or reject shadow. They may resemble fur or

The specific shape and texture of senecio is brought out here by the close-grouping of several specimens.

A strong architectural feature should be balanced by an equally bold group of planting. In this case, a group of *Phormium tenax* echoes the diagonal boarding of the summerhouse.

velvet, wool or suede, metal or even plastic, and all this has nothing to do with colour, although it may well affect the way in which the colour is perceived.

The shapes which have been previously arranged can now become clothed with texture. A fine textured, light-absorbent group will be needed to display a coarse, light-reflecting individual, the metallic placed against the feathery, the heavily ribbed against the smooth and so on.

Seasonal variations

These arrangements and decisions would be comparatively simple if it were not for the fact that garden design is an art form with four dimensions, the fourth being that of time. Nothing in the garden is static: constantly leaves expand and fall, plants grow or decline in response to the rhythm of the months or the advancing years. In the garden even time is not static for there is short-term time, with the changes effected automatically by

The striking vertical shape and woolly texture of the verbascum contrasts nicely with the horizontal lines of the brick wall and edging.

71

the seasons and constantly renewed, and the long-term time of the total growth-cycle of the plants, which may range from two years to two hundred or more. Inevitably this element of time influences both the arrangement of forms and the contrast of textures.

Even evergreens are not entirely unaffected by the seasons, for in spring they mostly put on new growth which changes both texture and colour to a greater or lesser extent. But it is among deciduous plants that the change is most obvious: certain subjects which create powerful sculptural forms for six or seven months of the year—for instance hosta or gunnera—can be almost totally absent for the remainder. Shrubs like *Rhus typhina*, with its strongly defined fern-like foliage, become so sparse in winter that they appear to have the bare elegance of a Chinese drawing, while a large philadelphus or deutzia is a solid mass of twigs and only semi-transparent. A dominant element of form or texture at one season can therefore be missing at another, while a fine textured, light-absorbent group which plays a supporting role in summer may have a powerful winter presence because it is evergreen, while its neighbours are deciduous.

These seasonal variations mean that there must be four, rather than one, sets of planting elevations made on which to define textural effects, since the balance and emphasis may change completely. There is a tendency to think that spring and autumn, when the plants are not fully clothed with foliage, will be much the same, but this is not the case. In spring a deciduous shrub or tree will be completely covered with small, partly unfurled leaves, giving a semi-transparent appearance to the whole. In autumn it will be irregularly grouped with full-scale foliage creating a different, more blotched and random appearance.

Planting for the future

In the long-term, the problem becomes not so much a question of the variation of texture as the progressive change of scale. The landscape designer has to ensure that a planting scheme is reasonably effective during its first year, but unless there is some specific cut-off point because the client will only remain in the house for a limited time, it must also be clear that in five, fifteen or twenty years the appearance, while changing, will steadily improve. A serious designer, properly attuned to the perspective of history, will also try to ensure the future of the landscape as a whole by planting well grouped trees and slow-growing shrubs, which will flourish far into the next century.

Such planting for the future can create certain problems. In general, long-lived trees and shrubs will take up considerable space but grow comparatively slowly. If they are planted at the correct distance for their eventual size, the grouping will appear sparse and flimsy for

The brilliant 'white washed' stems of the ornamental bramble (*rubus cockburnianus*) makes an unusual winter picture against an evergreen background. An effect which will last well into spring.

Left: In spring, the skeleton of the *Liriodendron tulipfera* is clearly visible through the young foliage.

Right: In autumn, the mature leaves which remain on the tree reveal some parts of the structure which gives a more random effect.

many years, but if impatience causes them to be placed too close together they will eventually become misshapen and possibly sickly. Fortunately there are a number of fast-growing, short-lived shrubs which can be used as fillers: there are also many fast-growing trees, but these take too much from the ground, and therefore from the development of the permanent plants, to be of much use.

When thinking about the time-scale, therefore, the first essential is to consider the long-term trees, when appropriate. They should be grouped carefully in relation to the contours, so whatever development occurs in the next two hundred years or so they are likely to be retained as being essential to the quality of the landscape. Where trees only are in question it may be possible to interplant with crataegus, malus, pyrus, sorbus and other more ephemeral subjects to give bulk and colour in the early years, but the wide-ranging shallow roots of birch and prunus are best avoided. Then come the large-scale, long-lived shrubs such as magnolia, camellia, rhododendron and many others. Spaced correctly for future growth they leave wide gaps which can be partly filled by *Lupinus arboreus*, plus species of cistus, cytisus, senecio,

spiraea, elder and other rapid growers suitable to the soil and situation. These will not only fill the bare spaces in early years but will give a degree of shade and protection to their slower neighbours, providing that sufficient space is allowed so they do not swamp or malform the growth of the permanent planting.

Bedding plants

Even so, the effect will still be thin in the first year or two, and that is where bedding plants come into play. To many people the word 'bedding' suggests only municipal flowerbeds packed with brightly coloured flowers, but because one has only seen a plant badly used, there is no excuse for not thinking of ways in which it could be better employed. A great flood of pale 'Cambridge Blue' lobelia will unite any number of young shrubs into a single, cool composition, while trailing nasturtiums quickly cover the ground with their strong textures and colours. Nicotiana, with its bold leaves and small spikes of flower, gives a satisfactory appearance of bulk—the dwarf variety, of course, must be avoided in this context—and careful analysis of flower-seed lists or boxes of plants at the garden centre will reveal hundreds of other possibilities according to the particular situation. It is important, however, not to choose plants of flimsy appearance—nigella or nemesia for instance—since these underline rather than conceal the thin nature of the permanent planting.

For the first two, or even three, years such instant solutions may be necessary to give an effect of unity, but by then the fast shrubs will have filled out and for five or six years they will hold the group together. Then they will begin to look poor and will have to be taken out gradually to reveal the increased stature of their slower neighbours. Even so, there will be spaces, but this time they can be filled with suitable ground-cover plants, choosing those which are not so rampant that they inhibit the growth of the shrubs. In the more open areas there may be bulbs for the spring or lilies to give spots of colour among the heavy summer foliage. Gradually, as branches from adjoining groups grow together, the ground-cover plants will be largely suppressed and shaded out, but this does not matter since the final effect is complete.

The character of plants

Ask any group of gardeners if there are any plants which they dislike, and they will come up with a dozen or more names of subjects whose only fault may be that they are so often badly grown or used in an unintelligent way.

To be a serious student of planting design it is essential to forget all preconceived ideas—this is a vegetable, that a herb, this shrub is ugly, that tree is commonplace—and see the plant as it really is. Note its habit of growth, its texture, its seasonal variations, its good habits and its bad ones. Plants do have bad habits, quite apart from the general one of not wishing to grow where we want them. Some, like camellias, have the annoying habit of holding their dead blooms, so that only the first flush of flower is effective while the remainder have to compete with a brown withering background. Others, including several conifers, are enchanting when young and very dowdy in middle age. Yet again there are plants with delightful flowers which are seen too briefly, leaving us with months of boring foliage and an unattractive habit of growth. The list is endless and needs to be compiled afresh by every student, for there is no substitute for looking at plants, not just when they are at their best but at every season. Preferably one should try to grow as many as possible oneself, since that is the way to know them best, and if this appears a counsel of perfection it is no excuse for not making the attempt. For a professional designer a year or two working in a good nursery garden with a wide range of plant material can be very beneficial. Not only the visual characteristics but also the cultural requirements, propagation, speed of growth, planting techniques and every other aspect of plant life can be studied at first hand. Above all never, ever choose a plant just on the evidence of a catalogue description or a brief sighting at a flower show. If you do, your scheme can only succeed by accident rather than design.

Colour in the garden

Another attribute, and generally the first to be considered, is colour. People have strange ideas on the subject, insisting 'I do like colour' or 'I must have colour'. But is not green a colour, or at least an infinite variety of colours of the greatest subtlety, from which any number of gardens of interest could be made, especially in the city where the eye is constantly assaulted by bright and everchanging hues? This obsession with colour is very strange, since colour, by itself, achieves nothing but hectic variety—an effect seen all too often in gardens. It is the way in which the colour is used, rather than the quantity employed, which is all important.

Foliage colour

The first thing to remember is that flowers—which are normally considered to be the main source of garden colour—are very ephemeral. Many of the species employed are only in full beauty for two or three weeks, while we have to look at them for fifty-two weeks of the year, so it follows that for continuity of colour we should rely upon foliage. There is, after all, a wide range to choose from: yellows and golds, reds, crimsons and purples, greys, blues and an infinite number of variations in anything from white and cream to copper pink and pale apricot. One can create very satisfying colour

A subtle arrangement of helleborus and euphorbia showing striking grouping which uses only shades of green to achieve its effect.

A single colour grouping arranged for effect. Here a red scheme is beautifully set off by the purple-brown leaves of the dracaena and *prunus pissardi* in the background.

Left: Simple colour themes and textures make successful compositions. Here the cool blue of the massed groups of *myosotis* unify the complicated patterns of the topiary specimens.

borders using no other medium than coloured leaves, both evergreen and deciduous, perhaps sharpened up in season by associated bulbs and lilies. But the colour-seekers are not satisfied by leaves, and if they must have colour they must also have flowers. The main continuity of the colouring, though, can be maintained through foliage, while the flowers ebb and flow, perhaps highlighting different areas at different times, just as spotlights will subtly change the emphasis of a stage set to accord with the action.

Colour and space

Colour is not simply an abstract quality but can be used creatively to change the apparent nature of a space. A cold looking, north-facing garden can appear much warmer if planted with all the fire colours—not merely golds and yellows, which can imply sunlight but not necessarily warmth, but also pale oranges, apricot pinks and flashes of scarlet. On the other hand, a south-facing courtyard, hemmed in by walls which reflect the heat, can feel degrees cooler with the use

of frosty silver foliage, cold blues and icy whites. If a boundary is too close it can be faded out and made to appear more remote by the use of 'distance' colours of misty blue and grey, while a small town garden can seem large if the edges are planted out with dim greens and purples, using leaves which hold deep shadow beneath them, to suggest a jungle clearing surrounded by mysterious hanging curtains of creepers which, at a touch, will swing aside to reveal further glades beyond.

Colour and light

Here again the question of light must be considered. In many northern countries, including Britain, the light is not only soft but is always tinged with blue, so all the rather faded colours—pale pinks, vague mauves and grey blues—gain vibrance from the blueness of the atmosphere. Under a more brilliant southern sun such colouring merely appears washed out and lifeless, while a dashing arrangement of orange and bright pink, wonderfully stimulating in the south, has

Opposite: An occasional clash of colour is very stimulating if carefully controlled, but only one should be visible at a time, and an arch of cool colouring is needed before the next bold grouping can be attempted.

77

a strangely flat and vulgar look beneath a northern sky. In general, pale colours need shade and brilliant hues require the fullest degree of light to be effective. A scarlet flower placed in shadow appears almost black, while a rhododendron which is palest pink in the woodland garden is seen as dirty white in full sun. The way in which light strikes a surface also affects its apparent colour. Holly and yew have about the same tone and depth of green, but because the holly leaf is shiny it appears to be much lighter.

In Britain the colouring of the different seasons is very distinctive. Spring is clear, pale and rather cold, with primroses, apple blossom, bluebells and the various white flowers of crataegus, prunus and others. Early summer is still clear but warmer, with rose pink and reds, clear blues and yellows, while by high summer the colouring is heavy and a little muddy, the rather mid-Victorian purples, oranges and crimsons. In autumn of course we have the warmth of bright scarlet, yellow and gold. Thanks to the activity of hybridizers we can completely ignore these traditional colourings in the garden if we wish, and have a scarlet spring or a cool pink autumn, but it is always worth considering if this is the most effective thing to do. Generally it is better to exploit the essential quality of each season to the full rather than fight against it, but in countries where the differences are less pronounced the problem does not arise.

Colour in context

Some thought should also be given to colour in the context of place as well as season. Within the garden there is no doubt that any form, however artificial, and any colour, however strange, may be used if it is part of a carefully considered scheme. But in, or even against a background of, a rolling landscape of green fields and woods, a golden chamaecyparis, blue cedar or purple acer looks distinctly out of place. It does nothing to

enhance the natural scenery and can only appear as an alien intrusion quite unrelated to its surroundings. Perhaps on a more subjective level, buildings with strong period characteristics such as a thatched Tudor cottage, or prim Queen Anne manor, seem to demand plants and colourings in tune with their particular style. Not necessarily only plants of that particular age—a far too restrictive aim—but at least those which are not strongly at variance with it. Scarlet rhododendrons against a background of beams and latticed windows are more suggestive of suburbia than Shakespeare.

Planting for colour effects

How then, should colour be used? The simplest way is to follow nature and do one thing at a time: nothing could be more perfect than a bank of primroses or wood full of bluebells. It may be argued that this shows a prodigal use of ground and is only possible in the large, landscaped garden, but this is not necessarily the case. Essentially there are four levels in the garden: bulbs, herbs, shrubs and trees. In its simplest form, therefore, four distinct effects can occur on the same area of ground and with careful mingling—for instance with autumn crocus as well as daffodils in the bulb layer—and the use of subjects which have both spring flowers and autumnal coloured foliage, this number can be greatly increased. The trick with garden-

Opposite above: The typical colouring of spring is pale and clear. Here the composition is helped by the blue door which adds a note of deeper colour.

Opposite below: As the season advances the colouring gets progressively warmer.

Below: The garden's context is an important factor in determining the choice of colour schemes. The soft tones of Gertrude Jekyll's planting do not distract the eye from the view beyond.

One simple effect at a time is often the most effective way, especially when garden and countryside meet. By skilful interplanting several separate displays can be obtained from the same area of ground.

ing of this kind is to keep the periods of display quite separate, rather than attempt continuity which will result in messy intermediate periods when one effect is going off and another beginning.

The next very simple way is to use only one colour at a time, perhaps with a contrasting or toning range of foliage as, for instance, grey foliage with a yellow scheme, or brown and purple with orange. The only difficulty then is to ensure a good balance between deep, medium and pale tones and an equally good balance of colour throughout the

area to be covered at any one time. It is quite difficult to make a bad mistake, and the effect is usually good. Yellow, red and orange schemes always work well, as can blue although it needs touches of palest yellow to bring it to life. Purple looks rather dead unless spiced with touches of crimson and magenta, and white is often misunderstood. White is a very powerful and positive colour, not a negative one as some people imagine, and attempts to use it as a neutral between groups of other colourings generally end with the white becoming too dominant for its surroundings. White schemes work well if they contain some off-whites and plenty of white variegated foliage to break the colour down at the edges, but hard white flowers in a setting of dark green leaves are more startling than attractive.

It seems that flower and foliage colours are based either on blue or yellow. In the blue range are all the hard whites—it is the blue undertone which makes them so brilliant—all the bluish pinks of old roses, magenta and fuchsia colours, crimson reds, blues and purples. In the yellow range are warm whites, creams, ivories, apricot pinks, scarlet reds, oranges and golds. Any of the colours within either group look well together and it is only between the groups that clashes can occur. Not that there is anything wrong with a good clash, but it should be designed rather than accidental and should not occur more than once in a single view.

Perhaps the most satisfying way is to create harmonies, building tone against tone, to some interesting climax and then descending the scale using a different set of tones to reach a period of quiet foliage before starting upon a different grouping.

Never be afraid to use unconventional material. Many vegetables such as beetroot, parsley or Swiss chard are very decorative, as are a number of wild flowers which can be grown from seed, or plants widely regarded as too ordinary. There is nothing whatever wrong with golden privet, speckled laurel or scarlet pelargoniums, for instance, provided they are not badly used, neglected or grown in a stereotyped manner which is not attractive. If the soil and exposure are correct—an important point since nothing looks worse than a collection of sickly plants—it is possible to use anything which will add to the quality of the scheme in question. The most dangerous element, which must be avoided at all cost, is the impulse buy: the pretty but irrelevant plant, bought on the spur of the moment, for which there is no designed place in the garden.

The soft English light, always faintly tinged with blue, gives added richness to pale colour groupings.

CHOOSING PLANTS

Every successful garden, no matter the size, should contain a variety of different elements, leading the observer effortlessly from one part to another. This is the true art of garden design, often difficult to achieve, especially when faced with a flat, featureless, rectangular plot. In design terms, the best way of approaching the problem is to divide up the garden into a series of different spaces each with its own character and identity.

Special consideration needs to be given, for instance, to the front as well as the back of the house, to the sitting-out area at the rear and to the more informal sectors towards the end of the garden. Other governing factors to be taken into account prior to planting are orientation, amounts of rainfall, exposure to wind, varying degrees of sunshine and shade and, of course, the nature of the soil.

These factors have already been discussed in some detail but it is worth repeating that it is vitally important to plot the north, south, east and west aspects, to establish which areas receive sun and which partial or total shade, to check the moisture or lack of it (remembering that rain seldom reaches beds adjacent to walls and under house eaves), and to assess the quantity and quality of the soil, assuming this has been thoroughly prepared, incorporating whatever additional nutrients and conditioning agents, such as peat, compost or well rotted manure, that may be necessary for optimum plant growth. Bear in mind especially that whereas most plants will grow in a neutral or moderately acid soil—which can be altered if need be with a little extra lime—no plant requiring an acid soil will really be happy in one that contains much lime.

Planting plan

We have already dealt with plant design in terms of form, texture and colour, suggesting harmonious combinations and seasonal effects. Here we give more detailed consideration to plants and planting effects for particular situations and conditions. You should already have a clear idea of a planting plan in general terms—the height and shape of trees, the visual weight of those masses which are to be represented by plant material, the texture of voids, and the impression which each part of the garden is intended to convey. You will also have taken account of the special factors described above. It is now time to give careful thought to particular areas, bearing in mind that no hard and fast rules can possibly apply to every situation and that every garden has an individual character.

The frontage

First impressions are important, setting the scene and providing a clue to the style of the garden and its owner. The approach and entrance, therefore, require special consideration.

In order to maintain a good impression throughout the year, it is a good idea to make use of evergreens and contrasting foliage, the solid and glossy against the light and feathery, the vertical forms of slender conifers against the rounded

Right: When space for an avenue is lacking, a dignified approach can be created by flanking the entrance path with rows of pleached lime trees, giving a similar effect on a smaller scale.

shapes of box or the horizontals of low cotoneasters or creeping junipers. As a general rule, bold and simple effects have the greatest impact and are the most appropriate.

A country property with a reasonably long drive can be dignified by an avenue of trees, the planting distance depending on whether the shapes are fastigiate or spreading. Handsome links between gateway and house are provided by avenues of lime (*Tilia* x *euchlora* is a variety which does not 'drip' in summer), the evergreen or holm oak (*Quercus ilex*), beech (*Fagus sylvatica*), Norway maple (*Acer platanoides*) or horse chestnut (*Aesculus hippocastanum*).

Avenues on a smaller scale might comprise the mountain ash (*Sorbus aucuparia*), flowering cherry (*Prunus avium*) or hawthorn (*Crataegus oxyacantha*), all of them charming in spring when flowering or in autumn when turning colour or laden with berries. The trees should be planted sufficiently far back from the drive to allow a generous sweep of grass, which can be close mown at the front and left longer towards the back, perhaps with bulbs and wild flowers for interest.

The house walls may form part of the planting scheme. Narrow borders beneath north-facing walls might be planted with *Skimmia japonica*, with a sufficient number of males to ensure a brilliant display of autumn berries, backed, if space permits, by groups of tall red-flowered varieties of *Camellia japonica*. Large groups of *Mahonia japonica* and *Aucuba japonica* 'Crotonoides' could effectively be backed by the dark foliage of *Garrya elliptica* or contrasted with the feathery bamboo *Arundinaria nitida*.

With white house walls effective seasonal colour can be supplied by pots of dwarf scarlet tulips in spring and scarlet geraniums in summer. If the walls are of red brick, white subjects can be used for contrast.

South-facing frontages would provide an opportunity to use the fresh evergreen

foliage of *Choisya ternata*, dark-leafed, white-flowered cistus and *Escallonia iveyi*, against the bold architectural forms of the loquat (*Eriobotria japonica*) and the evergreen *Magnolia grandiflora*.

Even with a town house where space is lacking for any grand garden gesture, the most windswept doorstep can generally support a neatly clipped pyramid box or bay, adequately fed and watered, and the foliage sprayed with water at regular intervals. If window boxes are used, it is important to aim at a simplicity in scale with the building, preferably choosing one type and colour of flower and one supporting foliage plant. Hanging baskets for a balcony or a large porch must be beautifully planted and maintained.

In a rural setting, in particular, borders should have a backbone of evergreens— lavender, rosemary, cistus or rue— perhaps punctuated by simple topiary in box or yew; and the house walls can be clothed in part by ivy or evergreen honeysuckle. Roses, where employed as a major feature on the front of a house, should be recurrent bloomers and perhaps semi-evergreen like 'Mermaid' or 'Albéric Barbier', rather than species with only one brief moment of glory.

Strong pyramids of box, backed by a yew hedge and linked by a simple planting of myosotis, give character to this path. A group of chairs and a table close to the front door suggest hospitality and yet are concealed from the street.

83

Terraces and patios

The sitting-out area of the back garden, perhaps in the form of terrace, court or patio, will necessarily be sunny and sheltered, either by walls and buildings or by hedges and shelter belts. This is a place for intimate planting. Striped roses, laced pinks and polyanthus, striped and feathered tulips, frilled double petunias and many 'artificial' looking flowers which might seem out of place in the open garden may all find an appropriate setting here.

Scent, too, is desirable near the house, and may be obtained not only from ephemeral plantings of nicotiana, sweet rocket (*Hesperis matronalis*), night-scented stock (*Matthiola bicornis*) and pots of lilies, but also from aromatic shrubs and those with sweetly scented flowers. Some of the best aromatics are rosemary and lavender, the gum cistus (*Cistus ladanifer*) and some of its hybrids, lemon-scented verbena (*Aloysia triphylla*), myrtles, *Choisya ternata* and, where there is room, the sweet bay. Although most of the shrubs with fragrant flowers bloom before it is really warm enough to sit out, it is worth planting *Viburnum carlesii* and its varieties, spicily scented clove carnations, and the delightful, neat evergreen *Osmanthus* x *burkwoodii*. There are also numerous varieties of philadelphus (the so-called mock orange), with heavily scented flowers in June, the spicy *Calycanthus floridus* in July, and the curious honey scents of buddleias in August and September.

A sheltered area near the house which receives late morning sun in winter might encourage the creation of a complete winter garden. Although blooms may be small and ineffective individually, when massed they can have a striking impact. For height there is the winter-flowering cherry (*Prunus subhirtella* 'Autumnalis') or, on acid soils, the witch hazel (*Hamamelis mollis*), whose thread-like flowers are pleasantly scented. Both the winter sweet (*Chimonanthus fragrans*), which needs a warm wall to ripen its shoots, and the less fussy *Lonicera fragrantissima* smell sweetly in the sharp, clean air, as do the almost invisible flowers of *Azara microphylla*, a handsome evergreen for a warm corner. In a shadier spot there might be a bold planting of the strikingly foliaged *Mahonia japonica*, with sprays of pale lemon-yellow flowers that smell strongly of lily-of-the-valley.

Walls and climbers

There are climbers suitable for walls of any aspect, but where there is little or no soil it is best to plant something like a fig, whose handsome leaves require little soil to support them, or Virginia creeper (*Parthenocissus quinquefolia*), whose over-enthusiasm can be curbed by restricted root space and poor soil.

Few climbers grow of their own accord. There are the so-called twiners, like the sweetly scented white jasmine (*Jasminum officinale*), and its handsome variants with gold or silver variegated foliage; and others, such as clematis, which cling by means of a specially adapted leaf stalk that wraps itself around small supports. In both cases vertical wires must be provided so that the plants can grown upwards; better still, the entire wall may be covered with coarse mesh wire netting, secured and held slightly away from the wall face by vine eyes driven into the brickwork. All twiners will quickly rise to the top of the wire and hang down in graceful festoons and curtains of foliage.

Of the true climbers, the best known is the ivy in all its many green and variegated forms. Provided the brick or stone work is sound, ivy will do no damage and is an excellent way of furnishing an otherwise bleak or shaded location. Other favourites are the various types of Virginia creeper, which cling by small suction pads and cover large areas with sheets of brilliant autumn colour. Ensure that there is sufficient space for

Many shrubs can be trained against walls with very good effect. Here *Hydrangea sargentiana* displays its fine foliage much better than if it were free standing.

the vigorous growth. Of these the most attractive is *Parthenocissus henryana*, which prefers a shady wall for its beautiful purple-backed leaves striped with silver.

For a shady wall, the climbing hydrangea (*Hydrangea petiolaris*), with creamy heads of flower and handsome chestnut-coloured stems in winter, is somewhat less invasive; and on sunny walls the trumpet vine (*Campsis radicans*) is spectacular with its great red and orange trumpet flowers and wisteria-like foliage.

The remaining plants described as 'climbers' are really twiner/clingers or trees and shrubs which must be trained in and secured to the wall or to wires mounted on its face.

Loquat, evergreen magnolia, the silver-leafed *Cytisus battandieri*, with yellow flowers smelling of pineapple, and the feathery mimosa (*Acacia dealbata*) are all suitable choices for the largest spaces on a warm wall, which is also the best home for the vigorous but thornless *Rosa banksiae* 'Lutea', with its fresh green leaves and sheaves of primrose-yellow double blooms in May.

Ceanothus, with small, dark evergreen leaves and flowers in various shades of blue, must be kept carefully pruned and held close to the wall. On smaller expanses of wall, try the semi-evergreen *Abelia* x *grandiflora*, with clusters of pinkish white flowers from midsummer until the frosts, or the evergreen *Carpenteria californica* which resembles a cistus, with dark leaves and brilliant white flowers with golden stamens. Rosemary, trained against a wall, can often be used to hide the bare lower stems of climbing roses or to shade the roots of clematis. Roses and clematis grow well together but make sure the colours complement each other.

Twiners and clingers for sunny walls might include the evergreen *Clematis armandii*, with white or blush flowers in early spring; the fern-leafed *C. balearica*, which is also a winter bloomer; the rampant, blue-flowered passion flower; and the evergreen *Trachelospermum jasminoides*, with fragrant blooms in late summer. Honeysuckles grow well on cooler, shady walls, provided there is sufficient room for a flow of air between the support and the wall; one of the most handsome is the scentless *Lonicera tellmanniana*, with wide heads of golden bloom.

Later flowering climbers can be trained through those which flower early in order to give a longer season of beauty and make the most of the available wall space.

Some of the more rampant climbers look best when grown through old trees and scrub or allowed to cascade down a rough bank or quarry face. Invasive rambler roses such as *R. filipes* 'Kiftsgate', *R. moschata* or *R. longicuspis* are excellent for this purpose; so too are the extremely vigorous Russian vine (*Polygonum baldschuanicum*) with its great froth of white flowers, and *Celastrus scandens*, which produces brilliant red and orange fruit from its insignificant flowers.

Climbers for smaller trees or rough hedges need to be less invasive but must always be planted away from the tree, with a well prepared bed free of tree roots. The climber should be placed on the windward side, as the prevailing wind will then blow it into the tree, to which it should also be led by a stout pole fixed securely to a convenient branch.

Shrubs

Shrubs will necessarily play an important part in the garden scheme. They are easy to grow and maintain, and nowadays there is an enormous choice. When creat-ing a shrub border, follow the same principles as for all other areas of the garden. Bear in mind the points concerning mass and void, the effects of time, contrasts of form and texture, and other factors already mentioned. Furthermore, do not attempt to do too much. It may be better for an area to be devoted to spring bloom and autumn foliage colour rather than try for flowering at every season. If you like a particular shrub or combination of shrubs, employ it on a large scale and then enjoy a quiet green garden until your next bold effect bursts into bloom.

Space permitting, it is possible to create shrub borders in the same way as herbaceous borders, packing in the plant material for notes of colour and texture, but this denies the essential nature of a shrub. Finer effects are generally obtained by planting groups and drifts of one variety at a time, close enough for the branches just to intermingle when fully grown.

Shrubs and roses are often used in herbaceous borders, where they are major elements of scale and solidity against which the frailer plants can be arranged, but certain shrubs and even trees with fine foliage can also be employed as a kind of semi-permanent bedding. Subjects such as catalpa, ailanthus, *Rhus typhina*, *Sambucus racemosa* and other vigorous growers can be planted in richly manured beds and cut down virtually to ground level every winter. They will then send up strong new shoots with exceptionally large leaves, producing an almost tropical effect, and will last for several years before needing replacement.

Bulbs

The first rule when planting bulbs is to avoid the 'mixed bulbs for naturalizing' trap. They are often inferior in quality and tend to produce a messy effect, with odd unrelated flowers and colours scattered about and opening a different times. It is far better to draw a rough plan

Bulbs should be planted in low drifts with sufficient grass between to show the blooms to advantage. It is best to keep the groups separate or only merge them at the outer edges.

of the area to be covered and work out a pleasing arrangement of drifts with sufficient space of grass or ground cover between to show off each group to advantage. Then decide whether all are to be of the same species—daffodils or tulips, for instance—or whether some will be of smaller bulbs with taller ones winding through.

For any one grouping it is advisable to work within a fairly small range of colours—white, off-white and pale sulphur daffodils, or white, pale and deeper pink tulips—than attempt dramatic colour contrasts which may look crude in the clear spring sunlight. Pale colours look more in harmony with the season. Try to arrange flowering times in a sequence so that, from the most used viewing points, the earliest are farthest away and the last are nearest; in that way one never sees a group in full bloom with a foreground of dying flowers and foliage.

In more formal areas and in small gardens a good show of colour can be achieved over quite a long period by planting in layers. Crocus, for instance, require only shallow planting while hyacinths and tulips can go deeper, and crown imperials (*Fritillaria imperialis*) deeper still. If you ensure that the earlier bulbs are smaller, the expanding foliage of each successive layer will tend to conceal those which are over, an effect which may be helped by a general ground cover of forget-me-not, which expands as the season advances and covers everything with a haze of blue. The old-fashioned, rather tall kind is better for this purpose than the modern dumpy varieties.

Ground cover

Ground-cover plants, which occupy space so that weeds cannot take hold, themselves take a great deal of nourishment out of the soil, and must be fertilized regularly if they and the trees and shrubs above them are to flourish. Indeed, it is not wise to plant ground cover until the main plantings are well established.

Choice is largely conditioned by soil and situation. Mainly evergreen plants will not require frequent lifting, division and replanting; and bold, shiny ground-cover species will display adjacent fine and matt-textured plantings to advantage as, for instance, a large-leafed glossy green ivy growing beneath conifers. If the major plantings are prominent and evergreen, the floor should be recessive—a good example might be *Epimedium perralderianum*, which is almost evergreen with divided leaves on fine wiry stems, beneath and in front of *Fatsia japonica*. Many such ground-cover plants—epimedium, *Vinca minor* and several of the lamiums—are better if cut right back in late winter; the blooms are then seen in a setting of fresh foliage with room between for drifts of bulbs.

Trees

Because trees are the largest and longest lived element in the garden, they need placing with the utmost care, since once established they cannot easily be moved. Broadly speaking, they are used for one of three purposes: to provide shade and privacy in a small garden or as a feature for a large lawn; as groups in conjunction with shrubs or as a spinney in rough grass; and (as already mentioned) in avenues or as woodland, which may double as a screen or shelter belt.

In each case it is essential to use material suitable not only for the soil and exposure but also for the scale of the surroundings. A young cedar, planted hopefully in a tiny front garden, will submerge everything else as it grows, whereas a magnolia or some pretty small tree of suitable form can occupy a confined space and give pleasure for years to come. Density of foliage may also create eventual problems. Beech (*Fagus sylvatica*), horse chestnut (*Aesculus hippocastanum*) and sycamore (*Acer pseudoplantanus*) all cast a very heavy shade which ultimately kills the grass or planting beneath, while the London plane (*Platanus* x *acerifolia*), a noble tree with large foliage, and the thin-leafed acacia (*Robinia pseudacacia*) have no effect on the ground below.

A small tree must have sufficient presence to stand alone. The placing of the tree in relation to the ground plan is of vital importance. There is an added advantage if it has more than one season of beauty.

A small tree, designed to stand alone, must have sufficient presence; thus *Sorbus sargentiana*, with a rounded habit and bold pinnate foliage that turns to brilliant autumn colour, might be better than a silver birch (*Betula verrucosa*), which looks better in a small cluster. Be wary, too, of flowering cherries which, although delightful in spring, develop invasive roots as they age, robbing adjoining beds, upsetting paths and creating unsightly humps on the lawn.

Although the conventional nurseryman's tree is a standard, with a clear stem of about 2m (6ft) before the first branches, it is possible to obtain and grow numerous small and medium-sized trees in bush form. The Japanese maple (*Acer palmatum*) and its many varieties, the snowy mespilus (*Amelanchier lamarckii*), with beautiful spring and autumn foliage, and *Parrotia persica*, which has fantastic autumn tints, are all splendid examples.

Fastigiate trees (with erect, parallel branches) come either in the form of slender conifers or as upright versions of species more normally seen with round heads, like beech, oak or hornbeam. They are useful as points of emphasis, perhaps to mark a door or step, or to contrast with a low range of buildings and rounded or horizontal shrubs.

The woodland garden

Provided reasonably fast-growing trees are used, it is not impossible to plant a woodland garden from scratch, as part of a shelter belt or screen. A semi-natural effect can be obtained by introducing a rather wider range of trees than would tend to grow wild in adjacent woodland. Trees such as beech or horse chestnut have leaves that create dense shade in summer only, but during winter and spring the light reaches the ground below, allowing bluebells, daffodils, cyclamen and other early subjects to flourish; species such as birch and rowan, with lighter foliage and casting only

dappled shade, offer more scope for underplanting throughout the year.

Seasonal effects can be exploited to the full as the plants are in a sheltered environment; this enables some quite tender and early flowering species, often heavily scented, to be grown. Bulbs, ferns and ground-cover plants, even ivy, can carpet and colonize the bare soil and stifle weeds, eventually creating a lush and entirely natural appearance.

When planting under trees, the soil must be thoroughly prepared with humus—compost, peat or leaf mould—as the tree roots use up most of the little moisture under the leaf canopy. If the soil becomes too rich and spongy, however, woody plants will tend to put on soft and leafy growth at the expense of flowers.

Simple planting looks best in the wild garden. Here, the bluebells flower before the chestnut leaves expand in an area which will become too overshadowed for later flowering plants to flourish.

89

Woodland gardens tend to rely rather heavily on spring flowering shrubs and become dull later, but in this example the bog planting (*Gunnera manicata*) will extend the season of interest.

Too many woodland gardens are only interesting in spring, so efforts should be made to extend the season with summer-flowering species and with trees that display outstanding autumn tints or striking bark and twig colour for winter. In sheltered, lime-free sites it is worth trying the holly-like *Desfontainea spinosa* with bright red and yellow trumpet flowers in late summer, the equally brilliant and hardier *Embothrium lanceolatum*, *Clethra alnifolia* with off-white scented sprays in August, and the various eucryphias, both evergreen and deciduous, with flowers like white dog roses. Many of the strong-growing species roses, such

as *R. moyesii*, are also appropriate for open glades.

Chalky soils are more restrictive, but many of the single-flowered philadelphus, pale-coloured weigelas and deutzias do well, as do species hydrangeas, provided the ground can be kept moist. In autumn *Euonymus alatus* and *E. europaeus*, with brilliant leaves and fruit, the sumachs *Rhus glabra* and *R. typhina*, and *Cotinus coggygria* all put on a brave show in sunny clearings, but do not colour much in shade.

Water gardens

Water, whether natural or artificial, running or still, brings a new dimension to the garden. Its reflective properties can help direct the eye to a particular place or planting, particularly areas of partial or total shade.

There are many interesting plants which need moist, or even submerged conditions in which to grow. Some, like the giant rhubarb, *Gunnera manicata*, require an uninterrupted source of moisture available to their roots during the growing season. Others do well if planted higher above the damp area, sitting on soil mixed with grit for quick drainage so the roots then reach down to seek out the moisture. Broadly, there are three types of water plants suitable for damp or water conditions: those which need varying degrees of moisture, those which grow completely submerged (water violets or Canadian pondweed, for example) and those which float (water lilies and water hyacinth, etc.).

Over-enthusiasm tends to result in over-planting, so that the water vanishes behind a barrier of iris and rushes and the surface rapidly becomes covered by shiny round leaves of water lilies. It is wise, therefore, at the outset, to prepare a diagrammatic plan showing the heights and general shapes of the marginal planting—both on the bank and in the water—and the exact amount of water surface (never more than one third of the total) to be covered by the eventual horizontal growth of such aquatic plants as water lilies. Depending on the effect you are seeking, there should be ample spaces where very low planting or mown grass reaches the water's edge in order to allow a good view of the fish or blooms of the plants, while at other points, the edge could be quite hidden by bold groupings of taller and more vertical planting.

Naturally the type and scale of the water feature will control the plant material used. A tank or pool in a formal garden would provide an excellent setting for some of the more artificial looking water lilies (*Nymphaea*) such as the red 'Escarboucle' or the coppery 'Sioux' in deep water—from 60cm (24in) upwards—or 'Froebelii' and 'Graziella' in shallower water. These might be allied with groups of the exotic looking Japanese iris (*I. kaempferi*) in blue or purple, blue-flowered *Pontederia cordata*, lavender-flowered *Mimulus ringens* and also the hardy arum lily, *Zantedeschia aethiopica* 'Crowborough'.

With a natural pond, particularly if on a large scale, it would be better to use white, ivory and pale pink water lilies, along with bold groups of some of the more striking foliage plants such as

Above: The formal water garden is an excellent place in which to display some of the more exotic water lilies and marginal plants.

Rheum palmatum with its large rhubarb-like leaves, *Rodgersia pinnata* with divided, slightly wrinkled leaves, or *Peltiphyllum peltatum* with circular shiny ones. Any of these would contrast well with the various rushes and irises, but beware of planting the native bullrush, *Scirpus lacustris*, as this will quickly colonize large areas and is very difficult to remove once it is established.

Areas for low planting might be filled with some of the many beautiful primulas which like damp conditions, in bold swathes of one kind at a time, with the pretty blue water forget-me-not, *Myosotis palustris*, which will spread out into the edge of the water, or the double marsh marigold, *Caltha palustris* 'Plena', which will sometimes bloom in spring and autumn. Where the ground is too damp for good grass by the water's edge, it can be covered by the creeping mint, *Mentha requienii*, which releases a refreshing fragrance when crushed by the foot.

Left: Water gardens should be planted so that the water surface itself becomes part of the composition. Here a bold grouping of *iris laevigata* 'Variegata' is nicely contrasted with a long drift of *alchemilla mollis* in the background.

91

GARDEN ORNAMENTATION

In the earliest gardens, ornamental features fulfilled a useful domestic role: sundials indicated the hour of day; dovecotes housed pigeons (a delicacy for the lords of the manor when fresh meat was in short supply), and wellheads supplied water for drinking or bathing. Pools were useful for cooling the atmosphere and raising fish, and arbours were constructed for seating and shade. In due course, such features, often imported from abroad, particularly from Italy and France, became an integral part of garden development, the original functional design being embellished or becoming more decorative as craftsmen drew attention to their skills and the objects they created.

Ornamental features

Most present-day gardens contain some decorative items, but the functional role has altered. Often, the object serves as a focal point, possibly at the end of a vista, or indicates a change of direction, attracting and diverting the eye from one place to another. In developing a design for a garden, the placing of decorative objects is as important as siting and choosing a tree—the effect depending on how it relates to the surroundings. When set into an existing framework, the comparative scale and proportion of such a feature will affect its impact. The backcloth often determines how an object is seen, and the statue or urn which looks impressive in front of a yew hedge may be almost imperceptible when viewed against a skyline on a grey cloudy day. A platform or plinth may help to show off a seat, statue or urn, providing a firm base that visually links it to the surroundings, instead of making it appear to float in space. The way an object is used, where and how it is to be sited, must be thought through as part of the general plan.

Before considering the more usual statues and urns that proliferate today, a

The vertical lines of this classical vase are emphasized by viewing it against the backcloth of upright kniphofia beyond.

This simple dovecote leads the eye through from the generously planted lower terrace to the restful expanse of lawn beyond, and is carefully sited to be just visible before mounting the steps.

less obvious source of inspiration may be gained from certain features of classic garden ornamentation, designed both to delight the eye and to serve a purpose, and adaptable for contemporary use.

Balustrades were used to emphasize the retaining walls of terraces or steps, and can still be bought today, often being made of reconstituted stone. They are lighter in appearance than a solid wall, allowing views through to the countryside beyond.

Belvederes—or look-outs—are open-sided buildings originally designed to give views over the surrounding landscape and to provide shelter or shade. The present-day interest in garden history and restoration has resulted in the restoration of several such dilapidated buildings and some of the charming ready-made garden buildings available today could easily be sited on a prominent position to serve the same purpose.

Cisterns, usually made of lead and generally for collecting rainwater, can occasionally be found at moderate prices

and either adapted for use as decorative fountains, or as plant containers, the height and width allowing the use of more soil than in most contemporary designs.

Clair-voyées, or wrought-iron grilles let into walls to give views through beyond the garden, can relieve the monotony of a solid wall. A small decorative metal gate can sometimes be used as an insert, but a good metal worker could easily make an interesting grille and relieve the boxed-in effect of being surrounded by walls. Nowadays, clear glass is sometimes used, but birds tend to attempt to fly through, damaging themselves or breaking the glass. Clair-voyées can also be openings or 'windows' cut into hedges.

Dovecotes—or pigeon houses—can be a very interesting addition to a large garden, particularly if some of the more unusual doves are collected. Housing is only required for two or three pairs, and can be constructed as part of a wall, or as a separate stone, brick or timber building; drawbacks are noise, which can be

93

This summer house, or belvedere, provides sheltered seating from which to view the surrounding landscape. The scale of the structure is in proportion to the woodland planting.

disturbing, and the untidiness of discarded straw and droppings.

Finials are ornaments to be set on piers, columns and walls. They can draw attention to a gateway or provide an interesting focal point to be seen against foliage or the skyline. Shapes vary from round stone balls to more detailed carvings.

Gazebos (gaze-abouts) or garden houses with a view, differ from belvederes in that they are closed on three sides. The present-day garden house can if necessary, be envisaged as a 'summer living' unit, perhaps situated near the swimming pool, complete with comfortable seating and cooking facilities. Constructed in stone or brick, the furniture and flooring can be hard-wearing rustic cane and sisal matting.

Grottoes, or caverns, are also experiencing a revival in popularity due to the interest in garden history. Often found

by the side of a lake or pool, the inside may be lined with shells, bones, segments of contorted wood, pebbles or glass. The exterior usually resembles a haphazard rustic pile of stones, but the

Stone ball finials placed on top of columns or piers make an attractive embellishment even for the smaller gateway.

This imposing stone lion lends importance to the steps with their wide treads and shallow risers. The eye is also caught by the carefully positioned sun-dial in the background.

construction is surprisingly exacting and laborious. A grotto can be a tremendously exciting place for children, more fun than a tent but often a bit damp.

Orangeries were the forerunners of greenhouses and conservatories, giving winter protection to citrus plants grown in ornamental tubs, to be placed by garden paths in summer. The winter fragrance of the flowers made the orangery a delightful haven, but they have now been replaced by glassed garden rooms not necessarily attached to houses, where people and plants can shelter from inclement weather.

Pots, urns and garden vases provide a way of growing plants when soil is not available in the open ground. Obtainable in a wide variety of shapes, sizes and materials, they must be sufficiently deep and strong to accommodate the plants' roots, and with drainage holes in the base. The more ornate forms can be used singly as focal points to arrest the eye, with the simpler designs arranged in bold groupings to give impact.

Statuary and sculpture—particularly if antique or a collector's item—can be very expensive, and it is difficult to establish authenticity. Obtaining a provenance of origin and a written guarantee of the approximate date will help. Genuinely old garden ornaments are costly, sought-after items, and many firms now supply excellent replicas in reconstituted stone. Manufacturers have different methods of composing this material, some more successful than others in withstanding elements, including frost, which can cause rapid weathering and deterioration. Suitably weathered versions, which have been allowed to stand outside, gathering moss and lichen, can often be seen in their showrooms or yards.

Ask particularly how any ornamentation on the item will react to harsh climatic conditions—it may be wiser to choose a less ornate design rather than see an intricate relief detail rapidly crumble away. The same precautions may be necessary with terracotta, which is often imported from continental countries where there is less risk of frost.

Metal fixings, used to secure one item of stone to another, must also be checked

95

This substantial urn, displayed to great advantage on an equally substantial pedestal, creates a focal point at the end of a vista.

because alloys have different chemical reactions and can be responsible for green discoloration or streaked rust. The way an item is to be set off or secured is important—a statue or urn may require to be set on a substantial octagonal plinth, or a stone ball ornament or finial decorating a gate pier or balustrade may need a collared base and block— both to unite it visually and to secure it safely.

Trompe l'oeil—or the art of illusion—is a simulation of nature, currently very popular as a painting skill, and employed in and out of doors, round swimming pools, and to relieve the boxed-in feeling in small gardens by creating an illusion of views beyond.

Garden furniture

There is an equally wide range of functional garden furniture available today— seats, tables, upright or lounging chairs, benches and parasols. Many designs are ugly and badly constructed. Notwithstanding the test of time, they are often an impulsive purchase but a poor investment, adversely affecting the character of the garden.

Reliable and talented cabinet-makers have copied the rather grand Lutyens designs, and there are many good contemporary designs in stone, timber, wrought or cast iron, metal or wirework. Octagonal seats which fit round the base of a substantial tree trunk can be very useful in an informal setting, and wooden arbours (or love-seats) can be a charming addition to a more classical design. Seek out what is available, make sure it is comfortable as well as decorative, and that the height, style and scale are suitable.

Natural treated timber will of course not require frequent repainting but should be given an annual coating of preservative, usually supplied by the manufacturer. Yacht paint will stand up to the most extreme weather conditions —a dark French green, black or grey blends in with paving and planting. Canvas 'director's' chairs which fold away when not required can be useful in town gardens, or as extra seating, versatile in conservatories or outdoors. The canvas can always be renewed when worn or dirty. Tough washable cushions are also useful, particularly when seats are wet; and as not everyone likes to bake in the sun, a large portable parasol may be welcome to provide shade.

However, old and worn garden furni-

A decorative garden seat which encourages progress through the garden, the curved form indicating that there may be more to see round the corner.

ture should not lightly be discarded— timber can be repaired, layers of old paint can be removed, and a de-rusting agent applied prior to priming with a lead-based primer, undercoating and repainting. The old, rejuvenated item will often perform better than the new.

A seat of striking design can terminate a long vista and suggests an air of finality.

MAKING UP THE BRIEF

There is one abstract component of major importance in any proposed garden design, and that is the character and wishes of the people who will be using it, which must be researched in depth before any plan of campaign is considered. This is no less true if the garden in question is your own, rather than that of a client since, for a successful result, any design problem should be approached with the same professionalism. It is curious how seldom people define exactly what they want from their gardens before they consider the layout, and when questioned they often retreat into vague generalities. When designing a garden for somebody else, therefore, it is essential to get a clear idea of the characters and lifestyle of the eventual users of the garden during the initial visit to the site.

Basic considerations

Firstly you should consider the ways in which the garden will be used. How many vehicles must be catered for, in general or on special occasions. Are they usually kept in garages or outside? Is there a need for games facilities such as a swimming pool, tennis court or croquet lawn? How old are the children, and do they want to play ball games, ride bicycles, have a sandpit, garden themselves, have swings or build a playhouse? How much entertaining is done outside, for how many people and how often? Should there be provision for the storage of barbecue equipment and garden furniture as well as tools, either separately or in the same building? Will the pets need any special facilities?

The nature of the garden too needs examination. Is it to contain vegetables, fruit and herbs as well as flowers? Will it contain flowers to be cut for the house (this will affect later considerations about the colour), or can they be grown in a separate cutting garden?

By asking these questions, and any others which may seem relevant to the particular situation, the designer can build up a picture of the way in which the garden will be used and what the owners hope to gain from it. At this stage it may be prudent to curb enthusiasm. It is easy to imagine the pleasure of an extensive or elaborate garden, and often the site will lend itself well to a number of ambitious schemes, but it is equally easy to brush over the cost, not only in terms of construction but of maintenance both in money and man-hours. Even though specifically asked to create a garden of a certain kind with particular features, no designer will be thanked when it proves difficult—even impossible—to maintain it with the resources available.

Cost and maintenance factors

After careful consideration the garden owner must set down exactly what can be afforded for the capital cost of construction—possibly spread over a period to ease the burden—and how much can be spent yearly on maintenance, bearing in mind inflation. There is a correlation between these two factors since a high capital outlay, if spent on good construction or labour-saving features, will result in the minimum of maintenance, whereas skimping on the construction can lead to ever increasing yearly expense. People who intend to remain in one place for many years will prefer the first option, in which case the scheme must be limited to features which can be really well built and easily kept. Those whose job perhaps entails frequent moves may well find it more convenient to take the second approach.

Then there is the question of who will actually do the maintenance, bearing in mind that this is always heaviest in the first years of a garden's life, before the plants have grown together to exclude the weeds. How much will the owner be able to do—we always think that we can manage more than is really possible— and how much must be turned over to a gardener or to contract maintenance? And what kind of labour is obtainable in that particular area? It is useless to design a garden requiring skilled upkeep or a sophisticated understanding of form and colour unless a knowledgeable person is available to look after it.

Formulating the design

After this the designer's own skill and knowledge of possibilities can be brought to bear on the problem. People tend to think only of stock solutions and forget that gardens are made for, as well as by, people. Is it really necessary, for instance, for the kitchen garden to be remote from the house? Why not place it outside the kitchen door where it would be far more convenient and need not be unsightly? Why should not certain household tasks take place out of doors in fine weather, in which case provision of permanent seating and a table in a warm corner becomes essential? With an outdoor electric point even the ironing can be done away from the hot kitchen: one of the author's favourite garden buildings was an ironing house equipped with an airing rack, concealed ironing board, electric power-point and benches on which to place the baskets of linen which were finished or were yet to be done. It was set in a lavender garden over which some of the linen was spread in the sun before being ironed.

Although children grow up rapidly, the garden can be designed to grow with them: today's sandpit can become tomorrow's lily pool, the formal beds containing the children's separate plots turn into the rose garden, while the paths, carefully graded to make easy runs for tricycles, are a permanent pleasure for the wheelbarrow. Even the swing, if sturdily made and attractive from the outset, will continue to have a strange fascination for adults.

Practical considerations

Just as a house needs an efficient kitchen, so the garden needs a well organized service area; some dark corner behind the bushes simply will not do. The first need is for a hard, easily cleaned surface, ideally concrete. Then there must be proper housing for tools and machines, well lit so that maintenance work can go on in winter, a glasshouse, if one is needed, a potting shed, and ample, well-made bins for peat, manure, compost and other necessities. Naturally there must be electricity and water, and if possible (and necessary) direct access to a road so that deliveries of manure, loam or peat bales need not be trundled through the garden. All too often this vital area is skimped or forgotten, leading to much wasted time and difficulty working in the future.

As people are usually at work all day, the garden must be enjoyable on fine evenings, so arrangements for lighting should be considered at the earliest design stage. Careful thought should also be given to the provision of any additional facilities.

The busy garden owner, who may frequently be away from home for days at a time, and those who need to maintain the gardens of a holiday house, will certainly require an automatic watering and feeding system. This, too, must be considered from the earliest stage as it may well control the shapes and sizes of lawns and planting areas, as well as plumbing runs and associated details.

Conclusions

With experience and practice, the designer will be able to assess fairly quickly the requirements of the garden owner, but until this becomes automatic, a general checklist can be compiled and taken on site visits. A glance through this before leaving the garden site will ensure that no obvious question has been overlooked.

WRITING A REPORT

When designing a garden for somebody else the first step is to write a comprehensive report, thus establishing a framework for a detailed consideration of the project. This report will enable you to recall your first impressions of the garden, its deficiencies and advantages; it will balance the existing potential of the garden with its long-term possibilities; and it will provide an honest assessment of the client's intentions. A written report may not be strictly necessary, however, if the garden is very small, or merely part of a whole, or if the client has already formed a satisfactory plan; in these situations your impressions can be summed up in a letter and planting can begin fairly quickly.

Sometimes the client will specifically ask for a report, and carry out the recommendations in his own order of priority. Or, having studied the document, he may ask the designer to concentrate on planning selected areas in detail. On other occasions the client may not be very interested in the report but it will still form an invaluable tool for the designer, both in the early stages of establishing a brief and formulating a plan, and also in later years if maintaining contact with the garden.

The procedure

Analyzing the site and assessing the needs of the family in one short visit is frequently a strain on the perception of the garden designer, especially if the clients are not themselves in complete agreement over the plans for the garden. But the prospect of writing a report will focus your thoughts and bring about a certain degree of objectivity. You should take care to. walk around the garden alone, making notes, taking photographs and sketching, and should also talk to the person responsible for the maintenance, whether it is the client or the gardener.

The content

The report should cover all aspects of the garden. It should analyze the brief; divide the site into areas; suggest alterations and improvements, clearly stating why and how these conclusions have been reached; suggest planting schemes; give guidance as to the programming of the work, maintenance and aftercare; and estimate the probable costs. It should be accompanied with a plan, sketches and photographs, the latter possibly having overlays of any proposals for the site.

Contractors and suppliers of plants can be recommended and catalogues of 'bought-in' items such as stone finials, statues, fountains, garden furniture and lighting will provide back-up information.

This report will eventually form a vital link between you and the client, saving time, expense and any possible misunderstanding about the project.

Summary
- Assess the client's needs and intentions.
- Make careful notes of all the features of the garden. Start at the entrance and work in logical order around the site. Take photographs as you go.
- Start writing the report immediately. Never leave an interval or too many details can be forgotten.
- A report must have a clear beginning, setting the scene as well as considering the practical details of soil and exposure.
- Set out the aims of the proposals for alteration, including suggested planting plans.
- Describe the proposals area by area in the same order as your original site record.
- The conclusion should also indicate costs, recommend the order in which the work should be carried out, and make suggestions for the future maintenance of the garden.

MEASURING THE SITE

Before any serious work can begin on altering and re-planning a garden, there must first be a survey of the site so that a plan can be prepared showing the existing situation. First find out what plans are already available: those which come with property deeds are too small to be of practical value, but if the house has been newly built or recently altered there may be the architect's plans, which not only give details of the building itself, with doors, windows and drainpipes, but may also show details such as manhole covers, boundaries, garden buildings and levels. Even so, it may be wise to make one or two check measurements to ensure that the building was actually constructed as shown on plan, since this is not always the case.

The simple, but expensive, solution is to have a detailed survey made by a professional land surveyor, and this may still be necessary if the area is exceptionally large or contains complex level changes. Otherwise it is quite easy to do it yourself, and far better since while you are measuring you learn a great deal more about the ground than might otherwise be noticed. You will need the equipment listed below:

Equipment check list

- Two 30m (100ft) tape measures, preferably the modern plasticized fabric variety. The old linen tapes tend to stretch and the steel variety are difficult to manipulate and prone to rust. When you get them, fix an ordinary metal meat skewer to the end of each: it can be stuck into the earth or any convenient crack and is a great help when working alone.
- A 2m (6ft) pocket tape. This will be used for short measurements and here the stiffness of metal is an advantage.
- A stiff, covered notebook or pad on which to do the drawings. (Squared or graph paper is often easier to use than plain.)
- An eraser.
- A ball of smooth, fairly thick string. This is often needed for setting out lines which may be too long for the tape measure.
- Some pegs to mark important points or to secure the string. Metal meat skewers are often better than wooden pegs as they are easier to drive into hard ground and can be carried strung together on a length of cord. A few garden canes are often useful too.
- If simple levelling has to be undertaken you will need a spirit level, a long straight lath of wood, some wooden wide-topped pegs and a mallet or hammer to drive them into the ground.
- HB pencils and a knife to sharpen them.

How to use tape measures

Before going out on site it is wise to practise with the long tape measures, since they are incredibly prone to tie themselves in knots or trip up the user. The trick is to keep the case under the left arm—if you are right-handed—and pay out or gather in the loose tape with the right hand, holding it evenly in the left hand as though it were a coil of rope. Once operations have started do not keep winding the tape back into its case, since this holds up proceedings and tends to get dirt and dampness into the case which will cause problems later. At the end of the survey, wipe all dirt and moisture from the tape and make sure that it is dry before winding it back. Never wind it in directly, but keep it running between two fingers, since there is a tendency for the tape to twist as it goes in which can cause it to get jammed. This may seem an unnecessary amount of caution for a simple piece of equipment, but it is expensive and inconvenient to have to keep returning your tapes to the makers for repair: well treated they give good service and last for many years.

The rough plan

Once on site the first thing is to make a simple plan on which to mark the measurements. This will not, of course, be at all accurate since it is done by eye, but try to keep the proportions and the relative positions of one thing to another correct. If the plot is large or complicated it may be necessary to make separate drawings of different areas with a rough map showing how the sheets fit together.

Then choose a base line: the largest unobstructed line from which all—or at least the majority—of the area can be seen. Sometimes a boundary can be used, or the edge of a long straight path or drive, but otherwise it will be necessary to set out a convenient line—which could be diagonal, running right across from corner to corner—using some of the pegs and string. This line will then be measured and entered on the plan. When entering measurements always try to keep the figures the same way up, and running along the line to which they refer, or they may prove to be ambiguous later.

The triangulation method

There are various methods of doing a survey but this one, called triangulation, is the simplest. A triangle is an absolutely stable figure: that is to say, if the three sides are measured correctly, they can only be drawn up to form that precise shape and no other. If the sides of any other figures are measured they can be put together in a number of ways, only one of which would be correct. The aim therefore is to divide the plot into a number of interlocking triangles, and build up the final picture from these. Before beginning to take measurements, work out the system of triangles to ensure that everything is covered, making sure that all the triangles are connected to the rest of the survey by two out of their three points. It is quite possible, and very annoying, to find that you know how a number of points relate to one another but are unable to relate them to anything else.

Supposing you have used a long boundary as base line, then the next measurement would be from one end, along the adjoining, probably shorter, boundary. The next measurement is taken between the two 'free' ends so completing the first triangle. Obviously many more than one measurement can be taken from one point, and as you get more expert you will work out how to complete the survey with the smallest number of moves. If the garden is a simple rectangular shape measurements along the other two boundaries will secure the complete outline. If the ground is of a more complex shape, or a view is obstructed by objects such as buildings or clumps of shrubs, more

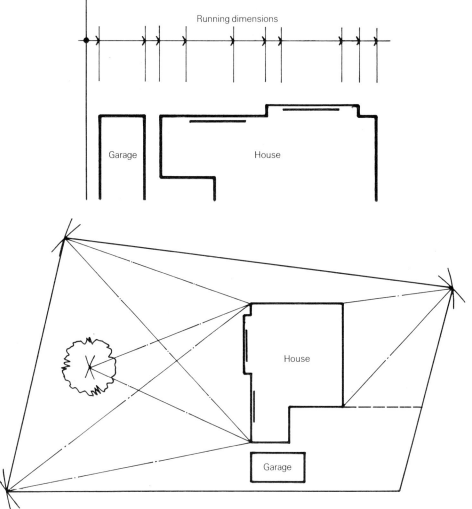

When measuring buildings, it is quicker and easier to take running dimensions, reading off where every window, door, or gap between buildings occur along the length as a whole. If this is being done without help, the tape can be laid flat on the ground, leaving hands free to write.

This method of triangulation divides up the awkward shape of the site into easily measured areas. The diagonals require plotting with compasses to locate accurately the corners of buildings and walls, or location of trees.

triangles will be needed to achieve the result. If a line such as a diagonal has to be measured across open ground and is longer than 30m (100ft), the ball of string can be used to set out the line first to ensure that it is straight. At regular intervals points can be marked by pegs, which may be helpful when measuring the smaller triangles needed to pick up internal features such as trees, beds of shrubs which are to be retained, manhole covers and so on.

Objects close to boundaries or on the lines that form the sides of triangles can be marked in when these lines are measured. If they are close by, a right-angled offset can be taken using the spring tape, since it is quite easy to judge a right angle correctly over a short distance—and no great harm is done if it is not quite correct—but not over a long stretch.

Where there is a curve, perhaps in the boundary or on a drive or path, a straight line can be laid down to join either end and then regular offsets taken from it to pick up the exact shape. Another, less accurate way is to mark the major changes of direction with pegs which are part of the triangulation system, and then fill in the curving line between them by eye.

Buildings

If there is no existing ground-plan of the house the building will need to be drawn separately on a larger scale, as there are so many detailed measurements between doors and windows, with downpipes, gulleys, chimneys, steps and recesses to pick up as well. Start at one corner and keep a continuous run of measurement all along that face of the building, avoiding the temptation to take separate individual measurements which, if not quite accurate, can accumulate a considerable degree of error when added together. Write in the measurements to the outer face of each window frame and doorway, noting the height of the sills above ground level and the height, as well as the position, of any steps. This information cannot be plotted on the plan but will be useful when you come to make design proposals.

Where there are recesses or projections they will have to be measured separately, triangulating from their corners to the main corners of the building or treating a recess as two triangles with a common diagonal base. The reason for this apparently unnecessary complication is that many old buildings, and even some modern ones, are not built with true right angles so errors can accumulate in the drawing up. However careful you are in making accurate individual measurements, it is always as well to take a check measurement from corner to corner along each side of the building, if these have not been made already as part of the triangulation system.

Simple levels

Few sites are absolutely flat, and although it is beyond the scope of this book to explain the taking of levels with theodolite and staff, there are several ways in which simple level changes can be indicated. If you have the levelling equipment itemized in the list, proceed as follows. Choose some level permanent feature such as a manhole cover or doorstep as datum and measure out from it a distance rather less than the length of your lath. At that point drive in a peg with its top approximately level with the datum and rest one end of the lath upon that, the other on the datum. On the lath place the spirit level, which will almost certainly show a necessity to move the peg up or down to get a true level reading. Once this is obtained, measure from the top of the peg to ground level, which will give the difference in level between the datum and that point on the ground. This is rather a tedious process and not one to extend over a large area, but it is a simple way of finding minor differences of level in a small garden.

If you are considering making changes in the level of the ground around the house, take careful note of the level of the damp-proof course of the building. This must be a minimum of 15cm (6in) above the adjoining ground level at all times. Old buildings may not have a damp-proof course at all, in which case it is most unwise to attempt to raise the level and, if the house is at all damp, it should probably be lowered. Equally, the ground must not be lowered so much that the foundations of buildings or footings of walls are exposed.

Existing features

The survey should also include the levels of water in ponds and streams, taken, if possible, during periods of drought, normal and high rainfall. The contours of the edges should be noted. The water should come up to the highest level possible and therefore the banks or sides may need adjusting so that they are uniform. The maximum depth of water should also be noted, and information obtained on underground water and springs. The natural water-table (the level at which water is naturally held in the soil separating the saturated level below from the unsaturated above) will vary according to the soil and geology, and excavation below the water-table can lead to flooding or seepage. In extreme cases, where fresh water is needed and difficult to locate, such as on land near the coast, a water diviner can be called in; he can also help determine the drainage pattern on fields and large sites.

All trees, except small, recently planted ones which are easily moved, should be marked on the plan, in addition to the spread of their canopy, the ground level around them, and their root system. If they are to be cut down the trees may be valuable for their timber.

Access

Access for heavy machinery for removing tree trunks or carrying in building materials is often overlooked in the survey. The width of paths between a public footpath or road and the garden at the rear, especially with semi-detached town properties, can determine how and what materials are brought on to a site, and with items such as columns or mature trees it is obviously very costly to use machinery to lift them over the house roof.

Other aspects

While you are on site taking measurements, take note also of other factors such as cold draughts of air, evidence of the prevailing wind, patches which appear ill drained or sunless, lack of top soil in parts of the site, and so on. It is as well to have a spade in the car and test in different places to discover the depth of the top soil, which even on a small site may vary, and at the same time take soil samples for testing, placing them in numbered boxes and marking the numbers on your sketch plan. Another useful piece of equipment is a small compass so that you can note the exact orientation, which is vital when it is time to consider what plants will grow where.

The final plan

All the information which you have gathered must now be drawn up accurately to produce a plan of the existing garden— or at least all those elements of it which you intend to keep—at a suitable scale. For very small gardens or courtyards and detailed areas around a building a scale of 1:50 may be suitable, but in general 1:100 or, for a large garden 1:200, will be best.

Having decided roughly how the garden will fit most conveniently onto your paper, draw in the base line and mark on it any intermediate positions which you may have taken when measuring along it. You will then need a pair of compasses with an extending arm long enough to cover the longest side of any of your triangles. Measure the other two sides of the first triangle which you took from the base line, and strike off the two arcs with your compasses to give you the position of your first measurement. If you had measured along an adjoining boundary wall, for instance, the arcs would meet at the further corner of the garden.

As each triangle relates to others, you can work on from triangle to triangle, drawing in only the lines which have to appear on the plan, since it is only these and the positions of the bisecting arcs which matter. In this way the plan gradually emerges, with the outlines of the various features being drawn in from point to point and detached items such as free-standing trees being indicated. At this stage the house will probably appear as a plain block outline which can eventually be filled in with doors, windows and other basic structural elements that have been the subject of your more detailed measurements.

It should be an invariable rule to draw up all this information on the day following the making of the survey. However careful you have been it is almost certain that you will have forgotten a measurement or made some error.

DRAWING UP A PLAN

A successful plan or design, which will transform an existing site into a pleasant workable garden, providing interest throughout the year, as well as accommodating practical features such as seating and storage, largely depends on satisfying the owner's requirements (or interpreting the client's brief) by adapting the site and surroundings accordingly. This procedure has already been explained in detail. The site has been measured and the next and crucial stage is to draw up a plan. The following description and accompanying diagrams relate to the hypothetical planning of a large town garden, from initial survey to completed design.

The Survey

This is a plan of the site as it exists, prior to any proposed work being carried out on it. The plan identifies natural features, records the horizontal distances between them, indicates the height and spread of major trees and shrubs, and draws attention to changes in level.

In this particular survey, the rear of the property is shown, prior to any alterations to the house. The boundaries are brick walls, the height and positions of the buttresses being clearly indicated. Areas of flower beds, bushes, paving and grass are also shown, in addition to a concrete pond sited in the middle of the lawn.

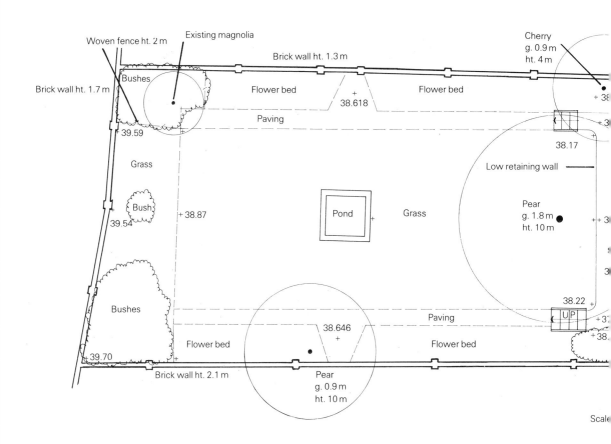

Low retaining walls and the direction of the steps indicate changes of level within the site, and the major trees are named, including their girth, height and spread.

Access is also shown, essential because in this case it is a narrow side alley. Not only is the front detailed on the survey, but also the pavement, road and any existing trees which overhang the property, particularly important in a conservation area where planning permission may be necessary before they can be lopped or felled. The position of manhole covers, the presence and directional flow of drains, and the location of rainwater pipes and downpipes are also noted.

The Analysis

This is a factual interpretation of the site as it exists, with diagrammatic indications to illustrate the various points, such as views, the present condition of the planting, the state of the boundary walls, or as an overlay on the survey. Sometimes it is easier to divide the garden up into imaginary sections, and describe the advantages and disadvantages of each in logical order. In our example the state of the boundary walls varied considerably. The south-facing wall was in reasonable condition, but was overlooked by the balcony of an adjacent house; the rear west-facing wall was dilapidated, and

The survey
A professional survey will detail the existing structures and planting, as well as underground services which may affect the plans.

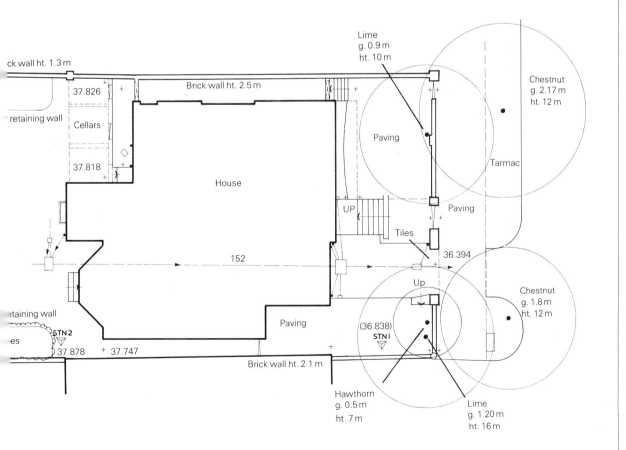

leaning suspiciously inwards into the owner's garden. The north-facing wall showed severe cracks, but was topped by a flimsy trellis. The garden had been allowed to deteriorate, and although a few good specimen shrubs, such as magnolia and lilac, remained, most of the planted areas were covered in brambles, nettles and polygonatum (a most invasive weed). The lawn had gradually grown over the paved paths, the York stone paving only being discovered when clearing the site. Closer inspection of the pond showed that the concrete lining had cracked, allowing the water to seep away, thus lowering the water level. A site meeting with the architect respon-

sible for alterations to the house revealed plans for demolishing the rear house walls, changing the existing layout and shape of the main rooms, and adding on a conservatory. Some dieback in the branches of mature fruit trees was worrying and therefore required reporting to tree surgeons.

The Appraisal

The appraisal assesses what, given the existing situation, can or cannot be done with the site. It should follow the same logical format as the analysis, progressing through the survey drawing in stages.

In our hypothetical case, the alterations to the rear of the building needed to be considered, making sure that the

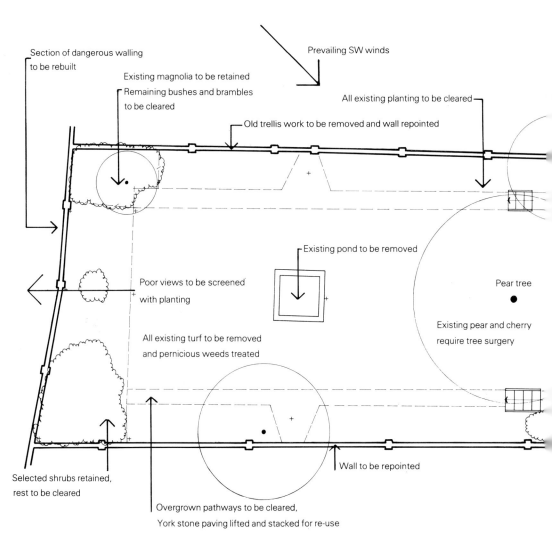

Section of dangerous walling to be rebuilt

Prevailing SW winds

Existing magnolia to be retained

Remaining bushes and brambles to be cleared

All existing planting to be cleared

Old trellis work to be removed and wall repointed

Existing pond to be removed

Pear tree

Poor views to be screened with planting

Existing pear and cherry require tree surgery

All existing turf to be removed and pernicious weeds treated

Wall to be repointed

Selected shrubs retained, rest to be cleared

Overgrown pathways to be cleared, York stone paving lifted and stacked for re-use proposals would help integrate the house with the garden. The floor of the conservatory was planned at the same level as the paving immediately outside, to make outdoor entertaining easier. The erection of a substantial trellis would prevent the neighbours from the adjacent house being able to see into the garden; the rear wall required rebuilding, but could, with the neighbours' permission, be raised to the same height as the other walls. The severe cracks in the north-facing wall required repointing to prevent it eventually collapsing into the newly designed garden, and the flimsy trellis needed replacing with a stronger type to support climbers.

Bad views could be partially concealed by planting or trellising, the good views being framed by planting. As this part of town had once been an orchard, many mature fruit trees, outstanding for their flowering in spring and for their striking leafless twig form in winter, were visible in adjacent gardens. The dieback, noticed in the two prominent pear trees, was diagnosed by the tree surgeons as due to stress and age, but the removal of some branches would lighten the canopies and help the trees cope with lack of sufficient water.

The few good specimen shrubs could be retained and moved to be shown off to better advantage, and the rest of the

Analysis and appraisal
It is often possible to put the required information together on one sheet, or overlay. This makes it easier to assess the potential as well as the limitations of the garden.

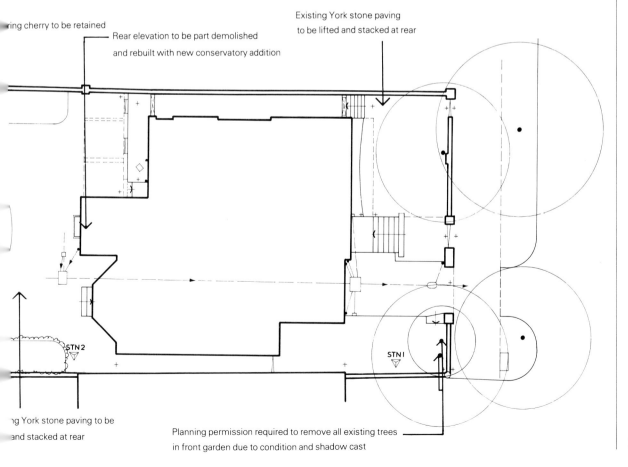

ring cherry to be retained

Rear elevation to be part demolished and rebuilt with new conservatory addition

Existing York stone paving to be lifted and stacked at rear

STN 2

STN 1

ng York stone paving to be and stacked at rear

Planning permission required to remove all existing trees in front garden due to condition and shadow cast

beds cleared of weeds. The existing but hidden York stone would be lifted and stacked for relaying. The pond needed either to be renewed and enlarged, to serve as a central focal point, with a fountain installed to help draw the eye, or removed altogether, in which case the focus could be directed to the far end of the garden by introducing a decorative 'Chinese' pavilion, useful for shade and storage.

Seating would be provided under the smaller pear tree for additional shade, and an urn or statue strategically placed within the border running along the opposite wall to break up the long vista. The existing patchy and weed-ridden turf would be replaced or renewed, or a bed prepared for seeding.

The existing garden must be cleared before the new design can be set out.

The Plan
Having completed the preliminary work —survey, analysis and appraisal—the owner or designer can now embark on the plan. People are often unnecessarily nervous about major changes, preferring to embroider what has been rather than create something entirely different. Even if the house and site appear to dictate a certain style, it is better to experiment with several different designs, if only to prove that the original concept is the most satisfactory solution.

Possible solutions
These diagrams show three different approaches to our particular problem:

1. a circular theme, using interrelated

and overlapping circles to disguise the rectangular shape of the garden;

2. a diagonal theme, making use of the longest distance from one point to another, and increasing the feeling of space;

3. a rectangular theme, dividing up the space with a series of interlocking, related shapes similar to the formality of the house.

In each case the garden is divided into three, almost equal, parts, attempting to make the most of the space available by creating different areas of interest within it, giving a logical progression through the garden.

The circular theme is, in this instance, discarded because it seems opposed to the shape and style of the house, creating a feeling of restless confusion within the garden. The diagonal theme, although workable, is also rejected because the clients prefer a classical English garden. The decision is therefore made to adopt the rectangular theme, which relates well with the proportions of the house, dividing the garden into an interesting but uncontrived series of spaces, the interlocking rectangles being allotted functional and decorative uses.

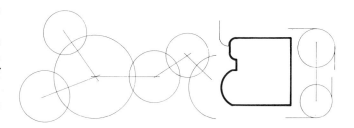

1. Circular theme

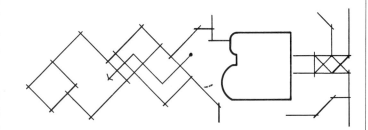

2. Diagonal theme

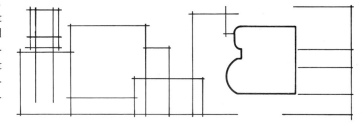

3. Rectangular theme

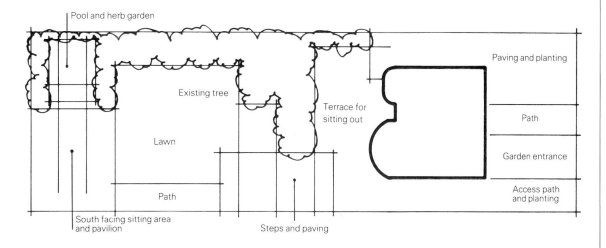

The adopted rectangular theme is now worked up, allocating areas of hardworks and planting.

Other considerations

The front of the house has been kept simple, with room for access, planting, paving and pots, while the plan for the rear has developed from the liaison between house and garden, the east-facing terrace linked with the conservatory being ideal for evening entertaining, steps coping with the change in level. The existing mature pear tree has become a dominant feature, and the largest single rectangle provides the lawn or 'void' necessary to balance the 'mass' of planting along the boundary walls. As the west-facing, or rear end, of the garden will receive sun during the afternoon, an area for sitting is provided there with a pavilion for shade, a pool and fountain for cooling and decoration, and planting which might include scented herbs. A path connects the two terraces, allowing people to use the garden without getting their feet wet or muddy.

The Sketch Plan

The basic division of space is now developed, with hardworks—paving, paths, steps and walls—receiving priority over planting. At this stage, although the areas for planting are allocated and the designer may have a clear idea of how this will eventually look, the construction must be thought through so as to enable a contractor to quote a price for building the garden, including the installation and fixing of the pool, pavilion or other decorative items.

The terracing is to be of existing York stone and to be relaid as shown, bounded by a low stone retaining wall for seating, drinks, etc. The steps are to be widened and located as shown for ease of circulation and to lead the eye from the drawing room to the view beyond. Paths of York stone will link both ends of the garden and continue round the existing pear tree. A stone seat backed by a yew hedge

Rubble and other waste material are used to infill the former pond. When burning rubbish, care must be taken not to scorch nearby trees or shrubs

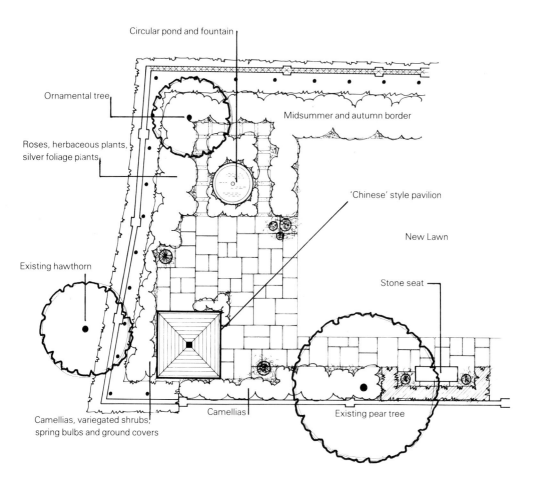

Circular pond and fountain

Ornamental tree

Midsummer and autumn border

Roses, herbaceous plants, silver foliage plants

'Chinese' style pavilion

New Lawn

Existing hawthorn

Stone seat

Camellias, variegated shrubs, spring bulbs and ground covers

Camellias

Existing pear tree

will allow people to sit in the sun, sheltered from the wind. A pavilion placed on a raised plinth of York stone at the far end of the garden will give a focal point, shelter, seating and storage. Lighting and irrigation will be finalized after discussion with the client or owner. A built-in barbecue is suggested adjacent to the terrace, and a conservatory will link the house to the garden. Trellis secured on top of the immediate boundary walls will maintain privacy. The garden at the front of the house is shown paved in York stone embellished with pots and urns selected to suit the architecture of the house.

Planting suggestions are made at this stage to give the client or owner an idea of the character and type of plants pro-posed. He may have some favourite varieties he wants included, but until the sketch plan is discussed and approved, there is no point in detailing every item.

The sketch plan is now ready for discussion with the client or, if prepared by the owner, for obtaining practical advice and costs from a contractor. This meeting should always take place on site, partly because a client often cannot vis-ualize a 'flat' plan in three dimensions and therefore the designer will need to talk him through the proposals, and partly because it is easy to be seduced by plan and graphics into accepting pro-posals which may seem perfect in the isolation of office or drawing room, but impractical when faced with cold reality on site.

The plan
The first plan includes a pool and a 'Chinese' style pavilion at the far end of the garden.

Revisions

This is the stage when the plan usually has to be amended according to what the client or contractor considers feasible. In this case, the built-in barbecue has been rejected in favour of a portable one, easier to clean, capable of being moved about to face the direction of the wind, avoiding smoke being wafted over assembled guests. The proposed stone seat is to be replaced by a classic treated timber 'Lutyens' style wooden bench—more comfortable to sit on than cold stone. In place of the 'Chinese' style pavilion, there will be eight stone Doric columns, recently acquired by the client, and the proposed pool and fountain are ruled out in favour of planting, to save the expense of installation and difficulties in maintaining an area of water. The proposed removal of the two mature lime trees in the front garden will require permission from the local authority, as the property is within a conservation area.

The Revised Plan

The stone columns have now been proposed as a pergola, with timber beams connecting them, providing overhead

The revised plan
The revised plan replaces the pavilion (which would not have been visible due to the canopy of the pear tree) with a stone-column pergola. Planting replaces the pool.

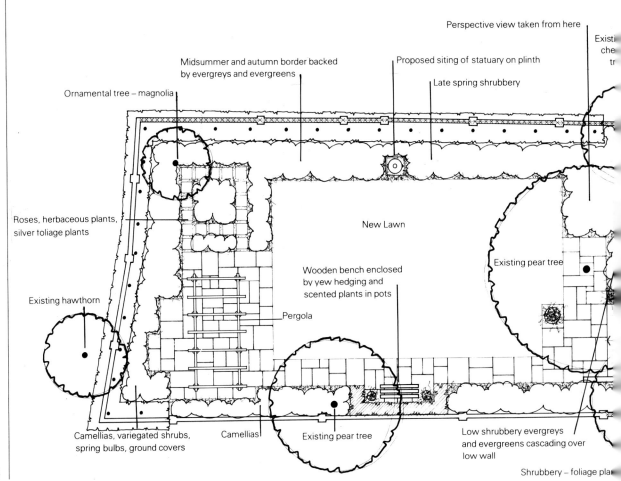

Perspective view taken from here

Existi
che
tr

Midsummer and autumn border backed by evergreys and evergreens

Proposed siting of statuary on plinth

Late spring shrubbery

Ornamental tree – magnolia

Roses, herbaceous plants, silver toliage plants

New Lawn

Existing pear tree

Wooden bench enclosed by yew hedging and scented plants in pots

Existing hawthorn

Pergola

Camellias, variegated shrubs, spring bulbs, ground covers

Camellias

Existing pear tree

Low shrubbery evergreys and evergreens cascading over low wall

Shrubbery – foliage plar

shelter and a means of supporting climbing vines or wisteria. To set off the columns and gain a more secure fixing, matching plinths for each are suggested—enabling steel reinforcing rods to be inserted through the centre of the columns linking the overhead timbers to the paving below, preventing any possible accidents caused by the columns collapsing. To help relate the columns to the rest of the garden, a stone statue, also on a plinth, is recommended as a central feature in the north-facing border.

Garden lighting, too, often introduced as an afterthought and usually overdone,

Left: The structure and planting of the new garden is completed. The mature pear tree provides an important focal point from the far end of the garden.

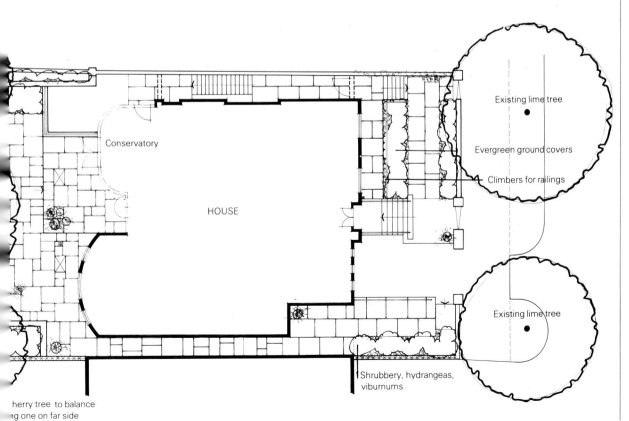

Existing lime tree

Conservatory

Evergreen ground covers

Climbers for railings

HOUSE

Existing lime tree

Shrubbery, hydrangeas, viburnums

herry tree to balance
g one on far side

has been proposed—including wall-mounted brackets on the exterior house walls to cast intimate shadows on the terrace, and a sturdy unbreakable fixture set into the turf *behind* the mature pear tree, to silhouette the outline of the tree against the darkness with no glare from the bulb. Unobtrusive lighting fixtures will be recessed into the steps or changes of level to prevent people falling or tripping in the dark, and lighting on spikes is suggested in the borders behind the pergola, allowing it to be lit up discreetly, showing both the handsome structure and the extent of the garden. For security or safety, an electric water-proof cable will be installed to extend round the base of the perimeter walls, with socket outlets to allow for additional spike lighting if necessary. Similar lighting will also be provided at the front of the house.

The Planting Plan

When the revisions have been approved by the client, and the amended sketch plan adopted, work can begin on the detailed planting plan. Frequently the client or owner is much more concerned and enthusiastic over this soft element than about the more expensive and less ephemeral hard construction, not fully understanding that if a garden is neglected for two or three years the planting may fail through lack of water and nourishment, or be overtaken by nettles, brambles and other invasive weeds, whereas the hard structure that forms the backbone of the plan will remain intact.

The concept

The concept of the proposed planting will have been established beforehand with the client. In our example, plants have been chosen to provide year-round interest, requiring little maintenance. Evergreens with strong foliage forms or distinctive outlines are to be used for structure planting, quick-growing climb-ers for covering walls and strategically placed trellis, and flowering shrubs, where possible, to offer the additional bonus of scent and textured foliage. Bulbs and annuals will accentuate the seasonal changes, herbs are provided for use in the kitchen, and suitable flowers and foliage for indoor decoration are also included. Clipped box and yew emphasize the formal design, their strong shapes leading and arresting the eye. The lawn is to be turfed for immediate effect, and pots and urns are positioned for decoration and to provide a planting medium where no soil is available. Planting at the front of the house is to be kept very simple, with shade-tolerant ever-green ground cover plants, and an occasional large shrub and climber.

Selecting plants

Before beginning any selection of plants, the areas of sun and shade must be established, these being governed by the orientation of the garden, the canopies of existing trees, and the proximity and height of adjacent walls and buildings. Here, the soil pH, being neutral, allows a wide range of plants to be considered. The general tendency is to cram far too many plants into too little space. In small gardens, each plant will occupy a valuable amount of soil and room; therefore anything chosen must have several points in its favour—possibly coloured bark, interesting foliage, scent, and continuous or recurrent flowering—before being worthy of selection. The colour ranges must also be established, so that the different shades blend and enhance each other.

Framework and structure planting

Framework and structure planting is chosen first to ensure that there is both a backdrop for more delicate subjects and that the overall effect will be well balanced and interesting. These plants are chosen for strategic places within the garden, either to focus attention on a particular spot, or, by creating an interesting 'eye-catcher', to detract or divert the gaze from something that would be better hidden. They also play a key role in forming effective plant groupings, usually being the primary subject around which the secondary subjects, i.e. the more decorative shrubs and herbaceous plants, are arranged. These groupings, or at least some of the plants in them, should be carried through and repeated in other parts of the garden, usually diagonally across from one side to another, thus achieving a unified whole.

Any existing trees and shrubs must be taken into account, whether they are to remain in situ or be moved to another part of the garden. The retention of some existing material, usually larger or more mature than the small plants offered by most nurseries, can help give the garden an established appearance, this older stock possibly being removed when the new planting has grown sufficiently to take its place. Shady areas may need to be furnished with light, variegated or golden foliage items if they are to be noticed, and sunny areas may need the coolness of greys and silvers.

Decorative planting

Having decided on these plants for framework and structure, the choice of decorative shrubs and herbaceous or ground cover items follows the same subjective approach. The function and role that the plants must play is as important as their height and colour; and the repetition of quite substantial groupings composed of three or five of the same shrub, underplanted with nine to fifteen ground cover or herbaceous items, weaving their way diagonally through the beds so that they appear to merge into each other, will give the planting a neat and comfortable feeling of cohesion.

Planting for seasonal effect

Seasonal effects can be achieved by grouping together plants which perform, either by flowering or by sending up new bracts, at roughly the same time of year. It is much more effective to concentrate on a few substantial groups which can be absorbed and enjoyed rather than to lose the impact by scattering them throughout the garden. This is particularly relevant when using bulbs and annuals.

Bulbs may be left in the ground from year to year, and can often be planted underneath herbaceous stock which will, as it comes into leaf, hide the yellowing bulb foliage as it dies down. Annuals give the opportunity of changing colour combinations according to fashion or whim, and sowing them in situ will cut down on expense. Pots and urns can also be planted with seasonal items for immediate colour effect. The addition of ferns, corms and tubers and low-growing or creeping items helps link hard and soft landscaping. These finishing touches can often elevate the garden from the mundane to the memorable, and can be added as the majority of plants mature.

Planting for immediate effect

Spacing is often a problem, and in this case, for purposes of immediate effect, the garden has been rather more heavily planted then necessary, but by rapidly covering the soil and leaving less room for weeds to gain a foothold, maintenance is reduced. Many books and catalogues indicate the height and spread after a period of a few years, but as most people are too impatient to wait that long, plants are often placed closer together than would ultimately be desirable. Major trees and shrubs should be planted in positions which give them sufficient space to develop fully, without being moved or pruned drastically, the space in between being filled by herbaceous or ground cover subjects that can easily be divided or removed when the main planting matures.

117

THE PLANTING PLAN

Ordering plants

The planting and ordering of plants is usually done well in advance of the proposed planting date, as otherwise the nurseries may be sold out of much of the stock. By using one supplier for the majority of items, the order is more likely to arrive in one batch, making it easier to set the plants out, still in their pots, in their proposed final planting positions, giving time to stand back and view what will be the final effect, and adjust it where necessary before committing the plants to the soil, as well as checking that those supplied are good specimens in a healthy condition.

The planting plan

The detailed planting plan pinpoints each plant or group of plants. These will take time to mature and merge. In the meantime, annuals and bulbs fill the spaces.

Trees or mature shrubs
1A. *Catalpa bignonioides* 'Aurea'
2A. Existing lilac
3A. Existing *Magnolia grandiflora*

Structure/framework planting
1. *Sambucus racemosa* 'Plumosa Aurea'
2. *Rubus cockburnianus*
3. *Choisya ternata*
4. *Cotinus coggygria*
5. *Rosa rubrifolia*
6. *Taxus baccata* (as clipped hedge)
7. *Sambucus racemosa* 'Plumosa Aurea'
8. *Amelanchier lamarckii*
9. *Viburnum plicatum* 'Lanarth'
10. *Prunus laurocerasus* 'Otto Luyken'
11. *Rosa glauca*
12. *Rosa* 'Madame Isaac Pereire'
13. *Viburnum rhytidophyllum*
14. *Rosa* 'Souvenir de la Malmaison'
15. *Arundinaria variegata*
16. *Amelanchier lamarckii*
17. *Choisya ternata*
18. *Rosa virginiana*
19. *Ceanothus dentatus*
20. *Mahonia* x 'Charity'
21. *Sambucus racemosa* 'Plumosa Aurea'
22. *Prunus laurocerasus* 'Otto Luyken'
23. *Amelanchier lamarckii*

Herbaceous/infill planting
24. *Buxus sempervirens*
25. *Iris germanica* 'Jane Phillips'
26. *Bergenia schmidtii*
27. *Artemisia* 'Silver Queen'
28. *Fuchsia* 'Versicolor'
29. *Lavandula angustifolia* 'Hidcote'

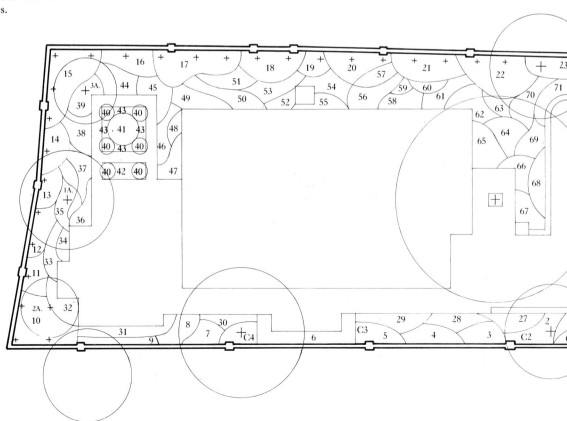

30. *Helleborus corsicus*
31. *Bergenia schmidtii*
32. *Alchemilla mollis*
33. *Iris germanica* 'Jane Phillips'
34. *Alchemilla mollis*
35. *Gypsophila paniculata* 'Bristol Fairy'
36. *Salvia officinalis* 'Purpurescens'
37. *Stachys lanata*
38. *Rosmarinus officinalis* 'Benenden Blue'
39. *Anemone* x *hybrida* 'Louise Uhink'
40. *Buxus sempervirens* (clipped into balls)
41. *Magnolia stellata*

42. *Rosa* 'The Fairy'
43. *Dianthus* 'Pink Mrs Sinkins'
44. *Caryopteris* x *clandonensis*
45. *Rosmarinus officinalis* 'Benenden Blue'
46. *Lavandula angustifolia* 'Hidcote'
47. *Salvia officinalis* 'Icterina'
48. *Ruta graveolens* 'Jackman's Blue'
49. *Alchemilla mollis*
50. *Hemerocallis* 'Pink Prelude'
51. *Phormium tenax*

52. *Hosta fortunei* 'Albopicta'
53. *Phlox* 'Norah Leigh'
54. *Rosa* 'Iceberg'
55. *Stachys lanata*
56. *Hemerocallis* 'Pink Charm'
57. *Phlox* 'Norah Leigh'
58. *Iris foetidissima*
59. *Artemisia ludoviciana*
60. *Phormium tenax*
61. *Fuchsia* 'Versicolor'
62. *Hosta sieboldiana* 'Elegans'
63. *Viburnum farreri*
64. *Hosta sieboldiana*
65. *Alchemilla mollis*

66. *Pachysandra terminalis* 'Variegata'
67. *Helleborus foetidus*
68. Ferns
69. *Daphne odora* 'Aureomarginata'
70. *Helleborus corsicus*
71. *Bergenia cordifolia* 'Purpurea'
72. *Camellia* 'Donation'
73. Ferns

Climbers
C1. *Lonicera periclymenum* 'Belgica'
C2. *Hedera colchica*
C3. *Clematis* 'Marie Boisselot'

C4. *Rosa* 'Wedding Day'

Front garden
1. *Hydrangea petiolaris*
2. *Bergenia schmidtii*
3. Ferns
4. *Pachysandra terminalis*
5. Ferns
6. *Magnolia stellata*
7. *Euphorbia robbiae*
8. *Euphorbia robbiae*
9. *Hosta fortunei* 'Albopicta'
10. *Hydrangea petiolaris*
11. Ferns
12. *Hosta ventricosa* 'Variegata'
13. *Daphne* x *burkwoodii* 'Somerset'

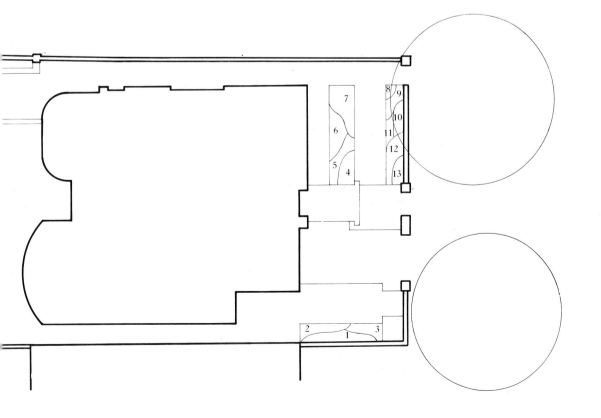

GARDEN DESIGN

AND CONSTRUCTION

HARD SURFACING
WOODEN STRUCTURES
WATER AND POOLS

HARD SURFACING

Paths and paving

The hard surfaces within the garden provide the basic framework of the overall design as well as serving various functional purposes. The pathways, for instance, link together the various elements of the design and should also provide a surface that is pleasant to walk on, well drained and relatively maintenance free. Other paved areas throughout the garden may be required for a variety of uses—for sitting out, dining or playing—and their design and construction should reflect their use.

Paving materials

When selecting materials it is important to ensure that the colour and texture will complement the soft landscaping or planting. Always err on the side of simplicity and subdued colouring. There is a wide variety of materials and finishes, including paving slabs, both natural and manufactured, bricks, concrete blocks, brushed concrete and a wide selection of stone and gravel. When choosing you should consider the cost of supply and laying as well as the colour and texture.

Natural stone

York stone is one of the most beautiful and commonly used natural paving stones. Its delicate colour and texture make it a popular choice; it looks good either wet or dry, and it combines well with traditional stock brick. Natural paving may be bought either in a range of cut sizes of uniform thickness or as 'random' sizes, i.e. a mixture of different sized squares or rectangular slabs of uniform or mixed thicknesses.

As natural stone is undoubtedly one of the most expensive forms of paving, it may be preferable to use recycled slabs which, apart from being cheaper, have the added advantage of a 'weathered' finish. Unfortunately, because of their popularity, recycled slabs are becoming more difficult to obtain and as a result a number of manufacturers are producing a range of reproduction slabs to look like natural stone. These vary greatly in quality and effect. It is always best to see a selection of slabs laid out before deciding, and also to see them when wet and dry as the colour and overall effect can change considerably.

Manufactured slabs are also available in different finishes and sizes, ranging from smooth-faced concrete slabs similar to those seen in most urban street pavements, through to the textured slabs using selected aggregates to give a variety of colours and effects. Furthermore, concrete slabs may be modified by the use of furniture wax which gives a warm honey-coloured finish. The slab sizes most commonly found are 600 mm², 600 × 300 mm, 600 × 450 mm, 450 mm², 450 mm × 300 mm, and 300 mm². The variety of uniform sizes allows one to create different patterns within the paving, but again it is best to keep this simple or it can become disturbingly overpowering.

Paving comes in many different sizes to create either random or uniform patterns:
a) Square slabs set in grid pattern
b) Random size pattern
c) Slabs set in herringbone pattern
d) Pattern made up of two-sized slabs
e) +f) Single size slabs with joints offset

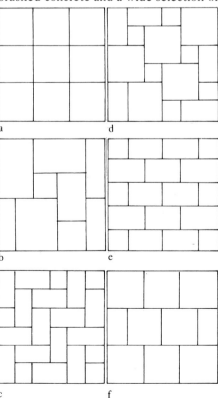

Laying paving slabs

Having selected the type of paving, you now need to decide the technique of laying. To avoid any problems of subsidence and drainage, you must follow the golden rule and first remove all the top soil from the area to be paved in order to establish a firm base on which to start.

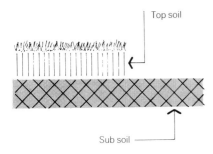

Top soil

Sub soil

Methods

There are three main methods of laying slabs. In the first, you excavate the area to the required depth and lay a bed of compacted hardcore approximately 75 mm (3 in) deep. This may be 'blinded' with either a layer of ash or sand. The slabs are then positioned on four spots of mortar, one on each corner, and gently tapped down to the required level. (Fig 1). In the second method, a weak mix of mortar is raked over the whole area of compacted hardcore. The slabs are then laid directly onto this and tapped down in the same way to the finished level. (Fig 2). The third method, used fairly frequently, especially with natural stone slabs of various thicknesses, is to lay the slab on a bed of soft sand approximately 50 mm (2 in) thick spread over the base of compacted hardcore. (Fig 3).

It is important when laying any hard surface to provide an even fall to aid drainage and avoid puddling. Usually the fall is directed towards planting areas, or in the case of large or enclosed areas, towards gulleys provided to take the surface water away.

For the final finish the slabs may be butted up against each other, or pointed-

up after a dry-mix of mortar has been brushed into the joints. It is important not to discolour the slabs with wet mortar. In some cases the joints may be raked out and dry sand brushed into the joints for a more natural look.

Natural York stone is one of the most attractive forms of paving. Its subtle colours and texture blend well with other materials and planting.

Methods of laying slabs

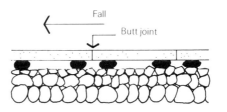

Fall

Butt joint

Fig 1: Slabs laid on spots of mortar

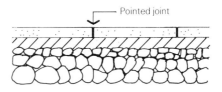

Pointed joint

Fig 2: Slabs laid on weak mortar mix

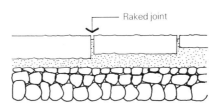

Raked joint

Fig 3: Slabs laid on bed of soft sand

Brick

Brick is one of the most traditional of all materials used in the garden. Its rich texture, varied colours and adaptable size make it ideal for paving, whether in a town garden or by a country cottage, and it can be especially effective when used in conjunction with other materials such as paving and gravel. It is important, however, that any brick selected is able to withstand the severe effects of frost, otherwise it will start to break up after a relatively short time. Although a number of house bricks may be used for paving, brick manufacturers have in recent years produced a range of brick paviours especially for the purpose.

Brick patterns

Like paving slabs, bricks can be laid to create a wide variety of patterns. The most common are variations on the basket-weave and herringbone patterns or various 'stretcher courses' in which the bricks are laid on their sides in parallel lines.

Basic brick patterns showing the different effect obtained by either laying the brick on edge or flat:
a) Basket-weave
b) Herringbone
c) Stretcher bond

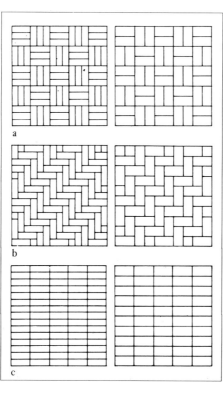

Laying bricks

Bricks can either be laid straight onto a weak mortar mix, or directly onto soft sand.

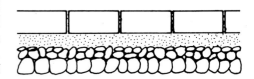

When laying bricks or concrete blocks on sand it is necessary to restrain the edge with either a line of bricks set in mortar or a length of treated timber set below the finished surface of the brick paving.

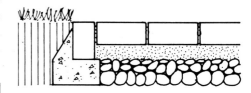

Concrete blocks

In addition to the traditional brick block, the concrete block has grown in popularity. It comes in roughly the same size as the standard brick, or in a variety of shapes that interlock to create a particular pattern. The blocks are relatively easy to lay, being bedded down onto a 50 mm (2 in) layer of sharp sand over a base of well consolidated hardcore. The blocks are simply butted together and 'vibrated' down until they are level with a special plate vibrator designed for the purpose. Sand is brushed into the joints as the vibrator passes over the surface. As when bedding bricks onto sand, it is necessary to restrain the edge.

In-situ concrete

This may seem to be a harsh and drab material to use within the garden, but it is possible to create very pleasing patterns and effects with concrete, especially when it is laid in panels bound by bands of another material such as brick or paving slabs. The areas should be designed in panels no greater than 3 m² (8 ft²) to allow for expansion and prevent cracking. A number of different finishes can be achieved; smooth or textured.

One of the most effective is known as the 'exposed' or 'brushed' aggregate finish. Here the concrete is laid and allowed to partly go off. When it begins to set, the top surface is brushed to expose the aggregate within the concrete. The size and colour of the aggregate may be selected to achieve the desired finish.

Gravel

This comes in two basic forms either as crushed stone or chips from quarries, or as rounded pea gravel from gravel pits. It can be laid either loose or compacted. If left loose, gravel has an informal character; it is also useful around trees as it allows the roots to breathe and avoids rigid paving lines around trunks. Loose gravel can look good with selected foliage plants set in pockets of top soil and growing up through the gravel. It should be laid on a well consolidated base of hardcore 75-100 mm (3–4 in) deep.

The traditional Victorian paths and driveways used a dry hoggin mix of clay and gravel to bind the gravel and prevent it from spreading. To achieve this, it is essential to consolidate each layer, using

a heavy roller up to 1020 kg (10 tons) for a driveway or a handroller up to 760 kg (15 cwt) for pathways.

Binding gravel

The specifications for this procedure vary greatly according to soil conditions, but the following method is fairly general: a hardcore sub-base of clinker or stone is laid, if required, and on this 50 mm (2 in) of gravel scalpings to form a base; then a fine gravel and dry hoggin mix is rolled on top to approximately 25 or 35 mm (1–1½ in) deep and, finally, a selected finish of gravel, fine grit, shell or stone chippings is well rolled in. It is important to create a fall of around 1:40 to allow for drainage and avoid puddling.

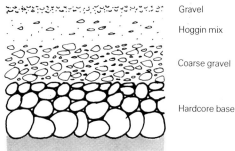

Gravel

Hoggin mix

Coarse gravel

Hardcore base

Cobbles

These beautiful smooth rounded stones come in a variety of sizes, and can be laid either in formal patterns or loose in an informal way. They are usually used in conjunction with planting and their rounded form contrasts well with the strong spikey foliage of conifers. They are somewhat uncomfortable to walk on when loose and may be used to deter people from crossing certain areas.

Fixed patterns can be created by setting them in mortar. They should be packed together as close as possible without any mortar showing. An alternative method is to bed them in a mix of dry mortar and then carefully water them to avoid any staining of the exposed surface of the cobbles. In both cases they should be set on a bed of compacted hardcore some 75 mm thick (3 in).

125

STEPS

A beautifully detailed flight of steps using York stone and brick. The brick risers have been laid with the headers showing to match the pattern of the raised brick planter.

garden are a different size to those found in a house, for example; the rise is shallower, 150 mm (6 in) maximum, and the tread is much deeper, usually a minimum of 450 mm (18 in); anything else feels cramped.

In a private garden the construction requires a foundation only at the base of the steps, but in a public park or garden a concrete foundation for the whole flight is necessary. Where there is a long flight of steps a landing should be placed at every twelve steps or so.

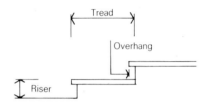

Steps within the garden should be of generous proportions and well integrated into their overall design.

Any change of level within a garden provides interest, and usually creates the need for a flight of steps to connect the levels. These steps need not be purely functional; they can often be designed as a feature in themselves. Steps in the

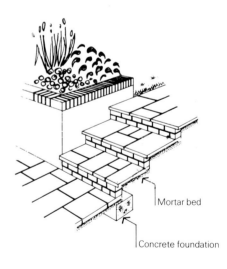

Sections of steps:
a) Brick tread and riser
b) Brick and paving slab combination
c) Pre-formed slab tread and riser

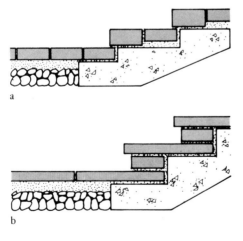

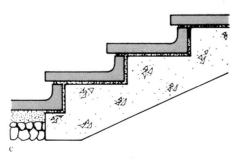

Materials

Steps can be constructed from any of the materials mentioned on pages 122–125 and should match or complement the adjacent hard surfaces. Such materials as brick, paving slabs, stone and pre-cast stone, or a combination of these, are effective. Wood, in the form of old railway sleepers, or log sections, is a versatile material and can also be used to good effect.

WALLS

Brick walls are either used to enclose a garden or to act as divisions between different parts of the garden; they may also be used to retain earth around raised planting beds or in areas where there is a change of level.

Before building a wall there are various stages to consider. First the foundations are formed in an excavated trench, the depth of which will depend on the height of the wall and the firmness of the subsoil base. On average the depth should be approximately 235 mm (10 in), and the width twice that of the finished wall size. A damp-proof course (DPC) should be included at the base of the wall, about 150 mm (6 in) above ground level. This is to prevent ground-water from rising up within the wall and causing damage, especially through the effects of frost.

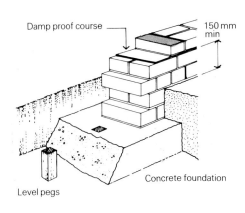

Damp proof course

150 mm min

Level pegs

Concrete foundation

Bonding

In a wall of double brick thickness the bricks are laid both lengthways (stretchers) and crossways (headers) to bind the wall and give it strength. This is known as 'bonding' and the various bonds create different patterns. The two most common are the English Bond, with alternate courses of headers and stretchers, and the Flemish Bond, where each course is laid with one stretcher followed by one header.

Bonds

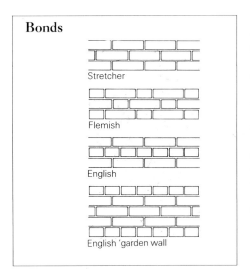

Stretcher

Flemish

English

English 'garden wall'

First ensure that the foundations are set on firm subsoil. If necessary a base of compacted hardcore may have to be put down. Bitumen-impregnated strips are usually used for the DPC, although several courses of high density engineering bricks or overlapping tiles can be used for decorative effect.

Pointing

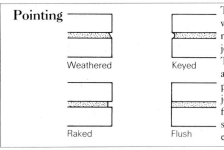

Weathered

Keyed

Raked

Flush

To ensure that the wall withstands the weather it is necessary to point up the joints between the bricks. There are various methods and the choice depends purely on aesthetics. The joints can either be finished flush or raked out to give a shadow line to emphasize each brick module.

Coping

To prevent water from seeping into the bricks, the top of the wall is finished off with a coping. A brick laid on edge is the simplest and perhaps the most pleasing of copings for a brick wall but there is also a variety of pre-cast concrete and dressed stone copings which can be used. It is important that the form and material used should, when appropriate, respect the predominant style in the locality. If the wall is over 10 m (30 ft) in length it will be necessary to provide expansion joints at regular intervals. This will allow the wall to expand and contract in different weather conditions without cracking.

Different types of coping:
a) Ridged stone coping
b) Bullnose brick coping
c) Ridged stone coping with overhang
d) Brick on edge

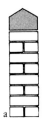

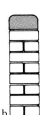

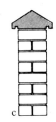

a   b   c   d

127

Right: A brick pier bonded into a single brick wall can provide extra stability.

Below: A single brick wall can be given extra stability by setting short sections of walls at right angles to each other. The bays created give added interest to the overall design.

Single-brick thickness walls, although cheaper to erect, present problems of stability. This may be overcome by incorporating piers at regular intervals. The wall may also be 'staggered' to form bays. Where the different sections meet, expansion joints—small gaps filled with fibrous materials—should be included to allow for expansion and these can be made a feature of the design.

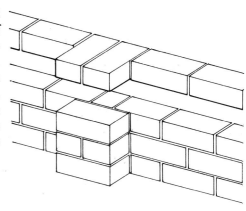

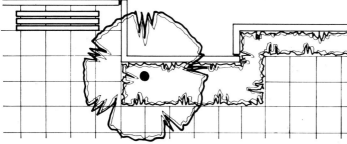

Retaining walls

Where a change of level occurs in a garden it is often necessary to provide a retaining wall to hold back the soil at the upper level. The design and construction of this is important as there will be considerable forces acting on the wall from the mass of the soil behind it and from the water within that soil. If there is to be a large area of retaining wall and it is more than 1.5 m (5 ft) in height it is advisable to consult a structural engineer.

The wall should be thicker at its base and built on adequate foundations to provide added strength and stability. An area of gravel or stone provided at the base behind the wall with weep-holes through to the front at regular intervals helps water to drain away. Where appropriate a land-drain can be included to carry the water away to a soakaway or existing drain.

Alternatively, a concrete retaining wall can be constructed and then faced with brick or stone. One advantage of this is that a 'toe' can be cast at the base of the wall to give extra stability so preventing the wall from being pushed over by the combined pressure of the soil and water. Natural stone is often used to form a retaining wall.

Right: A brick retaining wall will need to be wider at its base to give it extra stability (Fig 1).

A concrete retaining wall cast in-situ and faced with brick (Fig 2).

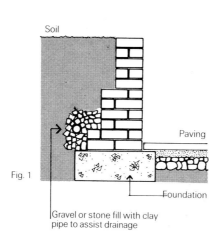

Soil

Paving

Fig. 1

Foundation

Gravel or stone fill with clay pipe to assist drainage

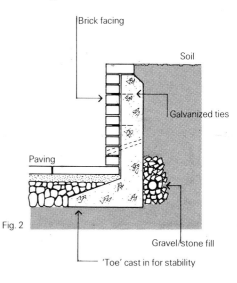

Brick facing

Soil

Galvanized ties

Paving

Fig. 2

Gravel/stone fill

'Toe' cast in for stability

Raised planting beds

These can be constructed in brick in the form of an open-topped box. The walls can either be single or double brick thickness and are usually lined on the inside with a waterproof cement render to prevent the moisture in the soil working its way through the brickwork and discolouring the brick face. Some people, however, like the mossy bloom that this forms on the brick so they omit the waterproofing.

It is important to ensure adequate drainage by placing a hardcore mix at the base of the box and, if necessary, to form weep-holes in the vertical joints of the brickwork to give extra drainage. However, the allowances for drainage should not be too generous as the soil may become excessively dry in the summer months.

Stone walls

Building with stone is a very old tradition and throughout each country, the appearance of local stone and the manner in which it is worked will vary considerably from area to area. It is important, therefore, to use the natural stone of the locality and follow local building styles. In urban or suburban situations, however, natural stone tends to look incongruous, and the imitation stone bricks that are now available are rarely satisfactory.

Though there are many styles and methods of using stone, the basic principles are the same: the wall is graded in size with the larger stones at the base to give stability, and the stone is either coursed in graded sizes to give a particular pattern or laid in a random way, the stones matched or dressed to size to give an overall pleasing effect. The building of stone walls is a highly skilled job and should preferably be undertaken only by someone who has worked with stone and who has a feeling for it.

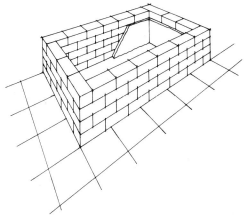

A raised brick planter with waterproof render on inside face. A raised pool can be created by adding a waterproofed concrete base.

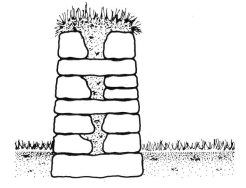

A dry-stone wall. This section shows the 'through' stones running from back to front giving added stability.

Below: The soil fill in a dry-stone wall makes it possible to establish planting to give added attraction.

129

Natural stone wall
Section of a natural stone wall using a mortar fill. The external joints are raked clean to give it the appearance of a dry-stone wall.

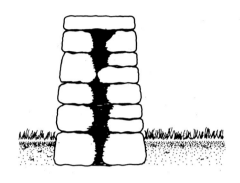

Ashlar
The centre of the wall is constructed of concrete blocks and faced with a selected stone with a coping to match.

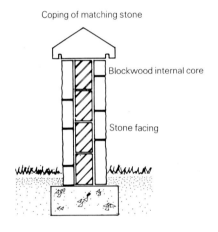

Coping of matching stone

Blockwood internal core

Stone facing

Dry-stone retaining wall
As with all retaining walls it is important to provide a back fill of gravel to prevent the build-up of ground water.

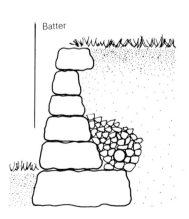

Batter

Types of wall construction

The traditional dry-stone wall uses no mortar and is simply built stone on stone with a clay and soil fill. The wall is usually wider at the base and tapers to the top. This angle is referred to as the 'batter'. At most, the bottom should be twice as broad as the top; a standard formula is that the wall should narrow by approximately 35 mm (1½ in) on each face for every 300 mm (12 in) in height. The large base stones or grounders are laid across the width of the wall onto a firm sub-soil base. It is important to have a number of cross or tie stones running from the back to the front of the wall throughout its height to tie it together and provide stability. As each layer of stones is laid, soil is used to fill up any gaps, especially in the centre. This is suitable for establishing plants within the wall.

Sometimes in a garden it is more appropriate to build a stone wall using mortar. This can be done to give the effect of a dry-stone wall by putting a mortar fill in the centre of the wall and raking the face joints out clean. Alternatively, the wall can be pointed up in the normal way, taking special care to avoid any staining of the stonework.

Retaining walls in natural stone can either be built using mortar or as a dry-stone wall. In either case it is necessary to angle the face of the wall against the retained soil. The same principles apply: placing large stones at the base and keying cross stones into the bank for added stability. As with all retaining walls, it is important to have an area of stone and gravel fill at the back of the wall with both weep-holes and a land drain to prevent the build up of ground water behind the wall.

One of the most pleasing, though expensive, uses of stone is where it is cut into blocks and used for construction. To lessen the expense it can be cut in such a way that it is used as a facing only. Known as ashlar, this is often seen in older houses and gardens.

WOODEN STRUCTURES

Wood is a sympathetic, versatile and relatively cheap material to use in the garden, appropriate for fences and trellises, pergolas and timber decking. Both soft and hard wood can be used; soft wood is cheaper, but hard wood lasts for longer. It will be necessary to protect all timber in the garden with a wood preservative to prevent rotting, and due consideration should be given to the various finishes available; darker colours such as browns and blacks provide a better foil for the brighter colours of the plants.

Fences

For the most part fencing is used to define the boundary of the garden and to provide a degree of privacy. A fence is cheaper than a wall, though less permanent and more trouble to maintain. It can often provide some shelter from prevailing winds, but will not act as a noise barrier as effectively as a wall or a thick planted hedge.

Fencing

In some cases fencing may be looked on as a temporary measure while planting and hedges establish themselves, or it may be designed as a feature in its own right. The more common forms of fencing, such as the vertical board and ubiquitous larch-lap, are hardly attractive features, but their impact may be lessened by the effects of planting. In a new garden the fencing often remains a dominant feature for a number of years, especially if the garden is small. So, although it is easier and cheaper to buy a panel of larch-lap from the local garden centre or supplier, it is better to devise an attractive fence which will create interest in certain areas and also act as a background foil to the areas of planting.

Since a fence is a free-standing and relatively thin structure it is prone to being damaged, especially in an area of high winds. It is important, therefore, that the main structure of the vertical posts and horizontal rails is well con-structed and firmly anchored.

The size of the fence post required depends on the finished height of the fence. For a normal solid-panel fence 1.8 m (6 ft) high, a 75 mm^2 (3 in^2) or 100 mm^2 (4 in^2) post is necessary. It should be about 600 mm (4 in) extra in length, allowing it to be set into the ground by about 550 mm (22 in) and to stand about 50 mm (2 in) proud of the top line of the fence if desired. For open-

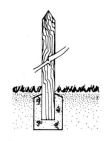

The fence post must be set firmly into the ground. If necessary include compacted hardcore to provide a firm base for the concrete.

Different ready-made designs of fencing:

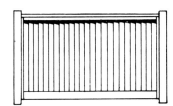

a) Traditional close-boarded

b) Spaced horizontal board

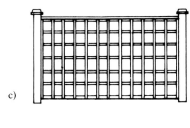

c) Square-grid trellis

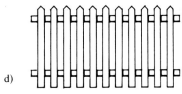

d) Top-pointed paling

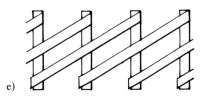

e) You may choose to design and construct your own variation on site. This is a simple angled board fixed to a series of posts.

Wherever possible fencing should be designed to give added interest and to act as a background foil to planting.

board fencing 100 mm² (4 in²) posts are preferable. With the lower post-and-rail or picket style of fencing, where the average height is 1 m, (3 ft) the post need only be set into the ground by approximately 450 mm (18 in).

All timber will need to be treated with a wood preservative to prevent the wood from rotting, especially at ground level. To prevent water from seeping into the end-grain at the top of the post, a small cap of wood can be fitted, or the post can be cut at an angle to shed the water.

The posts should be set into the ground using a strong mix of concrete: 1 part cement to 4 parts ballast. It is important to ensure that the bottom of the post is totally encased in concrete and not in contact with the soil, as water will rise up through the end-grain of the post and, in time, rot it away.

The cross rails of the fence can either be mortised into the post or fixed to the outside face. The particular design of the fence will determine the size of these rails but, in the case of picket fences, their size must be adequate to carry the weight of the fence boarding.

When designing a fence ensure that the timber sections used are adequate for the job and that the construction is not too complicated.

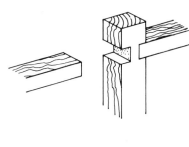

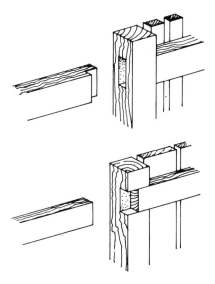

Gates

Gates are an important feature of any garden, and their design should complement the character of the house and the surrounding area. If the garden is enclosed by a particular style of fencing, the gate should be of a similar design.

A gate should be well constructed and able to stand up to constant use. It is important to ensure that the post on which the gate hangs is of sufficient size, especially in the case of a large five-bar gate at the entrance to a driveway, where it will need to be at least 175 mm^2 (7 in^2) and set 900 mm (36 in) into the ground. For a similar pedestrian gate a 100 mm^2 (4 in^2) post is adequate. Wrought-iron gates in modern styles have become very popular in town areas, but unfortunately they often appear to be flimsy, both in form and style, in comparison with their earlier counterparts. In recent years, however, craftsmen have started to make gates in more sturdy and distinctive styles, suitable for modern or period settings.

Trelliswork

The traditional diamond- or square-patterned trelliswork can either be used as a free-standing screen to separate areas within the garden, or as part of the boundary fence. Painted white or stained in dark colours, trellising can be very decorative in its own right, as well as providing an ideal support for climbing plants.

There is a wide variety of pre-fabricated trellises available today, ranging from rather flimsy types to beautifully made sections manufactured in the traditional styles. Unfortunately, the prices reflect the quality.

Trellises are basically constructed from thin laths of timber, so it is possible to experiment with diamond and square patterns, or variations on these. Trellis can also be tailor-made to suit the particular situation in the garden. As trelliswork is relatively light it is ideally suited to roof gardens, although due regard should be paid to the destructive effects of any prevailing winds.

Traditional trellis designs are now being manufactured to a very high standard, and can either be bought in a variety of standard panels or made to measure to suit a particular design.

Right: A traditional style of pergola using timber cross beams set on columns made up of clay tiles.

When designing a pergola or overhead beams it is best to use larger sections of timber to achieve a solid look. Figs 1 and 2 show two methods of fixing the upright so that it is set above the ground, lessening the chances of rotting.

Fig 3 shows a typical overhead beam construction. The upright is notched to carry the beams and the cross-tie fixed to both the beams and the face of the upright to make the structure rigid.

Pergolas and overhead beams

The design of pergolas should be simple and sturdy, with the overhead beams of timber and the supports of wood, metal, brick, stone or concrete, or, as can be seen in a number of Lutyens gardens, of tiles.

If the supports are wood they should be $100 \, mm^2$ ($4 \, in^2$) and set into the ground with concrete to a depth of $300 \, mm$ ($12 \, in$). If the pergola is free-standing the supports should be sunk deeper. In certain situations the base of the supports can be fixed to stand above the surface of the ground, making them less susceptible to rotting. This can be done by fixing them to a galvanized metal strap or dowel set into concrete.

The overhead beams may vary in size according to design, but they need to be sturdy enough over the given span to bear their own weight and that of future planting without bowing. A good guide is they should be strong enough to bear the load of a grown man. The beams can be fixed by notching into a tie beam or, as in the case of a free-standing pergola, directly into the face of the upright.

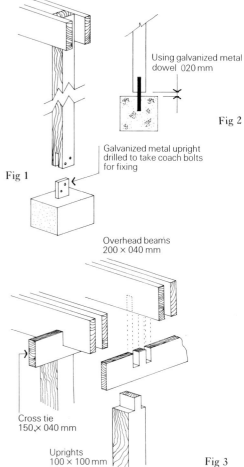

Using galvanized metal dowel 020 mm

Fig 2

Galvanized metal upright drilled to take coach bolts for fixing

Fig 1

Overhead beams 200 × 040 mm

Cross tie 150 × 040 mm

Uprights 100 × 100 mm

Fig 3

134

Timber decking

The use of timber decking creates a very distinctive modern character in the garden, usually associated with design in Scandinavia and the West Coast of America. The clean lines of the decking are particularly effective with the rounded forms of pebbles, stone and gravel and strong foliage plants such as hostas, bamboos and conifers.

Wood stains and preservatives are now available in many different colours, so different effects can be explored in relation to the surrounding plants and hard surfaces. Though the darker blacks and browns tend to look good and weather well, the silver greys, poppy reds and apple greens can often be used successfully, especially with the darker colours. Care should be taken that the brighter colours are not used where they might clash with existing or future planting. The wood needs to be sanded before applying preservative, but no other preparation is necessary. Two or three coats should be applied with a brush. Make sure each is dry before applying the next.

The basic construction of decking is very simple. It consists of joists or bearers on which is fixed the planking or decking. The bearers should be of suf-ficient size to carry the required amount of decking, but the size is also affected by whether the decking is built directly onto the ground or suspended. The spacing of the bearers should be such that when the planking is fixed it does not flex. This depends very much on the width and thickness of the planks used.

When designing decking, attention should be paid to its relationship with the rest of the garden. Where the space is enclosed or the garden small a narrower section of planking may be preferable to the heavier look of a wider section.

A variety of different patterns can be achieved with decking using different widths of timber and laying them in different directions, but avoid making the design too fussy. Planed timber should always be used for the top decking to avoid the danger of splinters, and it is advisable to run a sander over the whole construction when completed prior to staining.

Decking usually looks better with a slight gap between each plank. It is important to keep this small or chair legs will disappear and big toes will get trapped! Always use spacers when fixing to ensure that the gap between each plank is even.

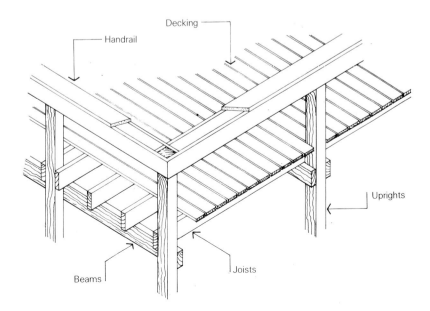

Avoid making the design and construction of decking too elaborate. Always use galvanized nails and bolts for fixing.

WATER AND POOLS

Formal pools

Most pools today are made with a flexible liner, but formal shaped pools can be constructed with waterproof concrete. Raised pools are usually made in brick and are similar in construction to raised planting beds, except that the inside is lined with either a waterproof liner or a cement render with a waterproof additive.

Ground-level pools

If a ground-level pool is to be built of concrete, timber shuttering will be necessary. First the area of the pool is marked out and excavated to the required depth, giving a finished pool depth of at least 450 mm (18 in), allowing for concrete sides of 100 mm (4 in) thickness and a foundation of 75 mm (3 in). To lessen the effects of damage if the pool freezes over, the sides should be angled to about 20°. After the hardcore foundation has been well compacted, place chicken wire over the bottom and up the sides to act as reinforcement. The concrete should be a standard mix of 3 parts aggregate, 2 parts sand and 1 part cement, with a waterproof additive.

Once the base has been poured and levelled, place the timber shuttering in position and pour in the sides. It is essential that this is done while the base is still wet, so the two run together and do not crack when dry. When the concrete has set, remove the shuttering and fill the pool with water. This helps the curing process of the concrete and makes it stronger. After a few days drain out the water and apply a 25 mm (1 in) thick cement render (1 part cement: 3 parts sharp sand) with a waterproof additive. The edging of the pool (see page 122 for materials) can now be added. This must be absolutely level as the water will show up any discrepancies. Overhang the edging by about 50 mm (2 in) to give a pleasing shadow line.

The pool cannot be stocked immediately as the water will become alkaline when the free lime in the concrete leaches out. One solution is to fill the pool and let it stand for a few days before emptying it. Repeat this 3 times over a period of 2 weeks, brushing out the pool each time. An alternative is to paint the inside of the pool with a couple of coats of a proprietary sealant.

Fig 1. Timber shuttering made up with a plywood face is positioned to ensure an even thickness of concrete in the base and sides.

Fig 2. A typical section of a pool showing the hardcore base, chicken-wire for reinforcement, concrete sides and base and the waterproof render.

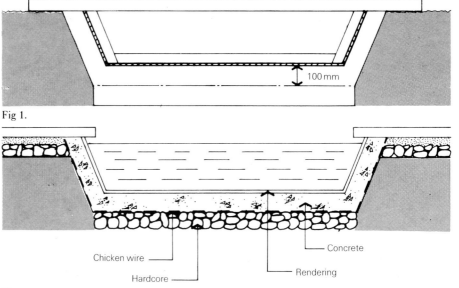

Fig 1.

Fig 2.

Chicken wire

Hardcore

Concrete

Rendering

100 mm

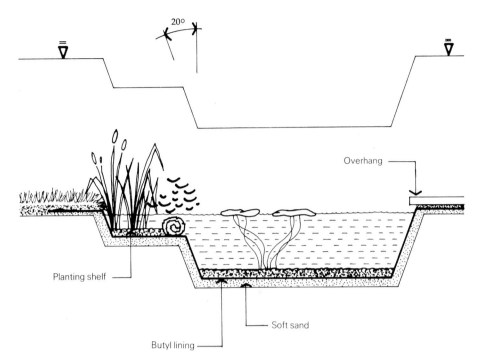

Fig 1. When excavating a pool it is important to ensure that the top surround is level the whole way round.

Fig 2. Soil and gravel may be spread over the bottom of the pool to help establish planting.

Informal pools

A flexible liner will be needed for the informal pool. The two most commonly used are laminated PVC and butyl rubber. The PVC liner comes in a variety of grades: plain, laminated and nylon-reinforced, the last being the strongest and most durable. The butyl liner is undoubtedly the most popular of liners as it is longer lasting and comes in various grades, ranging from a lightweight liner for a small pool to a heavy-duty grade suitable for a lake. It is more expensive, but easier to use than the PVC liner. To calculate the amount of liner required, measure the overall length and width of the pool, plus twice the maximum depth and twice the overhang around the margin.

Having marked out the area of the pool, a number of pegs should be driven in around the edge to indicate the finished level. It is important that this is accurate or there will be an uneven gap between the water and the edging. Excavate the area of the pool to the required depth, which can be between 450 mm (18 in) and 600 mm (24 in). If planting shelves are required these should be about 235 mm (9½ in) below the surface and at least 300 mm (12 in) wide depending on type of planting. A simple plywood template can be used to check the profile of the sides, which should be at an angle of about 20°.

Once the area is excavated, check that there are no loose or sharp stones projecting and then cover the bottom, sides and planting shelves with a layer of damp soft sand about 25 mm (1 in) thick. Place the liner over the pool and weight it down around the edges with slabs or stones. Fill the liner up slowly with water until it has taken up the shape of the pool. It may be necessary to adjust and tuck it in at certain places. When the pool is full trim the edge of the liner, leaving a margin of about 300 mm (12 in). Now the coping stones or slabs can be fixed in place using a 1:4 mortar mix (1 part cement to 4 parts sand), with an overhang of about 50 mm (2 in).

Planting in the pool can either be in plastic-mesh baskets, which rest on the bottom, or directly into a layer of soil and gravel spread over the bottom of the pool. Rolled up turves placed along the edge of the planting shelves help retain the soil until the plants become firmly established.

Garden Preparation
And Maintenance

Groundwork Preparation
Planting And Aftercare
A Year In The Garden

CULTIVATION

No garden, however well designed, will look its best if the plants are not healthy and carefully cultivated. Proper preparation and maintenance of a new garden will help it to get established quickly. Before carrying out any of the major practical tasks in developing the growing areas in the garden the ground needs to be thoroughly prepared. This groundwork cannot be over stressed. To overlook the importance of this operation will create great problems in the future.

Cultivation is the working of the soil. Even without man turning the soil with his spade the soil is being worked by nature: with dead material being decomposed by micro-organisms; with earthworms moving material around and creating aeration chambers; and with the roots of plants holding the soil particles together. So why is it necessary to cultivate the soil? As has already been stated on page 26 soils vary immensely and each soil type has its specific drawbacks: clay soils are heavy, lack air spaces and thus can have poor drainage, whereas sandy soils can lack organic matter and thus water-holding capacity. Cultivating a soil is the way to ensure that the correct soil improver is being added in the correct quantities at the correct time of year. By physically digging it into the soil the speed with which it will become part of the soil is increased.

As well as incorporating soil improvers and fertilizers, cultivation increases aeration (roots need oxygen and increased oxygen also stimulates the decomposition of organic matter); it buries surface annual weeds and removes the roots of perennial weeds; and it makes the soil surface uniform and easy to work for subsequent operations, such as planting, laying turf and seed sowing. On the other hand, cultivating the soil can bring fresh weed seed to the surface and, if done at the wrong time, cause the soil to dry out. It is also hard work.

The alternative to cultivating the ground is termed 'permiculture' in which mulches are regularly laid on the soil surface to be broken down by micro-organisms and worked into the soil by earthworms. In some situations this may be effective, but in creating a new area or when working on a soil that is poor in one form or another it is advisable to cultivate the soil to a minimum depth of 30cm (12in) to ensure regular incorporation of the soil improver.

Autumn cultivation

Cultivation is best carried out in the autumn to enable the winter frosts to break down any large clods, and to give time for the soil improver to work before the growing season begins. This is particularly important with lime, which if applied too late will 'scorch' the plants' roots. If the soil is cultivated when it is too wet then damage can occur to the soil structure, that is to say the way the soil particles are arranged and held together. If the structure is damaged the soil can turn to dust. The structure may also be damaged by compaction by heavy machinery and by over cultivation.

Cultivation can be carried out by hand (digging) or by machine, with a mechanical cultivator or plough. The choice of

Hand digging is the most thorough method of cultivation. It is designed to aerate, level and turn the earth.

method depends upon the size of the operation, accessibility and the available work force. Digging by hand is by far the most time consuming, but it is also more thorough as perennial weeds and debris are removed at the same time. Machinery can be quick and efficient, but it will chop perennial roots into many self-propagated pieces so the area should be weed killed in advance. There are many models of power cultivators on the market, displaying a wide range of sizes, depths of cultivation and ease of use, but hiring a model can be more practical for the occasional or 'one off' operation. Ploughing is only economical for the larger, accessible areas. Mole ploughs attached to the back of a tractor can be used to break up the subsoil.

Hand digging

In any garden there will probably be areas inaccessible to machinery so the gardener should have a good understanding of single and double digging. The cultivation of an area of ground to a spade depth (or one spit, which is 25cm or 10in) is known as single digging. For convenience the plot is divided down the middle and the contents of the first trench are placed in a heap alongside the last trench. The trench will be 25cm (10in) deep and 20cm (8in) wide. Organic matter is then placed in the bottom of the first trench. A second trench is then dug alongside the first, into which the soil is turned. This process is done with a spade, turning each spadeful over to bury surface weeds and debris. The process is then repeated all down one side of the plot and up the other.

On soils with heavy subsoils and where deep cultivation would be beneficial double digging is used. Again, a trench is dug running halfway across the plot, this time one spit deep and 40cm (1ft 3in) wide. The bottom of the trench is then forked over and organic matter is incorporated into this second spit. The second trench is then dug alongside the first, turning the soil over into the first. This process is then repeated all down one side and up the other side of the plot.

For both single and double digging it is important to maintain the size and line of the trench as you work down the plot. If you do not, the overall finish will be uneven. All annual weeds (not perennials) and manure should be buried and a rough clod finish should be left for weathering over winter.

Digging a plot (Fig. 1) Divide the plot down the centre lengthwise. Dig out the first trench up to the dividing line. Place the soil at the edge of the plot on the opposite side. Proceed down the length of the plot, then return up the other side. Fill the final trench with the soil from the first one.

Single digging method (Fig. 2)
1. Take out the first spit to the depth of a spade and 20 cm (10 in) width.
2. Organic matter is then placed at the base of the trench.
3. Soil from the next trench is turned over on top of the organic matter.

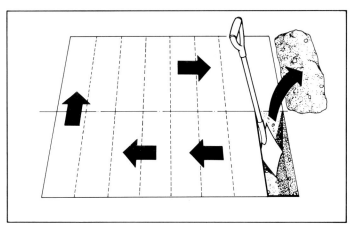

Fig. 1

Fig. 2

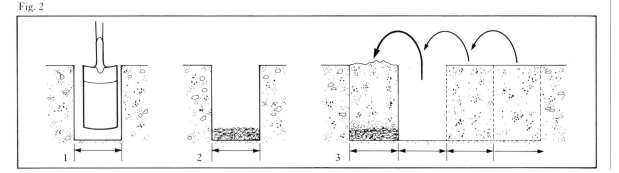

SOIL IMPROVERS AND MULCHES

Various materials can be added to the soil, either incorporated into it at the time of cultivation or applied to the surface later, to improve the soil structure and fertility. The choice of soil improver depends on the condition of the soil (see chart), and in some cases the addition of a bulky inert material, such as sand or clay, is recommended. In practice this is rarely done due to the difficulties of handling and incorporating such materials. It is much easier to dig in a bulky organic manure, which will improve the soil structure as well as the nutrient content.

Bulky organic manures

These help to improve the soil structure by increasing the humus content which binds the individual particles and increases the water-holding capacity of poor sandy soil. In clay soil humus binds together individual particles into larger conglomerates, thus creating larger air spaces and hence better drainage. Most bulky organic manures have the additional effect of increasing soil fertility by supplying the nutritional elements required for healthy plant growth.

There are various types of bulky organic manures. Farmyard manure should only be used when well rotted and no longer generating heat, or it will 'scorch' the roots of plants. Its nutrient content depends on the animals' diet; horse manure is probably the most socially acceptable as it is not so smelly, but its nutrient content is variable. With leaf-mould the end product should be moist and sponge-like, crumbling into small flakes and blackening on exposure to air. The time it takes to reach this stage depends on the type of leaf and the construction of the heap. Spent mushroom compost is nutritious and releases nitrogen slowly into the soil, but it contains gypsum which is alkaline so is not recommended for sites where lime-hating plants are to grow. Other bulky organic manures include garden compost

Soil types and how to improve them

Soil type	Temperature	Texture	Nutrition	Drainage	Weight	Improvements
Sandy	Warm in spring, cold in autumn	Coarse, with large particles	Hungry soil, nutrients are leached out quickly	Very fast, soil porous	Light and easy to work	Add organic matter (and possibly clay) to improve water and nutrient-holding capacity. Fertilize
Clay	Cold in spring, warm in autumn	Sticky, with small particles	Rich in nutrients	Poor (i.e. slow, soil non-porous)	Heavy, hard to work	Add lime and/or organic matter (and possibly sand) to improve structure. Lay drainage system if necessary
Peaty		Spongy, high in organic matter	Can be low in nutrients, low pH, i.e. acidic	Often waterlogged	Depends upon moisture content	Improve drainage, add lime to neutralize acidity. Fertilize
Chalky		Crumbly, high in calcium carbonate	Can be low in nutrients, high pH, i.e. alkaline	Good	Usually shallow	Add organic matter to reduce pH and to improve water and nutrient retention. Fertilize
Loam		Good crumb structure, equal amounts of sand and clay, plus 10% humus	Rich in all nutrients	Good	Fair	Periodically add organic matter and lime

(described at length below), composted sawdust, spent hops, shoddy and sewage sludge.

Lime

Lime is used as a soil improver, particularly on heavy soils: it benefits the soil structure by causing flocculation, making the very small particles of the clay soil stick together, thus forming larger particles and improving aeration and drainage. It also neutralizes the excessive acidity and supplies the plants with nutrient calcium in the form of calcium carbonate, which is essential for plant growth, though few soils are deficient in this element.

The major sources of lime for use in horticulture and agriculture are ground limestone and chalk. Lime is constantly being lost from the soil by leaching by rain, removal by plants, and by the process of neutralization of soil acids and of fertilizers. It should be applied in the autumn and should be roughly worked into the soil, not be mixed with fertilizer or farmyard manure. The time between applying the lime and sowing the crop should be as long as possible.

Garden compost

Compost produced from rotted organic matter is a very good bulky organic manure. The term compost in this context should not be confused with the composts, such as John Innes, used as growth media. By managing your own garden compost heap you have a free supply of bulky organic manure that is on hand, of a known quality, and made with the knowledge that it is ecologically sound in that garden and kitchen waste is being re-cycled into first-class humus. The ideal compost is dark, even in texture, weed, pest and disease free, and nutritious. Most garden compost heaps fail because they do not rise to high enough temperatures to destroy the majority of weed seeds, pests and diseases. In order to reach the right heat the heap needs to

breathe, for oxygen is used by bacteria which are vital in breaking down the raw organic matter. The energy released by these millions of active bacteria is in the form of heat, and this in turn kills most of the weed seeds, disease spores and pests at all stages of their life-cycles. Although the bacteria feed off the compost their action can be speeded up by adding an activator to the compost which adds nitrogen and phosphates. A well-made compost heap should reach 60°C (140°F) during the first few weeks. In the summer a compost heap can take two to three months to be ready for use but in winter the process is much slower, taking up to the following spring. The signs that the heap is ready are that it becomes cold and earthworms are found within it.

Any organic vegetable matter can be used for compost providing it is not too bulky, so kitchen waste, grass clippings, weeds, straw and soft hedge clippings are all suitable. Bulky materials, such as cabbage-stalks and coarse hedge clippings, can be shredded by a machine to make them easier to rot down. It is

In these compost bins, leaves and compost are kept separate.

important to have a high ratio of green leafy material to build up the high temperatures. Diseased plant material and parts of pernicious weeds that will propagate should be burned separately and not used on the heap.

It is advisable to have one clear area in the garden for compost making, and also to make special compost bins for these look tidier, are easier to manage, reach higher temperatures and make better compost. Open heaps, on the other hand, are more likely to dry out and cool down, and do not reach such high temperatures. Large piles will benefit by being turned to make sure all the material is aerated—in summer this should be done after the first month, in cooler weather after six weeks—so it is best to have two or three bins, which will leave one clear into which the others can later be turned.

The bin most economically constructed has walls of wooden slats or planks that either interlock at the sides or are slotted into place between stakes or angled metal. Bricks can be spaced around the base to hold the slats up and allow air to enter from beneath. The heap is best made in layers approximately 15cm (6in) thick. On top of the first layer a nitrogen-providing activator can be added (e.g. sulphate of ammonia at $15g/m^2$ or $\frac{1}{2}oz/yd^2$) or farmyard manure spread out evenly. Sometimes soil layers are added but these can hinder the rise in temperature, particularly in the case of dry soil. The second layer is again of vegetable matter and to this ground chalk or limestone is added at $135g/m^2$ ($4oz/yd^2$). These layers are then alternated up to the top of the bin. If dry the heap should be well watered. Without moisture the heap will not rot and a dry, brittle pile will be created. Do not go to the other extreme, because if the heap becomes waterlogged oxygen will be excluded, thus preventing decay and producing a sticky, smelly, slimy, amorphous mass.

Green manure

Another way to increase the organic matter in the soil is by growing a green manure of mustard, Italian rye grass, alfalfa or rape. This will rapidly break down when incorporated into the soil, increasing the amount of humus and

This system of working three compost bins allows one of the bins to be kept free for turning compost into.

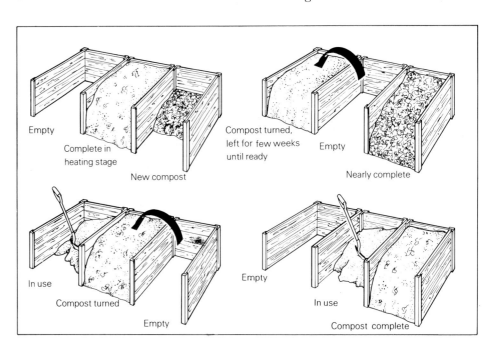

Empty

Complete in heating stage

New compost

Compost turned, left for few weeks until ready

Empty

Nearly complete

In use

Compost turned

Empty

Empty

In use

Compost complete

nutrients available to subsequent crops. When sowing a green manure the soil should be lightly forked and a nitrogen fertilizer applied at the rate of $33g/m^2$ ($1oz/yd^2$). The seed should be broadcast at $33g/m^2$ ($1oz/yd^2$), raked in well and irrigated. Then, when the crop is about 30cm (1ft) high, or before the flowers have opened, it should be dug directly into the soil.

Mulches

A mulch is a material that is laid on the soil surface around the plants in order to suppress weed growth and conserve soil moisture. The ideal mulch is too heavy to blow around, moisture retentive, looks good and is odourless. It is also cheap or free, and readily available in large quantities; free from weed seed, pests and diseases; has some nutritional content; and will improve the soil structure. The mulching materials displayed in the chart possess different combinations of these qualities; few contain them all.

The best time to apply a mulch is in the late autumn or early winter, but in practice a mulch can be applied at any time of the year, providing the soil is moist and weed-free and that the mulch can be applied without damaging the plants. The mulch must be applied thickly otherwise it will be ineffective as regards weed control. The ideal thickness is 8cm (3in). The mulch should be well rotted to prevent scorch and also to prevent the temporary loss of nitrogen, which is taken up by the partially decomposed organic matter in the decomposition process.

Mulches

Mulch	Nutritional value	Aesthetic value	Availability	Other comments
Gravel or stone chippings	None	Good	Local quarries and builders merchants; small quantities from garden centres	Excellent for alpines and dry gardens
Spent hops	Small	Fair	Breweries	Initially pungent, can blow around if dry
Leaf mould	Fair	Good	Own supply	
Lawn clippings	May detract nitrogen from soil	Poor	Own supply	Has been believed to reduce black spot when used as a mulch on roses
Well rotted farmyard manure	Variable/good	Good	Local farm or stables	Can smell unpleasant
Paper pulp	Small	Fair	Paper mills	
Pine needles	Small (acidic)	Good	Own supply	
Composted sawdust	Fair	Fair	Sawmills	
Black plastic	None	Poor	Hardware suppliers	Can be covered with an organic mulch to improve appearance
Mushroom compost	Good (alkaline)	Good	Mushroom grower	Gypsum is added by mushroom growers which makes it alkaline. Not advisable for acid-loving plants on near neutral soils
Garden compost	Good	Good	Own supply	Important that top quality compost is used; if it contains weed seed it will defeat the object
Shredded bark	Low	Good	Horticultural supplier	Expensive
Seaweed	Good	Fair	Own supply	Not easily available, at present only in coastal areas

FERTILIZERS

Major nutrients and fertilizers

Macro-element	Plant use	Deficiency/excess symptoms
Nitrogen	Part of every living cell, a constituent of chlorophyll	Deficiency – stunted growth, small pale leaves. Excess – soft, dark growth, retarded flower and fruit production
Phosphorous (Phosphate P_2O_5)	Part of every living cell; encourages root development and the ripening of seeds and fruits	Deficiency – retarded root growth, seeds and fruit slow to form, leaves turn yellow
Potassium (Potash K_2O)	Aids development of meristems; increases resistance to disease	Deficiency – dying back of shoot tips and leaf edges; lowers resistance
Magnesium	Used in chlorophyll production	Deficiency – leaf discolouration and premature defoliation; usually only on light soils
Calcium	Part of the cell wall structure, constantly needed by all growing plants	Deficiency – dye back, wilting, poor root production; deficiency is rare
Sulphur	Necessary for production of chlorophyll	Similar to nitrogen; deficiency is very rare

In discussing the addition of soil improvers, bulky organic manures have been mentioned not only as a means of improving soil structure and the water-holding capacity, but in some cases as a means of providing plant nutrients. The range and percentage of nutrients in these various manures varies greatly not just from manure to manure—for instance peat contains 1% nitrogen and horse manure up to 21%—but also from one source of a particular manure to another. Nutrient content fluctuates greatly according to the age, amount of leaching sustained, stage of decomposition and, in the case of farmyard manure, the diet of the animals.

A fertilizer on the other hand has the sole purpose of providing the nutritional elements required for plant growth. Most elements are found in the soil following the breakdown of the parent rock. They are taken up by the roots of the plants and in the natural cycle these elements are then returned to the soil on the death of the plant. However, if the plant is cropped or the dead material removed these elements need to be replaced. There are a number of nutritional elements essential for plant growth. These are divided into two groups: macro and micro elements. Macro-elements are required by the plant in large amounts, while micro or trace elements are only required by the plant in small amounts but are equally important for healthy plant growth. It is important that the elements are available in the correct proportions as plant growth can be affected by any deficiency or excess.

The macro-elements (not including carbon, oxygen and hydrogen) are nitrogen (N), phosphorous (P), potassium (K), calcium (C), magnesium (Mg) and sulphur (S). Sulphur, calcium and magnesium are readily available in most soils. The recognized micro-elements are: iron, boron, zinc, manganese, copper, molybdenum and chlorine. The availability of nutrients in acceptable form is

Natural source	Inorganic fertilizer	Organic fertilizer
Plants and animal remains, easily leached	Ammonium sulphate (20%) Ammonium nitrate (33%)	Hoof and horn (15%); Dried blood (10%); Horse manure (0.7%); Fishmeal (9%); Bonemeal (4%); Seaweed meal (3%)
Inorganic salts; most are unavailable to plants	Superphosphate (20%)	Bonemeal (20%); Fishmeal (4.8%); Seaweed meal (3%); Horse manure (0.3%)
Inorganic salts; most are unavailable to plants	Potassium sulphate (48%) Potassium nitrate (46%)	Fishmeal (5–7%); Seaweed meal (2%); Horse manure (0.6%); Fresh bonfire ashes
Inorganic salts and remains of plants	Magnesium, limestone, epsom salts	Farmyard manure
Inorganic salts	Lime	
Soil humus		

affected by the pH of the soil. Thus in alkaline soils rhododendrons and many other ericaceous plants turn yellow and chlorotic because the micro-element iron is 'locked up' and not available in an acceptable form for the plant.

Manures are normally of organic origin and derived from something that was alive—either animal or vegetable— whereas fertilizers are either organic, such as bone meal or hoof and horn, or inorganic and derived from a substance that has been either synthesized or of mineral origin. An organic gardener would only use the range of organic fertilizers and bulky organic manures, with the occasional use of a mineral fertilizer such as lime.

Fertilizers are either slow or fast release. There are advantages and disadvantages to both, but nowadays there is much demand for the fertilizers which will give immediate results. However, the disadvantage of these is that their action cannot be delayed and any fertilizer which is not used immediately is lost, perhaps washed away to cause problems elsewhere—nitrogen, for example, builds up in waterways and kills fish. This is ecologically destructive and wasteful of fertilizers. On the other hand, slow-release fertilizers are much more economical in the long run as they release small amounts over a long period, so they can be applied before planting as a base dressing or as a top dressing in the spring to last the season.

Application of fertilizers

Fertilizers can be applied by hand in the form of either base or top dressings, by a rotary distributor or by a diluter for liquid feeds. In base dressing the fertilizer is incorporated into the soil before planting, and in top dressing the fertilizer is applied after planting and watered into the soil surface. Liquid feeds are applied to the soil or to the foliage of plants. It is important never to apply a liquid feed to dry soil—always water beforehand.

WEED CONTROL

A simple definition of a weed is 'a plant out of place'. It is important to control weeds because they are unwanted competitors with garden plants for air, light, nutrition and space. They can harbour damaging pests and diseases and can look unsightly.

Weeds are generally plants that are highly successful in one form or other of regeneration, for example annuals which can rapidly produce an abundant supply of fertile seed. To control weeds effectively one must understand how they are so successful and their basic classification into perennials and annuals. The former last for many years, producing flowers and seeds each year. They may be woody or herbaceous, and they have roots or bulbs below the ground which enable them to survive a dormant period with no top growth. Perennial weeds include: bindweed (*Calystegia sepium*), dandelion (*Taraxacum officinale*), couch or twitch grass (*Agropyron repens*) and stinging nettles (*Urtica dioica*). Annuals are plants which grow from seed, flower, fruit and die in one growing season. Some annuals have more than one generation in one year and are called ephemerals. Examples of annual weeds are: shepherd's purse (*Capsella bursa-pastoris*), annual nettle (*Urtica urens*) and chickweed (*Stellaria media*).

Weeds can be controlled by either cultural methods or by chemical control (herbicides). Cultural methods are more time consuming in man-hours, but certain practices, such as mulching, can reduce the labour input immensely.

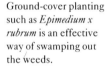

Ground-cover planting such as *Epimedium x rubrum* is an effective way of swamping out the weeds.

Cultural control

This can be achieved by a number of practices. Hand-weeding may be done with a dutch, draw or double-bladed hoe, or by a hand fork, which is useful for small areas such as rock gardens, or by a border fork, which is better for deep-rooted perennials and large areas. Hand-weeding is still the main method of weed control, but it is time consuming and can increase water loss from around the plants, bring fresh weed seed to the surface and damage roots. Weeds may also be controlled by the planting of ground cover, which fills all the available space with the desirable plants and leaves no room for the establishment of weeds. The disadvantages of this method are that it may take a while for the plants to become established and also it is difficult to incorporate organic matter into the soil. Mulching, too, will control weeds as discussed above on page 145.

Weed control

Common name	Botanical name	Cultural control	Chemical control
Couch	*Agropyron repens*	General for all problem weeds. Careful repeat forking may be the most effective way to control, followed by subsequent spot treatments for remaining fragments	Use glyphosate (e.g. Tumbleweed) at any time of the year apart from in severe weather in winter. Apply dichlobenil (e.g. Casoron G) in November–February, or dalapon when growing strongly
Dock	*Rumex spp*	As above	Apply glyphosate (e.g. Tumbleweed) when leaves have unfolded before the flower spikes emerge
Ground elder	*Aegopodium podagraria*	In a shrub border black polythene can be spread over area and covered with soil to weigh it down and improve appearance. If left in place for a number of years the polythene will kill any ground elder below it	Dichlobenil (e.g. Casoron G) can be applied in February and the glyphosate (e.g. Tumbleweed) as soon as the leaves have unfolded in May or June. On uncultivated areas repeated treatments of glyphosate May–June
Bindweed	*Convolvulus arvensis*	As couch	Apply glyphosate (e.g. Tumbleweed) in July–mid-September. If among other plants use Tumbleweed Gel to paint individual leaves
Creeping thistle	*Cirsium arvense*	Cultivate regularly	Spot treat with glyphosate (e.g. Tumbleweed) just before flowering in July. Dichlobenil (e.g. Casoron G) in February or spot treatments with 2,4–D
Oxalis	*Oxalis spp*	As couch	Spray glyphosate (e.g. Tumbleweed) onto the leaves in spring. May need a number of applications
Horsetail	*Equisetum arvense*	Improve drainage	Apply glyphosate (e.g. Tumbleweed) July–mid-September. May need repeated treatment
Nettle	*Urtica dioica*	As couch	Apply glyphosate or 2,4–D + 2,4,5–T (e.g. Boots Nettlekiller and Nettletex), preferably on spring growth (when 20cm/8in high)
Bramble	*Rubus spp*	Mow down with a powerful strimmer or large rotary mower to weaken plants	Apply glyphosate or 2,4–D + 2,4,5–T (SBK Brushwood Killer), preferably July–September

Chemical control

The use of herbicides for weed control is a relatively new practice. Although the first herbicide (sodium dinitrocresylate) was discovered in 1896, it was not until the Second World War that herbicide technology really developed.

In the 1940s the 'hormone' weedkillers (2, 4–D and 2, 4, 5–T) were discovered, so-called because they are related to natural plant-growth regulators or hormones. In the 1950s ICI discovered paraquat and diquat, both of which are contact weedkillers. In 1956, simazine, another well-known weedkiller, was marketed for the first time. More recently glyphosate (1971), a translocated herbicide, was discovered and in 1976 alloxydim sodium, a translocated grass killer; these are absorbed in the plant's system like a systemic insecticide. Herbicides can be divided into the various groups displayed in the chart, depending on the way in which they kill the weeds.

When using or purchasing herbicides (indeed any chemicals) it is important to distinguish between the 'active ingredient' and the 'tradename'. Different companies will sell products with different tradenames but containing the same active ingredient, for instance both Tumbleweed and Roundup contain glyphosate. The active ingredient dictates the way in which the weeds will be killed, and thus in which situation and on which weeds it will be most effective. It is also important to note that some products will have more than one active ingredient. Pathclear, for example, contains paraquat, diquat, simazine and aminotriazole.

Application of herbicides and insecticides

When applying any chemicals the following points should be strictly adhered to:

- Read and follow the instructions including the first-aid instructions.
- Prevent spray drift by not spraying on windy days, using a dribble bar, not using hormone weedkillers on warm still days as they will vapourize, and keeping the nozzle or the dribble bar as low as possible.
- Avoid spillage, and if it does occur wash immediately.
- Do not exceed the stated dose.
- Store all chemicals in a *locked* cupboard well away from food and out of reach of pets and children.
- Wash out equipment before and after each use.

Herbicides

Type	Effect	Use	Active ingredient	Trade name
Contact	Kills what it touches. Many become harmless on contact with soil	Annual weeds, seedling weeds	Paraquat Paraquat + diquat	Gramoxone Weedol
Translocated (Hormone)	Kills all parts of the plant, absorbed into and moved around the system. Can take a number of weeks for complete kill	Perennial weeds, spot weeding	Glyphosate 2,4,5–T + 2,4–D	Spasor Roundup Tumbleweed SBK Brushwood Killer Nettletex
Residual	Remains effective in soil for a period of time. Can be selective or total	Maintaining weed free areas	Simazine Dichlobenil Propachlor	Weedex S2G Simadex SC Casoron G Ramrod
Selective	Only kills certain weeds	Mainly for use on lawns	MCPA	MCPA
Total	Kills all weeds, indeed kills all plants	Neglected areas	Sodium chlorate	

- Keep a separate sprayer or watering-can for herbicides.
- Use recommended protective clothing—no harm can be done in being over cautious.
- Never transfer pesticides into other containers for storage.
- Safely dispose of all containers. Note special precautions on page 157

for use of insecticides.

There are various methods of applying herbicides: with a knapsack sprayer, a watering can with a dribble bar, with a mounted or mobile sprayer, or by Controlled Droplet Application (CDA) sprayers. The time of application and the choice of herbicide will depend on the particular problem (see chart).

Applying a translocated herbicide to broad-leaved weeds in the lawn with a paint brush.

Using a watering can to apply a selective herbicide to kill broad-leaved weeds in the lawn.

PESTS AND DISEASES

Plants under stress are more likely to be attacked by pathogens (pests or diseases). This stress may be due to a number of causes including under and over watering, wind scorch, temperature fluctuations, air pollution and nutritional imbalances. These environmental factors will also cause other symptoms of poor health, which should not be confused with a pest or disease attack.

The pests that attack plants are usually insects, but the term can also include slugs and snails, birds, rabbits, deer and livestock. They can be broadly divided into groups according to the damage they cause to the plant: the suckers, which include aphids (greenfly and blackfly), whitefly and scale, extract fluids by inserting a stylet between the plant cells into the phloem (the vessel that transports the sugars around the plant); the tunnellers, such as leaf miner and eelworm (nematodes), bite the tissue between the upper and lower cuticle of the leaves, roots or stems; and, finally, the chewers bite off whole chunks of the plant—the leaves are eaten by caterpillars, slugs, snails, pigeons, mice, rabbits, deer, and leaf cutters, the roots are attacked by chafer grubs, wire worm, cut worm, millipedes and leatherjackets, and the stems by cut worm and leatherjackets.

Diseases

Plant diseases are the result of infections by certain fungi, bacteria or viruses, all of which are termed pathogens. There are some 100,000 species of fungi known of which only a few do damage to plants. They are all related to the plant kingdom but differ in that they do not contain chlorophyll, obtaining their nourishment instead by secreting enzymes into dead or living organic matter and then absorbing the digested products. All fungi are made up of threads (hyphae) which join up to form a network (mycelium) from which the spore-producing reproductive structures are formed. The major fungal diseases include rusts, powdery mildew, downy mildew and blackspot.

There are some 1,600 known bacteria, and they reproduce by division, which in warm conditions can be very rapid. But they, too, cause few plant diseases, the major ones being fireblight, bacterial soft rot and bacterial canker.

The most important and widespread plant pathogens are viruses, which are named according to the effect they have on a particular plant. This can be confusing as the same virus can have a number of host plants and will affect them in different ways, for example the virus that causes cucumber mosaic also causes stunting in dahlias and woodiness in passion fruit. Viruses can cause many symptoms of ill health in plants—yellowing, mottles, ring spots, malformations and 'flower breaking'. Sometimes these effects can be desirable and cause attractive variegation, in *Abutilon thompsonii var. striatum* for example. A virus can also be present in the tissues of a host plant with no symptons visible. Viruses can be spread by vegetative propagation, vectors (such as aphids, beetles, mites and eelworm), pollen, seed, physical contact and cultivation.

Pest and disease control

The control of pests and diseases in a garden is necessary unless the habitat is so well balanced that the pests are controlled by natural predators (those pests which have been introduced from abroad do not, of course, have natural predators), or unless their presence is not considered a problem. It is often stated that pest and disease problems in our gardens have greatly increased over the last few decades. With the general increase in the use of insecticides and fungicides in agriculture—killing not only the pests but also the natural predators—the total ecology seems to have become unbalanced; with fewer predators around, the pests seem to be more adaptable, quicker to form resistance and to increase in number. Pest numbers have rocketed and the only immediate remedy is to use more insecticides.

Non-chemical methods

There are, however, methods of keeping pests and disease at bay without constantly resorting to chemicals. If the plants are generally healthy they will be stronger and more resistant to attack. Also, 'companion planting' is a method of protection that may be successful. The theory is that by planting a particular companion plant next to your crop plant, for instance marigolds next to tomatoes, the plant pests will be deterred from attacking the crop. Also, certain plants, for example *Convolvulus tricolor*, will encourage the predators that in turn will control your pest outbreaks. Many plants of the Compositae and Umbelliferae families will attract hoverflies, which will then feed off the aphids.

Biological control, which introduces a natural predator, sometimes obtained from specialist suppliers, is very effective in certain cases. *Encarsia formosa* is a parasitic wasp which controls whitefly in glasshouses; *Phytoselius persimilis* is a large wasp which controls red spider mite in glasshouses; ladybirds and hoverflies control aphids; and hedgehogs eat slugs.

Other methods of control in specific situations include spraying greenhouse plants daily with water to reduce outbreaks of mealy bug and red spider mite, or the use of specialized fencing to deter rabbits and deer (tying human hair on fences has also been known to repel deer). Also, pheromene sprays can be used to confuse the moth pest so it is unable to find its mate, and slugs can be caught in slug traps—the slugs will hide in half grapefruit skins and can be destroyed in the morning, or they will drown in jam jars filled with beer and sunk into the ground.

Finally, when an attack occurs, the pathogens can be picked off by hand (this is particularly effective in small areas and at the start of an outbreak), and diseased material should be cut and burnt immediately, making sure that the cut is below the visible infection for the pathogen moves ahead of the symptoms.

Chemical control

The long list of chemicals used in pest and disease control include insecticides, acaricides (for mites), molluscicides (for slugs and snails), and fungicides. Chemical control is not used in Britain against bacterial pathogens and as yet viruses cannot be controlled by a chemical. This barrage of chemical products includes some which are practically harmless and others which are potentially harmful if misused. The repeated use of the same insecticide can give rise to resistant species in the pest population, which will rapidly increase in numbers, (aphids, for example, can reproduce asexually and one can give rise to more than 100,000 in one month). Thus it is always advisable to rotate the insecticides used.

In AD 900 the Chinese were using Barsenic to control garden insects, and other pesticides have been used by man for many centuries. The use of insecticides derived from plant origins has been recorded since the seventeenth century, when tobacco extracts were used as a contact insecticide. Along with pyrethrum, quassia and derris, these 'organic' insecticides dominated the field until the 1930s when the search for new chemical insecticides was intensified. From the late thirties onwards a whole new breed of chemicals began to emerge, including DDT (1939), aldrin and dieldrin (1945), allethrin (1949) and carbaryl (1951). These chemicals are broken down into four groups: the organophosphates such as malathion, diazinon and aldrin; the organochlorines, DDT, chlordane and dieldrin; the carbamates, pirimcarb, temik and carbaryl; and the synthetic pyrethroids such as allethrin.

By the 1970s, however, the bad side of

153

Major pests and diseases of the conservatory and ornamental garden

Pest or disease	Plants affected	Symptoms of attack
Aphids, blackfly, greenfly etc.	Nasturtium, roses and many others	Distortion of growing points and leaves
Caterpillars (cabbage-white etc.)	The leaves of many flowering plants	Unsightly holes appear in the leaves
Leather jackets	Lawns and many garden plants	The roots are eaten just below soil level
Mealybugs	Major pest of perennial glasshouse plants	White insects with a powdery wax-like coating. Insects cluster on leaf axils and on undersides of leaves
Moles	Lawns and borders	Plants disturbed by tunnelling
Red spider mites	On glasshouse and outdoor ornamentals	Many small pale dots appear on the leaves. Fine webbing may also be seen. The tiny mites are active on the undersides of the leaves and can just be detected by the naked eye. They are yellow or red in colour
Scale insects	Found on glasshouse and outdoor ornamental plants	Brown scab-like insects often found in clusters or dotted along stems and leaves. Immature scales are soft and pale. The insects all excrete honeydew which in turn encourages sooty mould
Slugs and snails	Seedlings and young plants	Seedlings disappear and large, irregular holes appear in young plants
White fly	Range of glasshouse and garden ornamentals, e.g. fuchsias, pelargoniums, cucumbers	Small white flies found on undersides of leaves. They produce honeydew on which grows sooty mould. Eggs are small, rounded and pale
Wild rabbits	Many garden plants eaten, particularly in rural and semi-rural areas	Large chunks eaten off, sometimes sizeable plants eaten to the ground. Will also eat bark of young trees
Blackspot	Roses	Dark brown spots on leaves
Damping off	Seedlings and cuttings, mainly under glass	Seedlings and cuttings rot at soil level
Powdery mildew	Wide range of ornamentals	Powdery white coating develops on leaves and stems
Rust – many different forms	Roses, hollyhocks, fuchsias	Orange, powdery spots on leaves and stems
Viruses	Many ornamental plants	Various symptoms including mottled, stunted growth and distortion

Cultural control	Example of chemical control	Comments
Encourage ladybirds and other predators, e.g. hoverflies, birds. Discourage ants	Regular spraying with soapy water. Non-systemic insecticides: rotenone (derris dust), malathion, pyrethrum, permethrin, resmethrin. Systemic insecticides: diazinon, pirimcarb (e.g. Rapid), pirimiphos-methyl (e.g. Symbol 2), dimethoate	Important to commence control measures at very first signs of infestation
Examine regularly to pick off caterpillars and crush eggs. Grease banding is effective against the winter moths	Rotenone (derris dust), bioresmethrin, malathion, permethin (e.g. Picket)	
Leave land fallow for one season. Regular cultivation of ground reduces larvae	In October or April apply a soil insecticide like diazinon (e.g. Root Guard)	Often a problem in land newly cultivated from grass or waste land
Spray over with water daily – prevents heavy infestation	White mineral oil dilutions sprayed will penetrate the waxy coat and kill. On a small scale paint insects with methylated spirits. Systemic insecticides include pirimiphos-methyl (e.g. Symbol 2) and dimethoate (e.g. Keriguard)	
Trapping – 2 types of approved mole traps can be purchased, best done in early spring	Poisoning is highly toxic and not recommended. Repellants, e.g. mothballs, creosote and garlic, have been used with varying degrees of success	
Mist over daily with water. High humidity discourages infestations. Biological control with *Phytoselius persimilis*	Spray with a systemic acaricide e.g. dimethoate (e.g. Keriguard), demeton-S-methyl, dicofol + tetradifon, primiphos methyl (e.g. Symbol 2); or non-systemic, e.g. derris, malathion, diazinon	Mites rapidly become resistant to any one chemical spray
Carefully inspect all newly acquired plants. Wipe off insects with soft rag dipped in soapy water	Soft immature scales treated by non-persistent contact insecticide, e.g. diazinon, malathion. On adults use systemic insecticide e.g. dimethoate (e.g. Keriguard)	
Hand-picking; also placing grapefruit or orange skins upside down.	Trapping in beer-filled jars. Baiting with metaldehyde or methiocarb pellets	
In glasshouses use *Encarsia formosa* as biological control	Contact insecticides: malathion, pyrethrum (e.g. Big Gun), permethrin (e.g. Picket). Systemic insecticides: dimethoate. Under glass a smoke, e.g. Fumite, can be used.	Examine plants regularly
Individual tree guards. Fencing 30cm (1ft) below ground and 1–1.25m (3–4ft) above. Inspect regularly	Repellants – various degrees of success. Trapping, shooting and gassing – seek expert advice	
Make sure all infected leaves are cleared and burnt in autumn. Plant resistant cultivars. Improve drainage, avoid shading and high nitrogen feeds.	Sulphur, captan	Some cultivars show a degree of resistance, e.g. 'Charlie's Aunt', 'Chicago Peace', 'Peace'
Good hygiene essential, not too crowded	Treat seeds with Combined Seed Dressing or Liquid Copper Fungicide when watering	
	Dinocap (e.g. Campbell's Dinocap), benomyl (e.g. Benlate), bupirimate (e.g. Nimrod–T)	
Collect and burn diseased plant material in the autumn	Thiram, oxycarboxin, sulphur dust, bupirimate (e.g. Nimrod–T)	
Take out and burn	None	

this chemical breakthrough became apparent. DDT was banned on the British market in 1970 for its remarkable persistance, so remarkable that it had found its way to the top of the food chain to the birds of prey. It was accumulating in the bodies of peregrine falcons and making their eggshells very thin and weak, so breeding was impaired as the eggs broke during incubation under the parent bird. Despite this, DDT is still being used in some places in the world today.

New substances are still being produced and in Britain alone there are some two hundred garden chemicals available to the public (including herbicides), all of which comply with the government's Pesticides Safety Precautions Scheme. The range is much wider for professional users, the farmers and growers. The approved list is published annually by the Ministry of Agriculture, Fisheries and Food as *Approved Products for Farmers and Growers*, and included in this listing are a number of Part II and III substances which are all poisonous (Part I Substances are not approved for use, so they are not listed).

If it is necessary to use a Part II (e.g. aldicarb) or III (e.g. demeton-s-methyl) substance or a chemical subject to the poisons rules (e.g. paraquat), care should be taken to use the correct protective clothing and to obtain a copy of, and read, the official booklet, *A Guide to the Poisonous Substances in Agriculture Regulations 1984*, HS (R)20.

Types of pesticides

All pesticides have been divided into two groups according to the method in which they kill the pest or pathogen: the contact insecticides, for example derris dust, are applied to the plants or the soil around the plants and kill by directly contacting the pest; the systemic ones, such as dimethoate, are absorbed into the sap of the plant which the insects then digest.

They can be further broken down into organic or synthetic chemicals, the term organic being loosely applied to mean those chemicals that are derived directly from living material. These organic chemicals—though some, such as nicotine, are highly poisonous if misused—will rapidly break down into harmless compounds on use, and so leave no residues to build up in the food chain. One of the most widely used is derris, which is an alkaloid once used by the South American Indians to kill fish. The active ingredient is rotenone and it breaks down in forty-eight hours. It is harmless to warm-blooded animals and will control aphids, caterpillars, red spider mite and thrips. Pyrethrum is also harmless to warm-blooded animals but will kill ladybirds and houseflies; it remains toxic for twelve hours and is derived from *Tanacetum cineriifolium* (syn. *Chrysanthemum cinerariifolium)*. Nicotine is also derived from a plant, *Nicotiana tabacum* or the tobacco plant; it breaks down in forty-eight hours and does not kill ladybirds or houseflies. Quassia wood comes from the wood of the tropical tree *Picrasma quassioides* and spares bees and ladybirds, but not hoverfly larvae.

Other organic pesticides are not derived from plants but from natural products. Soft soap is based on potassium carbonate and is usually obtainable from ironmongers and chemists; it is effective against cabbage-white caterpillars. Potassium permanganate is also available and has insecticidal and fungicidal properties, but will not taint the crop.

These products are used by organic gardeners along with many of the cultural practices already mentioned. The synthetic products, on the other hand, are mainly derived from petro-chemicals and some of them are very persistent; most of them kill the insects by affecting the nervous system or digestive tract, although more recently the Japanese have developed compounds that act as an insect growth regulator, killing them by preventing their development.

The application of chemicals

Pesticides are available in various forms and these dictate the method of application. Many come as sprays, either ready for use or to be diluted, which are applied by a watering can, hand-mister, knapsack sprayer, mobile-sprayer, aerosol (which is not recommended) or tractor-mounted equipment. They may also be available as dusts; smokes and thermal vapourizers for glasshouse use only; granules, such as bromophos, for soil insecticides; or pellets, such as metaldehyde for slug bait.

When using pesticides all the precautions on page 151 applicable to 'herbicides' should be followed but certain special precautions should also be observed:

- Do not use anticholinestrase compounds (e.g. organophosphorous or some carbamate products) if under medical advice not to.
- Protect bees by observing the best times to spray in the day and in the stage of crop; do not spray when flowers are open.

Applying insecticide to mixed ornamentals with a knapsack sprayer. When using the most toxic chemicals it is essential to use a mask with filter.

157

PLANTING AND AFTERCARE

Many plants die or fail to grow as quickly as they might due to bad planting and insufficient aftercare. The methods and time of year in which to plant depend very much on the type of plant and the way in which it has been raised.

Prepared trees and shrubs

Trees are available from nurseries and garden centres in various forms and can be categorized according to their size, form and root preparation. The size is related to the height of the plant and the height of the clear stem from the ground to the first branches. Trees are usually described as 'light standards' (1.5–2m/5–6ft clear stem and 2–2.5m/6–8ft overall height); 'standards' (2m/6ft clear stem and 2.75–3m/9–10ft overall height); and 'heavy standards' (2m/6ft clear stem and 3.5–4.25m/11½–14ft overall height). The form or shape of the tree is either a 'feather' with a straight single leader, and the stem evenly spaced with lateral shoots, a 'bush' with no single leader, or a 'standard' or 'half-standard' with a head of branches on a clear stem, either full height (2m/6ft) or half height (1.2m/4ft). The root preparation of the tree can be either containerized, bare-rooted (the root exposed, with no soil), or root-balled (the soil held to the roots with sacking or some other material). Shrubs are not so easily classified by size or form, but are found in the same forms of root preparation as trees.

Bare-rooted material is the cheapest and most common preparation available for broad-leafed species. It is very important that the roots and the entire plants are properly protected in transit and storage. At no stage should they be exposed to wind, sun or frost. The material should only be lifted when it is dormant (between October and March), when the ground is neither flooded nor frozen. Planting of hardy material is best in the late autumn and of semi-hardy material in the spring. The time between lifting and planting should be as short as possible. Plants should be 'heeled in', with the roots covered with soil, should any delay in planting be unavoidable.

Root-balled material commonly includes conifers which have not been containerized, but have been field-grown, lifted with the root ball intact and wrapped up in hessian to prevent disintegration in transit. Conifers are best planted in the spring.

Container-grown stock is more expensive and usually takes longer to become established. Its advantages are that it is easy to handle and can be

Types of tree commonly available for planting. Note the standardized heights and circumferences.
1. Whip
2. Bush
3. Half standard ht: 2–2.5 m (6–8 ft); clear stem: 1.5 m (5–6 ft)
4. Standard ht: 2.75 m–3 m (9–10 ft); clear stem: 2 m (6 ft)

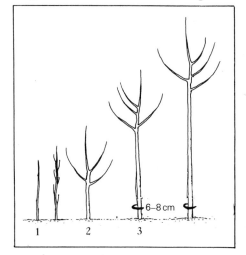

Typical root preparation for trees
1. Bare-rooted
2. Root-balled
3. Root-balled and wrapped
4. Container-grown

To check that a tree is being planted to the correct depth, lay a cane across the top of the soil. This should measure off against the nursery soil mark.

planted throughout the year, as long as it is well watered in dry conditions.

Planting trees and shrubs

For the standard method of planting a tree see the diagram. Another method that is used for large-scale planting of small trees is 'notch' planting. It is quick, cheap and efficient for large numbers of small specimens and is common forestry practice. Two notches are made with a spade at right angles to each other to form a shape of the letter 'L' or 'T'. The spade then raises a wedge of earth and the roots are slipped into the gap. The wedge is then replaced and firmed.

Trees should be staked to hold the root collar steady until the roots develop, to hold the developing crown upright, and to reduce wind and vandal damage. But damage can also be caused by improper staking and inefficient checking, so there is currently much debate about the best way to stake. The latest school of thought strongly advocates the staking of standard trees by holding the root collar with a short stake, reaching only about one-third of the way up the stem. This is then secured with a single tie to

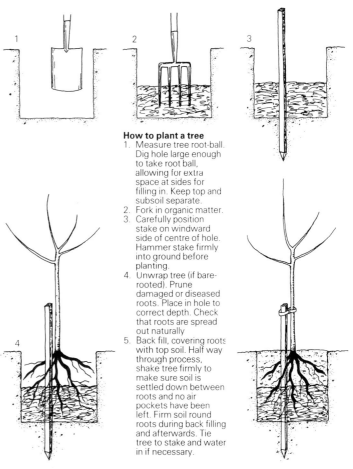

How to plant a tree

1. Measure tree root-ball. Dig hole large enough to take root ball, allowing for extra space at sides for filling in. Keep top and subsoil separate.
2. Fork in organic matter.
3. Carefully position stake on windward side of centre of hole. Hammer stake firmly into ground before planting.
4. Unwrap tree (if bare-rooted). Prune damaged or diseased roots. Place in hole to correct depth. Check that roots are spread out naturally
5. Back fill, covering roots with top soil. Half way through process, shake tree firmly to make sure soil is settled down between roots and no air pockets have been left. Firm soil round roots during back filling and afterwards. Tie tree to stake and water in if necessary.

159

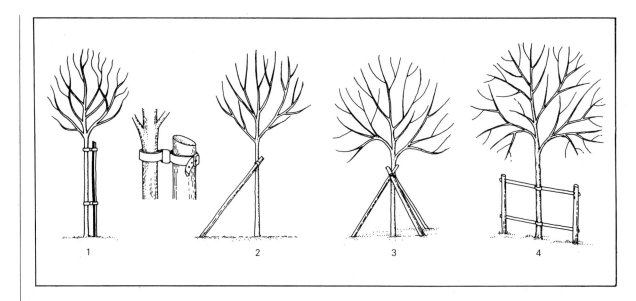

Standard trees need staking for the first few years after planting.

Methods
1. Traditional staking now replaced by method shown on page 159. Stake is placed on windward side of tree and reaches to the first branches.
2. Diagonal staking used for containerized material prevents damage to root ball when putting stake into position.
3. Tripod staking for large or unstable specimens.
4. Another method of staking large specimens.

be removed at the beginning of the second growing season after planting. This method is believed to encourage the tree to support itself by producing a better root system.

Shrubs are planted in the same way, as described in the diagram, but staking is rarely necessary. The younger the material the cheaper it will be and the greater its chances of survival.

Various forms of aftercare are important for the plants' longterm health. It may be necessary to irrigate them in the first growing season, and thereafter in severe droughts for the next few years until they become established. Weeds, which compete with the plant for nutrients, should be kept at bay by weed-killing a strip of ground 30cm (1ft) wide all around the base of the tree or shrub for the first few years. Formative pruning, for example removing the second leader of trees, if present, or reducing the size of shrubs to encourage bushy growth, may be beneficial.

Herbaceous perennials
Herbaceous plants are available in bare-rooted and containerized forms. As with woody perennials, containerized material is more expensive and slightly slower to become established. Its advantages are that it is easy to handle and theoretically it can be planted at any time in the year. In practice it should not be planted when the ground is waterlogged or frozen. If the material is flowering, the heads should be cut off. Additionally, many herbaceous plants are cumbersome to handle when the foliage has grown. The best time to lift and plant all herbaceous material is in the autumn or early spring when it is dormant.

When planting, dig a hole large enough to allow the roots to be well spread out. Some perennials—verbascum and hollyhocks for example—are very deep rooted so should only be transplanted when young; others, such as *Alchemilla mollis* and *Sedum spectabile*, have a very shallow root system. Choose your implement, a spade or a hand trowel, according to the size of the root system. Place the plant in the hole and back fill all around the plant. Firm well with your heel or hands, whichever is appropriate. Irrigate if the soil is at all dry, though in autumn or spring this is rarely necessary.

Irrigate when necessary, and mulch thickly to reduce weed growth and preserve moisture. Before applying the mulch, control the weeds. Some herbaceous plants need staking since they have very tall weak growth that will flop over untidily in the first heavy rain or strong wind. Stakes are best put in place in May or June when the plants are growing but not large. The plants will then grow through the stakes and have a rigid support system.

Staking can be done with birch sticks (pea sticks) pushed into the soil around the plants and bent over at the top to allow the plants to grow through. Another system is to use three bamboo canes for each plant, pushed firmly into the soil to form a triangle around the plant. The plant is then held up by strings wound from cane to cane around the plant. This method is best put into practice when plants are tall enough to stay within the strings. There are also many other proprietary staking systems on the market.

Bulbs and corms

A bulb is the perennating organ of a herbaceous plant that is formed from the swollen leaf bases. A corm is also the perennating organ of a herbaceous plant, but it is formed from swollen stem tissue. The difference can easily be seen when dissecting the two: a bulb always has layers, either in rings like an onion or in separate scale like a lily; whereas corms, such as cyclamen or gladioli, have even, starchy tissue.

When planting bulbs and corms the general rule is that they should be planted twice their own depth in the soil. However this rule is broken in a number of circumstances, for instance cyclamen are planted just below the soil surface. Corms and bulbs thrive in light, naturally rich soil. They can be grown from seed but will take from two to six years to reach maturity and flowering.

Staking in a herbaceous border using 'pea' sticks or birch twigs collected in winter and placed round plants early in the season. Herbaceous perennials will grow through the framework.

PRUNING AND TRIMMING

In their natural state most trees and shrubs are not annually pruned and will live quite happily. In gardens, however, pruning is carried out on some woody perennial plants and has many advantages. It maintains and improves the flower display by increasing the numbers and size of the blooms, or it may produce a better foliage or stem effect—*Cornus alba var. sibirica*, for example, should be pruned hard in the spring to produce new stems for winter colour. Pruning also improves the shape and form of the plant, removing crossing branches and preventing it from overhanging paths. Some shrubs, however, do have a naturally tangled appearance. Lastly, pruning increases the vigour of the plant and improves its health by cutting out dead and diseased material, or branches with active pest infestations to prevent their spread.

Different species produce their flowers on wood of various ages and this dictates the method of pruning. The first group flower on the current season's wood, and they tend to come into bloom between the middle and end of the growing season, from July to September. These are pruned in late winter or early spring before the buds break and some, such as *Buddleia davidii*, benefit from hard pruning. A few are winter-flowering plants like mahonia that require minimal pruning. The second group produce their flowers on the previous season's wood. This group includes many hardy deciduous shrubs and can be sub-divided into the very early flowering, such as *Forsythia suspensa*, and the mid-summer flowering like philadelphus. Most of these require annual pruning immediately after flowering, but a few (*Daphne mezereum* for example) should not be pruned at all. The last, and final, group flower from spurs produced on older wood and directly from older wood. This group, which includes malus, pyrus, prunus and chaenomeles, requires very little pruning, apart from some stopping to maintain the balance between flowers and growth, or the occasional cut to restrict size in confined areas.

General pruning rules

The first step in pruning any plant is to study it carefully, for so often secateurs are plunged into the shrub without any real understanding of the principles of pruning. First look for dead, diseased or weak growth. Using secateurs, a pruning saw or a knife, cut above the bud, making a clean, slightly sloping cut away from the bud. Do not leave a 'snag'. Then remove any branches that cross each other or are rubbing. Always cut to an outward pointing bud as the new shoot will follow the direction of the bud and a balanced shape will result. Never prune in frosty weather as the exposed cuts will freeze and be damaged, and avoid pruning live deciduous material in the weeks preceding bud-break to prevent excessive weeping.

Certain groups of plants will not fit easily into the above categories and

Correct pruning cuts slant down from the bud not so close as to prevent bud from shooting and not too high as to leave a 'snag' which will rot.

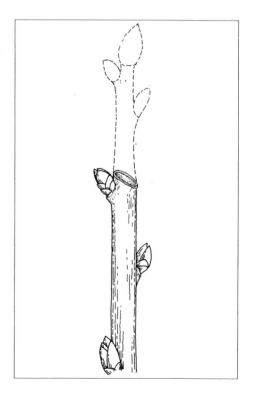

should be seen as special cases. Herbaceous perennial plants are normally pruned to the ground after the first heavy frost when the material is dead to tidy the beds for the winter. Also some herbaceous plants, such as *Alchemilla mollis* should be cut back after flowering to encourage a second flowering later in the summer. Conifers need no special pruning to enhance flowering and fruiting, but they may need to be trimmed to confine them to special areas or to shape them by removing the lower branches and thereby raising the crown, or if they have been damaged for any reason.

Roses

Roses consist of a very large and diverse group of flowering shrubs, which require specialist knowledge as to how and when to prune. The various types, which all need to be treated differently, include: bush roses (large-flowered or hybrid tea); bush roses floribunda (also called cluster roses); standard roses; miniature roses; ground-cover roses; shrub roses; climbing roses; and ramblers. (See the chart for further details).

Trees

The pruning of mature trees is a highly skilled and dangerous job. It not only involves working in awkward positions at high levels with dangerous equipment, like a chainsaw, it also requires a thorough knowledge of arboriculture. It should therefore be left to experts. On a small scale, however, when the trees are not very high you can carry out the pruning yourself, following the basic principles explained above.

Formative pruning of very young trees is carried out to shape the future tree. In nurseries this will involve the removal of side shoots (lateral growths) of seedlings, and the taking of softwood and hardwood cuttings; the trimming down of the rootstock after budding has been carried out; and the removal of all buds from the rootstock following grafting.

The young trees are then trained to produce specific types of tree (see the page 158): feathered, standard and bush. A feathered tree has a strong leader with laterals going all down the main stem. In this case the only formative pruning necessary is to thin some of the lateral

Pruning roses

Type of rose	Newly planted	Established (annual pruning)
Bush rose (large-flowered and hybrid teas)	Hard prune 10–15cm (4–6in) from ground to build up a strong root system	Moderate pruning. Reduce length of stems by 50% when dormant, preferably in late winter
Bush rose floribunda (cluster roses)	Hard prune 15cm (6in) from ground after planting to build up a strong root system	Moderate pruning as above except for the most rigorous cultivars, e.g. 'Peace', which should be pruned to ⅓ of their length
Standards	Hard pruning to 4–6 buds (not for shrub rose standards)	Moderate pruning to ½ length of shoot
Shrub roses	Do not prune	Remove dead and sickly growth
Miniature roses	As above	As above
Ramblers	Prune to 60–90cm (2½–3ft) from ground	All flowered stems cut to ground level in autumn if good, strong-growing replacements are in existence
Climbers	Do not prune. Remove dead tips only.	Little pruning is necessary. Remove dead and exhausted wood. Reduce laterals to 8cm (3in) in spring)
Ground cover roses	Do not prune	Remove dead and sickly growth only

Hedge maintenance

Hedge species	Usual number of cuts per year	Cutting season	Average height	Rate of growth and other characteristics
Deciduous foliage hedges				
Acer campestre Field or hedge maple	One	September–March	1.5–3m (5–10ft)	Moderate
Carpinus betulus Hornbeam	One	September–March	1.5–3m (5–10ft)	Moderate
Crataegus spp. Hawthorn	Two	July November–March	1.5–3m (5–10ft)	Moderate to fast
Fagus sylvatica Beech (also purple and copper-leaved cultivars)	One	September–March	1.5–3m (5–10ft)	Moderate to slow
Prunus cerasifera Cherry plum (also purple-leaved forms)	Two	June–July November–December	1.5–3m (5–10ft)	Fast
Rosa rubiginosa Sweet briar	Two	July November–March	0.75–1.5m (2½–5ft)	Fast
Rosa rugosa	Two	July November–March	0.75–1m (2½–5ft)	Moderate
Flowering deciduous hedges				
Chaenomeles japonica	Two	May December–March	1–1.5m (3–5ft)	All quite fast but discerning pruning is necessary to avoid cutting out all flowering wood
Cornus mas Cornelian cherry	Two	June November–December	1–2m (3–6ft)	
Forsythia spectablis	Two	May December–March	1–1.5m (3–5ft)	
Evergreen hedges				
Berberis darwinii	One	May–June	0.75–1.5m (2½–5ft)	Slow. Orange-yellow flowers. Lacks density
Buxus sempervirens Common box	Three/four	June–September	0.15m–1m (½–1ft)	Slow
Chamaecyparis lawsoniana Lawson cypress (and cultivars)	One	February–March	1.5–3m (5–10ft)	Moderate. Avoid hard cutting into old wood
× *Cupressocyparis leylandii* Leyland cypress	One/two	July–April	2–10m (6–33ft)	Very fast. One cut in March may be adequate for tall hedges
Elaeagnus spp.	One	August	2–3m (6–10ft)	Moderate. Informal hedge
Euonymus japonicus	Two	June–September	1.5–2m (5–6ft)	Moderate. Coastal areas
Ilex aquifolium Holly (and cultivars)	One	July–August	2–5m (6–16ft)	Slow
Ligustrum ovalifolium Privet	Four	May–September	1–3m (3–10ft)	Fast. Needs frequent clipping to keep shape
Lonicera nitida	Four/five	May–September	0.5–1.5m (1½–5ft)	Fast. Needs regular clipping
Osmanthus delavayi	One/two	May–August	0.5–1.5m (1½–5ft)	Slow. Scented white flowers
Osmanthus × burkwoodii	One/two	May–August	1–2m (3–6ft)	Slow. Scented white flowers

Hedge species	Usual number of cuts per year	Cutting season	Average height	Rate of growth and other characteristics
Prunus laurocerasus Common laurel	One	May–June	2–5m (6–16ft)	Slow. Prune carefully with secateurs– shears can disfigure
Prunus lusitanica Portuguese laurel	One	May–June	2–5m (6–16ft)	Slow. Prune as above. Not for cold areas
Quercus ilex Holly oak	One/two	April–August	1.5–5m (5–16ft)	Slow. Not for very cold areas
Rhododendron ponticum	One	July–August	2–4m (6–13ft)	Moderate. Acid soils. Purple flowers
Taxus baccata Yew	One	August–September	1.5–4m (5–13ft)	Moderate. The best architectural hedge
Thuja plicata	One	March	2–5m (6–16ft)	Moderate. Excellent hedge
Viburnum tinus Laurestinus	One	April–May	1.5–3m (5–10ft)	Moderate. Winter flowering. Resistant to pollution

growths. A standard tree has a strong central leader as above, but the laterals are removed from the ground upwards to leave a desired length of clear stem. The laterals are gradually removed over a period of a few years, starting with those closest to the ground. Each lateral is first shortened in the summer months to 13cm (5in) and then removed completely in the dormant season. Any rival leaders

are also pruned out and crossing branches are removed. A standard bush tree is generally a small tree. The main stem is cleared of lateral growths to the height of 30–80cm (1–2½ft) and the laterals are stopped in the same way as described above. However, with these trees no central leader is encouraged. Crossing branches are removed.

Hedges

Hedges can be trimmed or informal depending on the desired effect and the species planted. Informal hedges, such as *Rosa moyesii*, *Escallonia rubra var. macrantha*, *Viburnum tinus* and lavender, are rarely trimmed to shape, whereas formal hedges are regularly trimmed, the time of year and the number of cuts per year depending on the species (see chart). If you particularly need a labour-saving hedge it is best to select a species that does not grow too fast.

Hedges are trimmed by hand using shears or mechanically using hedge trimmers, which can be hired. To cut a straight, even hedge only those who are very skilled will rely on eye alone. Grids can be created by either setting up lines at the desired height or by constructing a frame on wheels which can be placed over the hedge and moved along as a guide for cutting.

Removing a small branch using a pruning saw. Note that the cut is made from above.

165

THE LAWN

In Britain particularly, where grass grows readily, lawns are a major feature of most gardens, offering visual relief from the busier areas of the garden and providing space for family activities. Some gardeners become passionately attached to the maintenance of a good lawn, while others regard it as a chore. In either case, a certain degree of forethought is necessary if the lawn is to be successful.

Establishing a new lawn

Before the seed is sown, or the turf laid, the ground should be thoroughly prepared, and if the subsoil or ground rock is impervious it may be advisable to incorporate some form of drainage system. The ground should then be levelled, not merely by moving around the top soil. Unless there is at least 15 cm (6 in) of good soil, it may be necessary to move the top soil to one side and level off the subsoil before replacing the top soil.

The ground will then need to be raked to remove stones and other debris. If it is going to be seeded in the spring it should be prepared in the autumn; and if it is to be sown in the autumn ideally it should be prepared in the spring. It is advantageous to leave the ground fallow for a period in order to destroy successive weed crops. The ideal pH is between 5.5 and 6.5, which is slightly acid. Lime may be added to correct excessive acidity and sulphate of ammonia if the soil is too alkaline, but the latter process takes a long time to be effective.

Laying turf

Turves are best laid between autumn and early spring. When laying them a board should be placed on those which are already in position. The turves should be arranged so the cracks between them are staggered, and then be topdressed with light soil, $1-2k/m^2$ ($2-3\frac{1}{2}lb/yd^2$), brushed into the cracks. Light rolling and later watering may be necessary. Banks can be turfed by skewering the turves into the soil with wooden pegs and laying them from the bottom upwards. Top quality lawn turf is now available in a number of garden centres—Rowlawn, for example, produce four grades, the most common being 'Medallion' which is ideal for the domestic garden. Large quantities can be purchased direct from the manufacturer.

Types of grass

Grass seed mixes and specified top quality turf contain various well tried mixes of grasses for a whole range of situations, from hard-wearing sports fields to the

Unrolling turves into position.

domestic back lawn. There are over 10,000 grass species in the world, of which ten to twelve are commonly used in turf production, and of these few species there are many hundreds of cultivars, thirty different browntops for example and eighty different rye grasses. In addition to grass there is always the choice of a herb lawn, such as chamomile, thyme or clover, but this can be hard work to establish because so much weed control is necessary.

Grass lawns can be made by seeding or by turf. Turfing gives an instant effect that may be used almost immediately, while seed may take several months; also, the ground preparation need not be so thorough, the turfing can be done in the winter months when more labour is available, and there is less chance of losses due to 'damping off' or birds. Seeding, on the other hand, is cheaper than turf and is less likely to be affected by drought; reliable seed mixtures are available for any situation, whereas turves can be of poor quality.

When sowing a new lawn the seed mix should be carefully chosen for the particular situation, the most usual being 70% chewings fescue (*Festuca rubra var. commutata*) and 30% browntop bent (*Agrostis tenuis*); for dryer soils the proportions should be 80:20. Hard-wearing areas such as cricket grounds and tennis courts need more resilient grass, a suitable mixture being 55% chewings fescue, 35% crested dogstail (*Cynosurus cristatus*) and 10% browntop bent. Rougher areas like road verges need 60% perennial rye grass (*Lolium perenne*), 20% chewings or creeping red fescue (*Festuca rubra var. rubra*) and 20% browntop bent. Also, other cultivars can be introduced to the mixes in special situations: crested dogtail in limy soil; wavy hair grass (*Deschampsia flexuosa*) in acid soil (below 5.5 pH); rough-stalked meadow grass (*Poa trivialis*) in wet heavy clay; smooth-stalked meadow grass (*Poa pratensis*) in very light soils; and rough-

stalked meadow grass, wood meadow grass (wavy hair grass) or perennial rye in shaded areas.

Sowing seed

The seed should be sown between April and September on a dry, still day when the soil surface is dry but moist below. If more than one species is being sown, bought in two or more bags, they should be sown separately. If the seed is ready mixed the bag should be shaken to

The turf is carefully laid on to prepared ground which is forked and then raked level. To avoid damage, turf is laid from a board.

167

ensure an even distribution of the seeds within the bag, as the smaller seeds will tend to segregate out.

Before sowing the seed the site should be consolidated by trampling or 'trodding'. It should then be raked level in the opposite direction to the trampling to obtain a good tilth, and the stones removed. Then mark out strips 1–2m (3–6ft) wide and sow the seed in two opposite directions. The normal rate of sowing is 17–49 g/m² (³⁄₈–1½ oz/yd²) for coarser mixes and 49–66 g/m² (1½–2oz/yd²) for finer mixes. The seed should be raked lightly into the tilth, in the opposite direction to the last raking, and, if on a small scale, protected from birds with black cotton suspended over the area. If no natural rainfall occurs the site should be watered within two to three days.

Later the site should be irrigated again if necessary and a fungicide like Benlate applied to control damping off. Good germination should be rapid and annual weeds will be controlled by mowing, but Morfamquat may be useful if the problem is acute. Five to eight weeks after sowing, the area should be lightly rolled to encourage tillering and to firm the soil. Two to three weeks later the grass may be given its first cut, removing the top of the grass with a sharp rotary mower to the height of 4cm (1½in).

The established lawn

A neat lawn should be cut once or twice a week in the growing season, but the extent of the mowing really depends on the time of year and the desired finish. As well as keeping the area neat and tidy, mowing stimulates 'tillering', causing new shoots to be produced from the base of the plant, which makes the grasses denser and mat-forming.

For most lawns the choice of mower lies between a cylinder or a rotary type. The cylinder mower is more suited to fine turf and the more blades per cylinder the finer the finish. The cutting height should not be too short as this will cause 'scalping', encourage moss and cause poor grass growth. Clippings are best removed from top quality turf as they will encourage disease, worms and weeds. However, in a drought the clippings can be left to act as a mulch.

To keep the lawn as healthy as possible other operations, too, are advisable. The thatch (dead leaves, moss and clippings) should be removed by hand or machine in the autumn or spring. This process, known as scarifying, allows air and water to penetrate freely into the surface and thus lessens the chance of disease. Spiking and hollow tining with the prongs of a border fork also allow more air and water into the soil, as well as relieving compaction and creating the spaces that are to be filled by the top dressing. They are best done in autumn and can be carried out by hand, a pedestrian machine or a motorized machine. Rolling is not necessary if a roller mower is used.

Top dressing should be done in autumn to fill in the hollows and level the surface, and to incorporate loam, peat, sand and fertilizer after spiking or hollow tining. Fertilizers should also be applied, in spring a general balanced one, in summer a high nitrogen one such as sulphate of ammonia, and in autumn a high phosphate one like bonemeal to encourage root growth. Do not use alkaline fertilizers, and do not fertilize flower meadows as this will encourage grass in preference to flowers.

Weed control

Weeds can be controlled with a selective herbicide such as MCPA or Mecaprop but these will work best when the weeds are growing vigorously. Moss is a symptom of poor cultural conditions and can be controlled by improving the drainage, not mowing too low, allowing more light to the lawn, increasing the soil fertility and reducing the soil compaction. If the soil is too acidic correct the pH with lime. Additionally a lawn sand can be applied in dry summer weather.

A YEAR IN THE GARDEN

January
Send orders for seeds and materials if not yet done. Send mowers for servicing and shears etc. for sharpening. Keep garden tidy.

February
Begin to sow seeds of half hardy annuals and glasshouse crops under glass. Check ties securing plants to stakes.

March
Plant root-balled conifers. Complete all planting of non-containerized woody material. Continue sowing seeds and begin pricking out germinated material. Make first cut of the lawn. Begin weed control in earnest. Prune roses early in the month.

April
Having cleared weeds, mulch borders when ground is moist. Continue sowing seeds under glass, sow hardy annuals in-situ outside. Keep a sharp eye open for pests and diseases and take necessary action.

May
Remove all unwanted suckers e.g. on lilacs and fruit trees. At end of the month remove spring bedding plants, fork through the beds and plant summer bedding. Take soft-wood cuttings. Sow outside half hardy annuals. Stake herbaceous plants as necessary.

June
Sow spring bedding material for flowering the following spring. Dead head roses and herbaceous material weekly. Begin cutting flowers for drying.

July
Mow the spring flowering wild flower meadow and spring flowering bulbs planted in grass. Continue dead heading. Begin taking semi-ripe wood cuttings. This is the best time of year to begin any construction work e.g. paths and patios. Trim hedges and topiary.

August
Continue construction work. Plant lilies. Begin to plan for following year if not done already. Place orders for trees, shrubs and herbaceous material to plant at the end of the year. Order spring flowering bulbs.

September
Complete construction work. Clean glass-houses and gutters. At the end of the month (after first frost) remove summer bedding and prepare ground for planting spring bedding. Weed growth should now slow down if not yet under control.

October
Plant spring bulbs and bedding. Cut down herbaceous plants to the ground. Planting season begins for non containerized dormant woody trees and shrubs. Lift tender material. Lightly prune roses. Plant new herbaceous material, propagate existing by means of division. Take hard wood cuttings.

November
Begin digging in organic matter or lime to borders and new areas. Rake up fallen leaves. Provide winter protection for in-situ tender species and lagging for pipes etc.

December
Send orders for fertilizers, seeds, summer bulbs and other materials and plants needed. Major tree work should be carried out while the plants are dormant.

SPECIAL STUDIES

TOWN GARDENS

CONSERVATORIES

ROOF GARDENS

ROSE GARDENS

SUMMER COLOUR

HERB GARDENS

KNOTS AND PARTERRES

HERBACEOUS BORDERS

CONTAINER PLANTING

TOWN GARDENS

A town garden, in our present context, is an outdoor area varying in size and shape, but usually rectangular or L-shaped, at the rear of a detached or semi-detached house, where soil is available for growing plants. All too often it comprises an unattractive area of paving surrounded by narrow raised beds containing a few spindly plants fighting for survival. Yet with a little patience and imagination such a space can be organized to function as an extension of the house or as an outdoor room—transformed into a place that will both look decorative during most months of the year when seen from indoors, and also provide a refuge from the noise and bustle of city life.

Even within an urban garden, interest can be maintained by careful use of detail and division of space. Here, the brick-edged lawn and paved terrace provide a neat framework for the planting. The opening at the far end of the garden, marked by two terracotta pots on either side, suggests that more lies beyond.

Site analysis

You can quickly sum up the potential of your site by listing in diagrammatic form the visible disadvantages and advantages *beyond* the perimeter walls. Start with the drawbacks. Is the garden overlooked by other houses or office blocks? Is the area particularly noisy, and if so where does the noise come from? What are the neighbouring gardens like? Do they lie at the same level on either side? Do they contain trees that cast shade, and if so where and at what times of the day? Are they used for keeping pets, or for hanging out the washing? Then examine the view. Is there a good tree or shrub next door which could be made to form part of your own garden design, or an interesting architectural feature—a sloping roof with decorative tiling—that may be worthy of 'framing' with plants.

Having surveyed the site, move closer in and examine, in the same way, the perimeter walls and contents of your existing garden. Do the walls need re-pointing? Are they high enough or will they require trellis to support climbers and ensure privacy? Is the garden wind-swept or sheltered, dry or damp? Do the plants look sickly or healthy? This will indicate the state of the soil; pale, yellow specimens are probably protesting against poor soil lacking in nitrogen, while flourishing camellias and azaleas indicate absence of lime. What aspect does the garden face in relation to the sun and how does it vary from season to season? It is important to resolve all such matters before any detailed planning.

Practical considerations

There are also a number of general problems applicable to most town gardens, which, if not considered at the outset, can have detrimental or disastrous effects on any planting scheme. Often builders' rubble lurks close to the soil surface and unless this is disposed of properly—a lengthy process—only the toughest plants will eventually survive.

The question of access to the site should also be considered. It may govern the choice of plants: even semi-mature trees or shrubs may have rootballs and stems which cannot be manoeuvered through narrow halls and stairways. Very probably, too, because of the perimeter walls, there will be some areas receiving a lot of sun and others that are generally in the shade; this will affect the choice and relationship of plants and planting.

The style of the garden

The question of style must be settled before you get down to a detailed design. There are really only two options, (though both can be successfully combined as long as one or the other is dominant): the garden can be designed either to echo and extend the interior of the house, or to create an illusion of space. This decision must be taken at the beginning, because it will affect the treatment of the boundary walls. If the garden is to be treated as an outdoor room, the walls may need to emphasize the feeling of enclosure, perhaps by being painted and played off with plants, urns and sculpture, the interior style being repeated outside. If a formal illusion of space is wanted, a variety of architectural trellis is available, giving an impression of false perspective or trompe l'oeil—in this case, the walls usually

Trellis and trompe-l'oeil can be used to create a formal illusion of space or to draw the eye to a particular part of the garden.

require painting to show off the panels of trellis ('treillage') to advantage. If an informal illusion is desired, it may be necessary to 'lose' the walls among the plants, borrowing and accentuating views wherever possible.

How to create a sense of space

Town gardens are often long and narrow, but by foreshortening them, or building a wall or trellis concealing the true end, the property will seem wider and more spacious, the left-over space being used for storage, or even concealing a greenhouse or toolshed. If a door is necessary, its presence might be disguised by painting it to simulate a statue in a niche.

In order to make the garden seem larger than it actually is, emphasis must be placed on the longest dimension, or, for example, on the diagonal from the near right-hand corner to the far left-hand corner. Try not to reveal the whole of the garden at once, but to change direction and position plants so as to heighten the sense of mystery. It is worth trying to use false perspective either with plant material or statues and urns—the nearest plant or object being almost identical to, but much larger, than that at the far end—this will give the impression that the two objects are the same size, but that the distance between them is much greater—a cunning device which could be carried even further by using, in conjunction with statue or urn, a large-leafed ivy in the foreground, and an almost identical small-leafed variety in the background. Similarly, a path, at the point nearest to the house, can be 1m (3ft) wide, decreasing gradually in the distance to 75cm (2½ft)—a theatrical device perhaps, but very effective in a small space.

Design features

The garden floor can be broken up with patterns or panels of brick, paving, slate, stone or concrete in a crisp design relating back to the proportions of the house.

A rectangular, diagonal or circular pattern, repeated most successfully by dividing up the garden into three, and integrating or connecting each third with the other, can be a foil for planting. Gravel or pea shingle is more suitable than grass, particularly for a soft, informal effect and is easily maintained. Any spoil left over from digging out foundations can be used to change levels, by building up the area at the rear, possibly elevating it from a damp, dark, overshadowed space to a sunlit platform, and using low retaining walls as informal seating. The area immediately adjacent to the house cannot normally be built up in this way because the level would then be above the damp-proof course.

Water, provided it reflects the sky, can help to enliven a monotonous space, but must be used, if at all, with discretion. Many different shapes and sizes of pools are possible; and thanks to modern pumping equipment, water is easily circulated for fountains and overspills, or for mini-cascades. Watering is always a problem in town gardens and a tap will also be needed for irrigation, possibly in conjunction with a fixed trickle hose system, placed at the back of the border, supplying water and nutrients.

Shade from the midday sun—its heat exaggerated by lack of air flow and absorption by paving or other hard materials—can be provided by pergolas and arches connected to the house, or freestanding in the sunnier part of the garden.

Colour effects

Probably the greatest pleasure in town gardens is being surrounded by green things—planting is really the 'icing on the cake', and as such the decoration should have a theme. Keep the colours simple and muted—a mixture of unrelated colour looks uneasy and will make the garden seem even smaller. The foliage itself will provide a wide range of greens, which can be 'lifted' by using

plants which have white, cream or pale yellow flowers over as long a period as possible, or those with pale shades of blue or pink. Too much white tends to look cold, while deep reds and purples tend to disappear in shadow at night. If there is insufficient light available to the plants, the bed can be raised—even a foot or two makes a surprising difference.

Choosing a tree

As space is so precious, every plant in a town garden must earn its keep. The scale and proportion of the planting must not dwarf the size of the house and garden, but if it is too small it may be reminiscent of 'toy town'. The first item to choose is usually a tree—the height and spread must be related to the size of the garden and a species with slender form and delicate leaves will not rob the garden of light. There are any number of small ornamental trees to choose from. An informal rounded shape can be achieved by using a member of the rowan family—*Sorbus aucuparia*, *S. vilmorinii*, *S. hupehensis* or *S. discolor*—all with white flowers in spring, and outstanding coloured berries and foliage in the autumn. The wild gean or bird cherry (*Prunus avium*) is delightful in spring with masses of white blossom. Drooping trees, such the birch (*Betula pendula* 'Dalecarlica') with light coloured

bark and delicate branch tracery, or weeping pear (*Pyrus salicifolia* 'Pendula') with soft green foliage and white flowers followed by tiny fruits, may be useful adjacent to water or seating. If more room is available, perhaps the golden acacia (*Robinia pseudacacia* 'Frisia') may light up a dark corner, or the Peking willow (*Salix matsudana* 'Tortuosa') with its twisted branches and slim, medium-sized leaves, will attract attention.

Whichever tree is chosen, it will usually be the main focal point within the garden, acting as a pivot to the surrounding shrubs and perennials, and as such it must be carefully placed. The balance and composition of the planting beds can be rearranged, but a tree does not take kindly to being uprooted, so make sure it is in the right place to begin with. Possibly it will need to stand out, showing off the vertical line of the trunk against background planting. A stout stake can be driven into the ground, moved and viewed from many angles, prior to actually preparing the planting hole.

Far left: An architectural feature such as this pergola will provide a shady area for entertaining, once the climbers are mature.

Left: The luxuriant foliage in this garden conceals the adjacent buildings.

Wisteria, decorating the top of the boundary, hints that a garden lies behind and softens the forbidding street entrance.

Designing with plants

Due to restricted space in the average town garden, coordinated mixed planting of shrubs and herbaceous species is difficult to achieve, since not only do the beds tend to be too narrow but some are inevitably in sun and others in shade.

A deeper effect can be achieved by using the perimeter walls to support climbers and wall shrubs at the back of the beds, literally clothing the walls. The early and late-flowering Dutch honeysuckle (*Lonicera periclymenum* 'Belgica' or *L.p.* 'Serotina') are not too invasive and have a wonderful, pervading scent. Repeat-flowering climbing roses can be used in conjunction with clematis, chosen either to flower simultaneously, or to fill the gap when the roses are over. *Clematis alpina* has long, hanging blue flowers borne on slender stalks during April and May; *C.* × *jackmanii* 'Superba' has enormous, profuse purple flowers from July to October; *C.* 'Duchess of Edinburgh' has large, scented, double rosette-like white flowers with green shading in May and June; and if the garden is relatively sheltered, *C. armandii* is a strong growing evergreen with creamy white flowers from March till June—best planted against a warm, sunny wall. The gaps can be filled with

ivy (*Hedera*), which will provide an evergreen backcloth, or even the golden hop (*Humulus lupulus* 'Aureus') which, although it dies down in the winter, makes a rapid soft yellow covering to lighten up the garden.

Arranging the planting

Arrange the shrubs loosely, allowing them room to develop their ultimate height and spread, grouping them strategically round the garden so that an evergreen shrub is in front of a deciduous climber, and the deciduous shrubs are backed by the ivies or other spreading evergreen material. A unified appearance can be achieved by selecting a few shrubs which tolerate sunny and shady conditions, and placing them in juxtaposition.

Massing all the taller shrubs at the back is a common fault—it is far more natural to allow some to flop forward at the front, and to fill in with herbaceous perennials, which can be removed as the planting matures. Tall architectural herbaceous subjects, like acanthus or fennel (*Foeniculum vulgare*), are sufficiently strong to be used at the back of the border, without support, allowing shrubs like *Elaeagnus angustifolia*, lavender, potentilla or senecio to filter through to the front. ·

Occasional taller shrubs like the purple smoke bush (*Cotinus coggygria* 'Royal Purple'), with amazing autumn colour, or the medium-sized, variegated, red-stemmed dogwood (*Cornus alba* 'Elegantissima') can act as a contrast to the other shrubs, while low ground-cover subjects such as *Bergenia cordifolia* 'Silver Light', with red-stemmed white flowers, and large reddish-green leaves, or *Pachysandra terminalis*, a luxuriant evergreen, can be used in front.

The evergreen box (*Buxus sempervirens* or the smaller *B. suffruticosa*) is a marvellous fresh-looking plant for edging borders, clipping into shapes, or using in pots; and, of course, annuals such as the scented tobacco plant (*Nicotiana*) or ferns can fill up left-over spaces.

Any basic colour scheme can be enlivened by using annuals—wallflowers for early spring, petunias for later on, harmonizing or contrasting according to fashion or whim. Bulbs can be planted underneath hostas, the dying bulb foliage being hidden by the leaves of the hostas as they appear in late spring. Hostas are very rewarding plants for shady gardens, and have a huge range,

A colourful collection of flowering plants and foliage frames the terrace of this small-scale garden and gives it an added air of intimacy.

from the enormous glaucous green *Hosta sieboldiana* to the smaller *H. fortunei* 'Albopicta', with pale yellowish young leaves which turn to green in summer.

The overall design can subsequently be enhanced by the addition of carefully chosen seating, lighting and containers, discussed elsewhere.

Basements and garden flats

Some town houses have basements with direct access to a lower-level, confined garden area; alternatively, they may have been converted into flats, the bottom one perhaps described euphemistically as a 'garden flat', even though the 'garden' may be dark and dingy, full of rubbish,

In a confined, rectangular area, reflected light from painting walls white helps create a sense of space. The array of pots and containers provides the necessary alleviating shapes and colours.

In this back garden, surrounding walls provide a sheltered microclimate in which less hardy plants flourish. The climbers are easily supported by the decorative trelliswork which relieves the starkness of the bare walls.

litter and fallen leaves. Yet for a keen gardener even this can have enormous potential. It is amazing how a few coats of white or cream paint, good lighting and a bit of imagination can transform this sort of space. Fine-mesh netting will keep out much of the windswept litter, and the light, newly painted area can be enlivened with plants growing in containers, in raised beds, or against trellis. Access can be from inside or by a metal, timber or stone staircase, preferably with generous treads and shallow risers. Wisteria or honeysuckle will soon twine up the handrail.

Occasionally basements back on to garden squares, and with a little expense and imagination, a substantially larger space can be dug out or excavated, the garden at ground floor level being supported by a strong retaining wall, perhaps with a subsidiary lower wall at basement level for growing plants. More often, space is limited by surrounding buildings, where low walls are equally useful; here weep-holes will be necessary for

drainage, and the inside of the wall should be painted with bitumen or waterproof paint to prevent nutrients leaching through, leaving a 'salty' deposit. The crossfall of the 'floor' should be carefully checked to ensure that water runs away quickly—often there will be a labyrinth of pipes, cables, manhole covers and gulleys beneath, which cannot be moved. It may be best to lay strips of timber decking over the area, as these strips are easily lifted for cleaning and for access to manholes or blocked drains, or a concrete screed with a gravel or brushed finish can be laid to relieve the starkness, plant containers being strategically placed to hide any offending objects.

Planting suggestions

As with any town or roof garden, soil and plants may have to be brought in through the house or via a narrow alley, but the plants, once there, will have a very secluded microclimate, making it possible to grow unusual, spectacular semi-evergreen climbers like *Solanum jasminoides* 'Album', with profuse white flowers lasting from midsummer until checked by autumn frosts. Ornamental vines, such as *Vitis coignetiae*—a strong-growing climber with large, handsome leaves turning crimson and scarlet in autumn—will soon cover the walls, and ivy will remain evergreen. A tough shrub such as *Fatsia japonica*, with polished palmate dark green leaves, gives a sub-tropical effect and succeeds in semi-shade. Bamboo (*Arundinaria japonica*) or the more elegant variety (*A. murielae*) forms tall arching clumps, excellent for growing in shade in good soil or large tubs, and will continue the jungle-like atmosphere. The firethorn (*Pyracantha*) is tolerant of all exposures, boasting flowers and fruit, and the long growths may be cut back immediately after flowering if they are becoming too tall; or try

the more delicate *Jasminum mesnyi*, with bright yellow semi-double flowers produced from March to May. It is well worth experimenting with some tender species as basements are rarely affected by general exposure to wind or frost, the surrounding walls keeping the ground warm. The biggest drawback is the tendency for plants to become leggy as they reach up to the sun.

Basements can also be transformed by trellis, trompe l'oeil or mirrors, or they can be glassed over, like a conservatory with walled sides. A storage cupboard for barbecue, tables and chairs can often be built in under the steps or stairs, and the garden discreetly lit to double as an outdoor dining room. A long-neglected space can quickly be transformed into a delightfully quiet and private outdoor living/dining room, the still air perfect for appreciating scented flowers or foliage.

Pale flower colours lighten this low-level garden. The perimeter walls are almost imperceptible behind the masses of green foliage, while statues and ornaments focus attention within the garden.

CONSERVATORIES

In the seventeenth century the term conservatory was used to describe those elegant buildings in which orange and lemon trees were accommodated in the winter. Unlike greenhouses, however, conservatories were not merely functional and were also used for pleasure. The same is true today, but conservatories now house a wide range of tropical, sub-tropical and alpine plants and, due to advances in technology and materials, they have recently become cheaper and very popular, providing an opportunity for relaxation in warmth and sunshine, surrounded by plants, even in the winter months.

Basic considerations

Conservatories can either be designed and constructed from first principles, or they can be bought in kit form and put up either by the supplier or by the purchaser. Prefabricated conservatories come in a wide range of styles, and a suitable design should be chosen with some care, bearing in mind its possible use for recreation; and the type of plants it is to contain. All these factors will affect the overall size and shape, and such details as the flooring and width of shelves. Some conservatories may be built with particular plants in mind— palm houses, for example, are immensely tall, while those designed for the tropical waterlily, *Victoria amazonica*, are wide but not tall.

The style should be related to that of the house, repeating such characteristic features as materials, doors and windows, for a unified effect will always be the most pleasing. Even small details, such as Gothic-style windows with stained glass insets may be repeated to give an air of authenticity. Ideally, the conservatory should appear to be an integral part of the original architecture. Whatever

A few small details, such as the glazing pattern and the design of the ornamental cresting on the roof, can make the house and its conservatory a unified composition.

design is chosen it should not be allowed to detract too much from the house itself.

It is more economical to construct a conservatory in an L-shaped corner, with two existing walls, and the ideal situation will also be warm and sunny. If, however, the only available space faces east or north, certain measures will make it warmer and lighter: the walls can be painted white or off-white, which is less glaring, or they can be covered with tinfoil which will trap the heat and also make the conservatory look bigger. The time of day when the conservatory will be used should also be considered, as adjacent buildings may screen out the sun.

Planning permission

Once the design and position have been decided, planning permission should be obtained, which may take some time, and neighbours should be consulted first since their objections may be difficult to overrule. (See page 214 for further details on the legal position.) Formal applications take time, experience and money but, fortunately, if an architect or specialist firm is employed they will apply on your behalf. If, however, the planning authority is first approached with rough diagrams and dimensions, photographs of the existing house and some projected designs, the likelihood of succeeding with the formal application will be increased.

Insulation and heating

Traditionally it was the high cost of glass and heating that made conservatories the sole preserve of the wealthy, but many of the problems of condensation, heat loss and heat gain have now been solved. Double or even triple glazing in the walls and roof will increase insulation, and factory-sealed units are also available. The gaps between the glass may be filled with argon gas which reduces the transmittance of heat from the warmer inner pane to the colder outer one, and special types of coated glass will reflect heat back into the room.

Heating is not absolutely necessary but if it is not installed the choice of plants will be greatly limited to those that are hardy or nearly so. Conservatories are classified by their minimum temperature and it is this that determines the plant range. Succulents require a minimum temperature of only 4°C (40°F) and many temperate plants are happy in a cool conservatory at no less than 7°C (45°F). The warm or tropical conservatory, though, must be kept at a minimum temperature of 18°C (65°F).

If tropical plants are to be grown, the heating bill could be something of a shock; a warm conservatory will be roughly five times more expensive to heat than a cool one. There are a number of ways in which heat loss can be reduced, but even so the cost of heating has persuaded many owners to abandon tropical plants in favour of those that are more hardy.

Numerous heating systems are available but some can also restrict the choice of plants. Dry hot air systems will not act kindly on the majority of tropical plants from humid environments; and paraffin and bottle gas after regular use will cause many plants to suffer premature senescence and loss of leaves. Hot water systems, if practicable, are the best.

The maximum temperature in any conservatory should never exceed 24°C (75°F), but in summer months it is not easy to achieve this. Temperatures can be reduced by ventilation, and by shading and spraying the paths and plants with water, which obviously may not be practical in some conservatories.

The interior of the conservatory

The interior style of the conservatory will depend on its function, but if it is connected to the house it may become an extension of a living room or kitchen. In this case it is advisable to link the two together visually by repeating colours,

fabrics and even plants—if two or three plants are placed in the adjacent room, the transition between the two zones will appear more gradual. The lighting, too, should be continued and will discreetly emphasize the shadows cast by the foliage in the evenings.

The flooring should be washable and waterproof so as to be resistant to watering, high humidity and general planting activities; and, as in a bathroom, the floors should be safe when wet, a slightly rough surface being more secure than a smooth one. Quarry tiles, available in various sizes and finishes, make a sympathetic transition from the house, while brick pavers (which are lighter and thinner than ordinary brick) and paving slabs might be compatible with an adjoining terrace. Some of these are very porous and many need to be sealed, if used indoors, to prevent them from becoming wet and stained. If the finish is not to be continued outside, linoleum, vinyl or cork may be used, but they should be well laid and sealed from moisture or they will swell and lift from the floor. Rush or sisal matting can be laid temporarily on top of harder materials to give a softer effect.

Methods of growing and arranging plants

The plants may be grown in containers or in plant beds, depending to some extent on their particular range. Containers are easy to handle and move around, but will restrict plant growth after a while, so that a certain amount of work is involved in potting on the plants. They can be arranged on slatted wooden shelves, which allow excess water to escape, and if they are placed on metal or plastic trays filled with 25mm (1in) of fine gravel or pea shingle, the plants can soak up surplus water gradually and will not dry out. Ordinary clay or brick-coloured plastic pots are preferable to the more fancy designs which detract from the foliage and flowers. A thin layer of gravel sprink-

Left: A garden room, furnished as an extension to a house, provides extra space for year-round use amongst the plants.

led on top will give a uniform appearance, and weeds will be unable to root.

If the plants are placed in beds, they can be arranged more naturalistically and can grow unchecked, which is less labour intensive. On the other hand the beds may be messy and encourage disease. The choice between the two depends upon the plants, the available labour and the aesthetics.

The arrangement of plants in the beds or on the standing-out area for the containers follows the same rules as exterior planting. Spend time thinking of plant associations, looking at colour, texture and form. Keep the taller plants at the back or middle, and at the front use plants that will soften the edge of the bed or the pot. Have a framework of plants that are interesting throughout the year—evergreens, such as the parlour palm (*Chamaedorea*) or the panama-hat plant (*Ficus*)—through which the temporary 'exotics' can be placed when at their best.

Choosing plants

A very wide range of plants can be grown in conservatories, but the final choice must be determined as much by the particular environment as the aesthetic factors. Certain plants will be required for particular purposes: a good climber, such as *Allamanda cathartica*, to screen an ugly corner in a warm conservatory; an effective ground-cover plant, perhaps the strawberry geranium (*Saxifraga stolonifera* 'Tricolor'), to cover soil below trees and shrubs; or a strong architectural plant, like *Cycas revoluta*, to prevent people from cutting corners.

All the environmental factors required by a plant—space, temperature, water and light—are determined by its native habitat. These can, however, be altered to some degree and many of the plants used in interior landscaping have been acclimatized to grow in lower light levels. All such factors are interrelated, and if one is changed then it will probably alter

Opposite above: Apart from a few permanent plants such as the palm in the background, a small conservatory can be kept bright and interesting with pots of seasonal flowers which can be replaced when they have finished blooming.

Opposite below: Geraniums and fuchsias can be trained up the roof supports to make the best use of space.

one or more of the others. Cacti, for example, tolerate very low rainfalls in their native state, where their roots are spread over a large area to absorb as much water as possible; but when they are grown in pots the root spread is limited, so that a higher proportion of water is required.

As in the garden, the eventual size of the plant should be borne in mind, for if it proves large for the conservatory it will either have to be pruned or removed altogether after a number of years.

Temperature, too, is vital and the minimum temperature that each plant can withstand should be noted. *Primula malacoides*, poinsettia, freesias and bougainvillea require a minimum temperature of 10°C (50°F), while pomegranate, *Passiflora coccinea*, *Thunbergia mysorensis* and *Cycas revoluta* need at least 13°C (55°F).

Conservatory plants need water both in the form of irrigation and atmospheric humidity. If only 'hard' water is available, the choice of plants may be limited, because some, such as ericaceous plants, will not tolerate the high pH of limey water. Additionally, limey water deposits an unattractive white film on the leaves.

Seating is essential if one is to use the conservatory to the full, and sculptures which might be damaged by the weather are best enjoyed within its shelter.

Mobility is solved in this example by the wheel so that the seat can be trundled into the best position for sun and shade.

Non-limey water may be obtained from rainwater butts, collecting the water off the roof, or in the form of treated water from which the calcium carbonate has been removed, but this source can be expensive.

Plants originating in humid tropical climes require an atmosphere with a high relative humidity. This can be achieved by regular dampening down of paths—up to four times daily in the height of summer; regular misting over of plants; arranging the plants together so that they create their own microclimate; and installing an automated electric humidifier.

Plants have adapted to grow under a wide range of light levels depending on their native habitat—those from the ground floor of a tropical rain forest, for example, have adapted to grow in very low light levels. It is a fair generalization to say that flowering, coloured and variegated foliage plants require higher light levels than all green non-flowering plants. The amount of light in a conservatory will depend upon its orientation, construction, and amount of natural sunshine. Unless supplementary lighting is to be used, north-facing conservatories are best planted with shade-loving material.

Plants can be acclimatized to grow in lower light levels, but those that require high light levels include cacti, many succulents, some cycads, hibiscus, pelargoniums, bougainvillea, many alpines and canopy palms. Plants requiring lower light levels include ferns, orchids, dieffenbachia, ficus, *Fatsia japonica*, philodendron, gesneriads, some smaller palms, and tender camellias.

Lastly, you may like to grow a particular group of plants—insectivorous or fragrant ones, or those native only to Australia, for example—and will need to adapt the conservatory specially for them. Such theme planting will give an extra dimension to the conservatory and create inner coherence.

How to keep the plants healthy

Bad watering (normally too much rather than too little) is probably the greatest culprit in killing off plant material in the conservatory. Watering is a skill that is learnt mainly by experience, but a few guidelines should be followed. Observe the colour of the compost; feel the weight of the pot; make sure the plant is not placed under a drip; observe changes in the plant; and ensure adequate drainage is provided.

Containerized plants will require repotting periodically. Make sure the new container is not too large or too small—it should be large enough to be able to firm the compost around the roots with ease. The composts can be either peat or loam based, but a loam-based compost provides maximum nutrition. The plants should be fed fortnightly in the growing season with an organic liquid feed through a diluter or by watering. Inorganic fertilizers may have an accumulatory toxic effect if over supplied. The unused nutrients are held within the compost and with each feed the levels build up, eventually becoming toxic.

The main criteria for keeping the plants healthy are to observe the environmental needs of the plant: get the temperature, watering, atmospheric humidity, light levels and compost right.

Raised beds give the planting greater importance. Pots can be sunk into the soil or hidden behind the wall and replaced when the flowers begin to fade.

185

ROOF GARDENS

In cities, where space is at a premium, roof gardens may provide the only opportunity for private gardening. They have always been popular in warmer climates, but even in more temperate zones roof gardens can provide additional space for recreation, in a secluded position surrounded by plants. Furthermore, there may be the bonus of a fine 'bird's-eye' view over the city.

As private roof terraces can range from small balconies to large roof gardens with paving, water, grass, low planting and trees, the general design procedure is similar in many ways to that for most gardens. Privacy, views, shelter, orientation and harmony with the architecture and environment should all be considered. In addition, however, there are factors unique to roof gardens which need particular attention: support, shelter and access.

The construction

Whether the roof garden is to span the top of an office block, or whether it is simply a small balcony, the first thing to establish is that the roof will support the extra weight of masonry, paving, plants and soil. If the structure is unable to bear the weight, severe damage may occur in the building below and legal problems could ensue. Expert advice should be obtained from an architect, engineer or building surveyor before work commences. Sometimes, too, planning permission may be required, and it is wise to check on this at the outset.

The construction of the roof terrace should provide for adequate drainage and waterproofing, as well as being as light as possible. The roof should have a 1:60 fall and then should be protected by a layer of asphalt, followed by a protective cement screed to prevent plant roots from puncturing the asphalt. In permanent planting beds a 100 mm (4 in) layer of rounded aggregate will be required for drainage. On this is placed a 15 mm (½ in) fibreglass blanket to prevent soil particles from silting up the drainage layer, and then a 100 mm (4 in) layer of

An imaginative roof garden exploiting changes in level between the pitched roofs. The trellising and planting give it complete privacy.

compressed granulated peat. The top soil, light or sandy loam, should be a suitable depth for the proposed plants. Great care must be taken not to perforate the waterproof layer during planting, whether with heavy machinery or garden tools.

Planting beds and their retaining walls should be sited around the edge of the roof terrace, where they will receive extra support from the walls, or above columns or pillars. As in general construction work, weep-holes should be provided for drainage, but the gulleys to carry away the excess water should not be located in the corners or they will soon be blocked by piles of driven leaves and debris.

Access

A roof garden is often reached by a narrow spiral staircase that is difficult to climb at the best of times and almost impossible for someone carrying food, plants or soil. Access should be as easy as possible, ideally on the same level as an

adjacent living room. If the levels have to change, the step risers should be shallow and the tread wide. If a staircase is really unavoidable, it should be a simple timber one with generous proportions, turning points and landings, perhaps covered with pots or climbing plants such as wisteria so as to blend into the surroundings.

This striking balcony display is delightful when seen from the adjacent drawing room or the street below. The planting of wallflowers in shades of orange, yellow, cream, and white, is replaced in summer by an equally harmonious grouping of geraniums which, in the sheltered town microclimate, flower until Christmas.

Timber trellising and balustrades provide an architectural element as well as support for climbers, while the trees, shrubs and herbaceous plants thrive unsupported in this sheltered roof garden.

187

Shelter

Shelter is often a serious problem in roof gardens, and the higher the garden the more shelter will be required, both for plants and people. To some extent, shelter may be provided by the plants themselves, but only the tougher plants, resistant to wind and sun scorching and the resulting transpiration, will survive without some protection; and even these will become established quicker if protected from the wind. Larger shrubs or trees will need to be staked to prevent the wind uprooting them, but if smaller stock is used the roots will become established without requiring any extra form of support.

Shelter is best provided by constructing slatted fencing or screening blocks.

These structural additions must be sturdy and secure enough to withstand buffeting from the wind, and if they are designed to filter the wind, rather than simply resist it, they are less likely to be destroyed in a storm. Filtering the wind also reduces the unpleasant eddying effect so prevalent between buildings. The proposed shelter should be as high as possible, though the actual height may depend on local regulations, and the protected area on the leeward side will be up to ten times as long as the height.

Overhead shelter from rain and sun may also be necessary as roof terraces can be baking hot in summer. A pergola with a translucent or corrugated perspex roof will be light, decorative and waterproof, and useful as a shady dining area.

Slatted fencing provides an easily erected, light and inexpensive screen, giving privacy and shelter from wind. Although not long-lasting, this natural material makes an unobtrusive foil for plants.

Flooring

It is possible to establish grass on a roof terrace, but it is difficult to maintain and tends to dry out easily. It is better to use some kind of hard surfacing, which can be laid directly on the asphalt and should be related in its design to the surrounding roof or townscape, as well as the interior of the building. Changes in level will add interest to a potentially dull site, and if expansion joints are necessary in paving, they should form part of the overall design.

A number of materials can be used for flooring. Quarry tiles are light, suitable for inside and out, and will harmonize with the rich colours of adjacent roofs; asbestos tiles are also light, but not so attractive, though if laid diagonally they are more acceptable that the usual rectangular design; and hollow tiles with open joints will allow water to drain easily. Other suitable materials include patterned or textured cement screeds, lightweight paving slabs, loose gravel and tarmacadum with a rolled-in dressing. Wooden decking or duckboarding is very attractive and is less hot in the summer, but tiny gaps must be left for drainage. Treated with wood preservative, the timber will weather and develop a mellow colour.

On this roof terrace, the planting will soon grow over the removable trellis, which hides access to the lift shaft. The view of green trees in the adjacent park is played up, while the safety railing is painted a dark colour to merge into the background. The striped cushions and garden furniture give foreground interest.

189

Walls and trellising

Timber trellis, simple or ornate, can be fixed along the perimeter of the property or in panels on the walls. Several manufacturers now make trellis with interchangeable sections, so the design can be varied according to the proportion of the building. Painted in dark colours, such as matt black or French green, the trellis will merge into the surrounding trees or the townscape beyond. Expandable trellis is unsuitable as it is flimsy and prone to deterioration, so ultimately more expensive. Interwoven wattle or larchlap is also short-lived, though it has the advantage of being inexpensive.

Often the trellis will have to be attached to iron balustrading, but this is quite easy and simply requires U-bolts and screws. It may be worth having the trellis tailor-made for the site, using brass screws that will not rust. Alternatively, the uprights of the trellis can be sunk into large planters, and pyramid-type timber structures, incorporating planters or Versailles-type tubs, can act as focal points and relieve the monotony of the planting.

The spacing of the laths of the trellis should be considered in conjunction with the scale of the proposed planting. Delicate climbers such as clematis will not be able to cope with widely spaced frames, and vigorous plants such as rambling roses will destroy a lightweight framework.

The walls of the terrace may be painted a colour, or off-white which will reflect the light but is less glaring than true white. In some cases, painting one wall and leaving the others as natural brick can reduce a box-like appearance. Trompe l'oeil effects, in which a Tuscan landscape is framed by living foliage or a drainpipe becomes the trunk of a tree complete with nesting birds and foliage, are currently fashionable and can be an amusing diversion.

Treated timber trellis and garden furniture blend with the brick walls and terracotta pots, and do not detract from the planting or view beyond. Sweet peas give quick growing cover to this recently planted corner. Drainage has been simplified by standing the pots and containers on terracotta supports.

Lightweight asbestos floor tiles and garden furniture help reduce the danger of structural damage caused by overloading the weight on the roof terrace. Permanent evergreen planting provides a backcloth for a colourful seasonal display.

Containers and other items

Most plants on roof terraces will probably be grown in containers (see page 210) and it is important that these are as light as possible. Vermiculite and peat can be mixed with soil to retain moisture and make it lighter. Since containers tend to dry out very quickly in these exposed conditions, it may be necessary to install a fixed irrigation system. Liquid fertilizers can be added to the water and the system can operate automatically to save time and trouble, particularly if the owner is often away from home.

Storage, in the form of a shed or of built-in seats with lift-up lids, is useful for tools and barbecue equipment, and lighting is also indispensable, so allowance should be made for cables and wiring. The finishing touches can then be provided by garden furniture, appropriate to the character of the terrace, and ornament in the form of statues or wall-mounted masks and plaques.

ROSE GARDENS

Roses, and their proposed inclusion in a planting plan, arouse more enthusiasm and interest than any other garden plant, and the dozens of new varieties which assail us every year make the final selection even more difficult. The role that the rose is to play in the garden will determine what class of rose is wanted.

Hybrid teas and floribundas
Hybrid tea roses are the most popular, closely followed by floribunda or cluster roses—both these 'classes' can be grown in bush or standard form, and are as invaluable for cutting as for display in borders, when they should be arranged in groups of three or five of a single variety, the colour chosen to harmonize or contrast with the rest of the planting. The lovely single varieties 'White Wings' and 'Lilac Charm' will bring a certain quality of lightness and charm to any arrangement. There is little demand nowadays for the once fashionable rose bed, usually a mottled collection of colours best confined to the kitchen or 'utility' area, unless the garden is large enough to devote one particular place to a single variety—perhaps around a formal pool or urn. The beds may be edged with box (*Buxus*), and a few strategically placed standards, possibly planted in pots, will give height around the perimeter. The creamy coloured 'Elizabeth Harkness' or pearly 'Margaret Merrill' are more effective when massed than most brighter colours.

Climbers and ramblers
Climbers and ramblers need a support for their display. An invasive species rose such as *R. filipes* 'Kiftsgate' and the larger ramblers such as 'Albéric Barbier' and 'Bobbie James' are splendid for growing through trees, while the more moderate 'Phyllis Bede' (valuable for long flowering) and 'Paul Transon' are very suitable for covering house walls or buildings.

Climbers have much stiffer stems and are less rampant, making them more suitable for walls or trellis—the buff-coloured 'Gloire de Dijon' flowers over a long period while the white, flushed pink 'Madame Alfred Carrière' will quickly clothe a north-facing wall. The climbing versions of hybrid teas or floribundas are often disappointing, not being such prolific flowerers as the bush forms.

Shrub roses
The informal use of shrub roses is a comparatively recent development, and today the designer's skill is not so much directed towards intricate rose gardens of dramatic display as involved with creating beautifully integrated gardens of roses. To achieve this, two basic principles have to be considered: arrangement and associated planting.

Taking shrub roses chronologically—perhaps for those planning a garden contemporary with a period home—the first group for consideration comprises the old 'summer' varieties, flowering from around midsummer through July. Five classes produce low-centred, intensely fragrant blooms ranging from

Many of the large shrub roses, such as 'Céleste', can be kept in check and displayed better if they are trained over tripods of wood or ironwork rather than allowed to sprawl at will.

A formal Victorian-style rose garden in which nineteenth-century varieties are displayed in a correct period setting.

white and blush through every shade of pink to crimson, maroon and purple. Their height varies (and should be carefully noted when selecting from catalogues) as does their habit, all-important in mixed planting.

Gallicas make medium, compact bushes of clear green foliage, contrasting with the glaucous tones of taller Albas. Soft green, downy leaves of lax Damasks form open bushes, while substantial Centifolias (full-petalled heavy Cabbage Roses) have coarser foliage, as do the Mosses, evolving from them. The largest varieties are displayed to advantage tumbling from a tripod frame against a dark background of yew or conifer. If starting to grow these roses, a representative quintet would be 'Tuscany Superb', 'Maiden's Blush', 'Madame Hardy', 'Fantin Latour' and 'William Lobb'.

At the turn of the eighteenth century hybridization with long-flowering roses from China led to an enormous number of newcomers for Victorian gardens. One of the first, the deep red Portland Rose, compact and floriferous, makes a useful small hedge. Bourbons, of Damask strain, tend to be weak-stemmed, but can be supported on a wall; thus the fragrant cerise 'Madame Isaac Pereire' can be savoured through the window. Noisettes, of China/Musk relationship, are true climbers: 'Alister Stella Gray', opening paler from deep yellow buds, flourishes in confined town gardens.

Hybrid Perpetuals combine many qualities of the new roses: sturdy plants, large blooms and dramatic colours. They respond well to being tethered to tent pegs, forming decorative arches of bloom along the front of a border. Many Teas, like soft yellow 'Safrano', once thought to be too tender for the English garden,

193

Above: Striking red hips are a feature of many of the shrub roses. Those of *R. rugosa* are almost as large as small tomatoes.

Right: Some of the more rampant growers look effective growing through strong shrubs or small trees. In this case the blooms of *R. helenae* are set off by the foliage of the purple *prunus pissardi*.

will thrive in a southern aspect or can be grown in pots and removed to shelter in winter. But more suited to container growth on patios are the small Chinas and Polyanthas.

With Victorian roses, emphasis is on beautiful blooms for close viewing, but we owe to the Edwardians the overall decorative aspect. Encouraged by Gertrude Jekyll—supreme arranger of roses—they used exciting new ramblers to adorn pillar, pergola and trellis towards the end of July. To emphasize ramblers in mixed planting today, train them as a pillar ('Sander's White' is splendid) or integrate 'Apple Blossom' and 'Violette' on a wall.

At the beginning of this century, the qualities of species roses were recognized for the wilder garden, having much to contribute with their whole graceful form, foliage and fruit as well as simple flowers, as *R. webbiana* and *R. willmottiae* demonstrate. Cream *R. dunwichensis* makes useful ground cover; Rugosas (unrivalled for hips) and Scotch Briars thrive in wood or heathland; *R. virginiana* and *R. nitida* are exceptional for fiery autumn foliage in a shrubbery and through old orchard trees; and lasting interest is provided by *R. longicuspis* or *R. helenae*. If a garden has a distant borrowed landscape the outline can be echoed by billowing forms of large species roses in rough grass to integrate the whole vista. Along banks of a stream or pond, long white trails of invasive *R. wichuraiana* will flow most appropriately.

For backing wide borders, Hybrid Musks flower early and, pruned back with care, perform equally well in autumn. Kordes' *pimpinellifolia* hybrids are more lax, but graceful, arching stems of bloom complement any early summer planting scheme. Three rewarding smaller shrub roses—blousy 'Ballerina', compact 'Yesterday' and low-growing 'The Fairy'—are also available as half-standards, to be prettily poised above other plantings. Finally, try to ensure that any rose chosen possesses the virtues of fragrance, frequent flowering, good foliage, vigorous growth and a healthy resistance to mildew and black spot.

Associated Planting for Roses

This very general survey has so far considered informal arrangement of roses in garden design, to be maintained by cutting out old wood from the base and carefully shaping new growth to suit the scene. Once the layout has been established, thought must be directed towards the choice of companion plants for appropriate backing and for complementary

Climbers should always be chosen to relate in colouring to the walls and adjacent structures. Here, *R.* 'Reveil Dijonnais' picks out the tones of the tiled roof.

Below left: Pergolas, or a series of linked arches, allow one to use many more climbers and ramblers. Wherever possible it is best to choose those which can be encouraged to flower low down, such as this 'Lawrence Johnston'.

Below right: Some sprawling roses, in this case *R.* 'Raubritter', can cover quite an area of ground but are better surrounded by gravel to avoid painful weeding.

The detailed pattern of the flower in many old-fashioned roses, such as *R*. 'Comte. de Chambord', is particularly usful as it blooms late in the season.

accompaniment.

With the old summer roses, scale is an important factor and to appreciate their splendid flush of flowering, overpowering neighbours, both in bloom size and colour, must be avoided. Cottage garden favourites—pinks, sweet williams, violas and aquilegias—are admirable. Herbs are historically correct, and both foliage and flowers of rosemary, sage, borage, hyssop and lavender are right for the purplish-red tones of these roses. The other important aspect to remember is that once the roses are over, nearby infilling colour is imperative. Sedum are most useful here; glaucous foliage is an excellent foil and flowers linger long into the autumn. Phlox and penstemon will also stand by for August and, as neighbouring shrubs, hebe and hardy fuchsia are reticent until the right moment, while earlier their foliage provides good backing. Old-fashioned sweet peas, planted late below Gallicas, will find in them support to flower decoratively amongst rose foliage, and, grown through the taller roses, late-flowering clematis are rewarding.

With leggier Bourbons and Hybrid Perpetuals, underplanting is essential;

both as camouflage for bare stems and as ground cover. All campanula and taller silver foliage plants are useful, while annuals like larkspur and love-in-the-mist add delicate accompaniment to these Victorian roses.

Solid mats of ground cover will balance heavy-headed bushes: *Tellima grandiflora* 'Purpurea' and *Heuchera* 'Palace Purple' for pale tones, and fresh green *Tiarella cordifolia* or *Tolmiea variegata* for darker. All border geraniums infill rewardingly: *G. sanguineum* 'Lancastrense' and *G. grandiflorum alpinum* for pink or blue flowers.

With a sheltered, southern aspect, Tea and China roses are almost self-sufficient, but a few clumps of sun-loving allium provide subtle, yet reticent, contrast with compact flowers and linear leaves. *A. pulchellum*, *A. senescens* 'Glauca' and *A. tuberosum* are correct scale. For a collection of small species roses, perhaps in semi-shade, primroses and violets add sympathetic ground cover, ferns and hellebores bring foliage and hips to dominate in the autumn. New ground-covering, small-flowering roses will present a dense picture in summer; and to fill the winter void, plant small bulbs below—muscari, scilla or crocus—to flower effectively through bare stems. When selecting a tree host for a rose, consider foliage contrast to prolong the picture: pale apple for dark *wichuraiana* ramblers and purple prunus or dark conifer for the fresh green of certain Noisettes; and a honeysuckle to flower and scent before or after the rose.

Roses need a setting of low ground-cover to reduce the stark appearance of the beds. The colouring of both flower and foliage should be carefully chosen to harmonize with the roses.

Old fruit trees, no longer productive, make a host for rampant roses which force their shoots up through the branches to tumble out in curtains of bloom.

Planting suggestions

In conclusion, a few specific planting suggestions may be helpful. For a dramatic mix of gold and purple, bend 'Reine des Violettes' over *Lamium maculatum* 'Aureum', and behind let 'Cardinal de Richelieu' associate with *Ribes sanguineum* 'Brocklebankii'. Conversely, foliage foil can be the darker: purple sage to echo the lilac tinge of 'Ballerina' and *Berberis thunbergii* 'Atropurpurea' to provide a contrast backing for 'Buff Beauty'. For a quieter scene of white and green, try *Viola cornuta* 'Alba' below 'Yvonne Rabier', surround 'Horstmann's Rosenresli' with masses of *Nicotiana affinis* 'Lime Green', and behind them let 'Nevada' fall with abandon against an evergreen background. To balance this large rose, the others must be in groups of three.

Although the following pink/silver arrangement, with a touch of blue, is designed for a 3m (10ft) × 7m (23ft) border, individual combinations can be selected for smaller situations. In mid-

front plant a group of 'Old Blush' China, with 'Hidcote' lavender; flank these with 'The Fairy' (two) falling on *Hebe* 'Pagei' and with prostrate 'Max Graf' to twine about *Stachys olympica* for good foliage texture contrast. Fill the middle area with an abundance of nineteenth-century roses: 'La Reine Victoria', 'Madame Pierre Oger', 'Louise Odier', 'Comte de Chambord', 'Marbrée', 'Vick's Caprice' and 'Jacques Cartier', with attendant *Artemisia ludoviciana*, *Santolina neapolitana* and *Senecio maritima*; ground covering *Nepeta nervosa*, *Anaphalis* 'Summer Snow' and *Geranium renardii*; neighbourly *Campanula lactiflora*, *Caryopteris* 'Kew Blue' and *Salvia haematodes*. At mid-back 'Blairii Number 2', a floriferous climbing Bourbon, would grace a trellis tripod if there is no wall, with 'Felicia' and *Ceanothus* 'Gloire de Versailles' on one side and 'Isphahan', a billowing Damask, threaded with *Clematis* 'Perle d'Azur' on the other. This informal, rather romantic rose arrangement will delight for many months of the year.

SUMMER COLOUR

For a concentration of colour through the summer months, there is no substitute for bedding plants—those half-hardy subjects raised in the greenhouse and set out at the beginning of June when all risk of frost is past. Given a reasonable amount of sunshine and warmth, lobelia, geranium, begonia and petunia will bloom until the late autumn, provided they are fed and dead-headed at regular intervals. Even in small gardens, a few such plants, carefully arranged, can have a major impact.

Generally it is best to aim for a concentrated effect immediately around the house rather than attempt a more general coverage. Much depends on house style and location. A black front door flanked by handsome stone urns filled with crimson geraniums against a painted stucco wall would provide a welcoming entrance to a formal town or country house, while single white petunias in plain oak tubs might be more suitable for a cottage.

Any scheme of planting, however ephemeral, should always be worked out carefully beforehand. Account should be taken of the building, the exposure, the amount of attention that can be paid to plants in pots and containers (which dry out very quickly in summer), the colour scheme of rooms which may open directly on to the area concerned, and so on. Having decided on the theme—in colouring, form and texture—stick to it and do not be diverted by the impulse buy or the wish to accommodate a surplus of plants from elsewhere. Often the simplest idea will prove the most effective: a few pots of vibrant scarlet geraniums, suitably grouped around a doorway or a central feature such as a fountain, will make a more lasting and powerful impact than geraniums of mixed colours or a muddle of variegated potted plants.

Planting in containers

Despite the problems of drying out, planting in pots and containers has much to commend it. Firstly the plants are easier to tend, and secondly they may be moved around at will and individuals replaced where necessary. Nowadays an almost infinite number of containers is available and, as always, it is generally the simplest designs which are best. Ordinary large clay flower pots, possibly standing on clay saucers to help conserve moisture, can have an excellent effect and look particularly well if banked up either side of a wide garden stairway leading down from a terrace. They are also effective used on the outer side of an iron fire-escape where, planted with trailing plants such as nasturtiums, they will largely conceal the utilitarian nature of the structure.

Additional colour

When preparing in advance for some special event such as a wedding or summer party, or to create an effect of luxuriance in an entirely new garden, many of the hardy annuals and biennials can be very useful in conjunction with bedding plants. Sunflowers, lavatera, tall

Containers of bedding plants provide additional colour on terraces and in corners where permanent plants are not possible. Lilies, planted in pots, can be set out when in bloom and removed to a reserve garden when they are over.

Ordinary runner beans trained round a simple pergola of wire and bamboo create an instant effect of maturity and shade even in a new garden.

nicotiana, *Campanula pyramidalis* and larkspur will all add height, while the canary creeper *Tropaeolum canariense*, *Cobaea scandens* and ordinary runner beans provide good wall coverage or furnish a temporary screen or pergola made from bean poles and bamboo canes. Large pots of gladioli or cannas, brought into flower in a reserve patch and then placed behind lower subjects or even dropped in between small shrubs, can have a striking effect, as can pots of lilies treated in similar fashion. To some extent, the time of flowering will be controlled by the time of planting, but much must still depend upon the vagaries of the weather.

Bedding plants

Given a frost-free greenhouse—the small amount of heat needed to keep the frost from a well-built greenhouse is not very great—geranium and fuchsia cuttings can be overwintered. The majority of bedding plants can be sown in early spring, to be potted on and set out at the beginning of the summer. There is a tendency, fostered by garden centres, who seem to get their bedding in far too early, to plant bedding in late April or early May. This is seldom wise, since the soil is still cold and frosts can occur at night which will put back the plants even if it does not kill them. The only possible exception to this rule is in large cities, where the atmosphere is several degrees warmer than in the more exposed open country.

When buying from garden centres or markets, look for short, sturdy plants well spaced out in their box, rather than tall overcrowded specimens forced into premature flowering, which will never come to any good. Remember, too, that flowers of a complicated type—frilled, striped or edged with a contrasting colour—may look very attractive on the stall, but will look muddled and ineffective in a mass or at a distance. However, such highly detailed flowers may prove very suitable for filling window-boxes and containers.

HERB GARDENS

One of the greatest problems confronting the maker of an ornamental, as opposed to a purely practical, herb garden is the rampant growth of so many of the herbs. For this reason it is generally wise to contrive a pattern in which each variety can have its allotted place, divided from its neighbours by a band of paving or at least a row of brick or stone on edge, to stop the spread of roots. Such hard divisions are better than hedges of hyssop, lavender or dwarf box which, however attractive and appropriate, can get invaded and swamped by the plants that they are intended to confine.

Whereas many herbs, such as thyme and rosemary, need sun, poor soil and good drainage, others, like mint, balm and bergamot, require rich, damp ground and light shade. These two conflicting needs are difficult to encompass within a small area, but much can be done by creating well-drained raised beds for the sun lovers and exploiting the shadows cast by a tree or building for the others.

Herb borders

Of course, there is no need for the herb garden to be a purely formal area, since the shapes, textures and leaf colour of herbs are very varied and they can equally well be grown in a herbal version of the herbaceous border. In fact, the very tall herbs such as angelica, fennel and lovage are rather out of scale with the average small formal garden, and are

Herbs can be grown informally and used as though they were plants in an herbaceous border. Such planting is appropriate at the edge of the kitchen garden where it can form the transition between decorative and practical areas.

A large formal herb garden where the beds of herbs, separated from one another by a pattern of brick on edge, are punctuated by square beds of santolina centred on clipped pyramid bays.

better displayed towards the back of a border. Although this would largely be a composition of green, several herbs, such as bergamot, have quite striking flowers, while the quieter blooms of rosemary, mint, hyssop, chives and many others add soft notes of colour from time to time. Quite apart from this, the variegated foliages of golden balm, mints (both gold and white), gold and silver thyme, bronze fennel and purple basil add more permanent notes of colour through the season. It must be admitted, however, that such a border would be quite difficult to keep in order, and would not be very practical from the point of view of gathering the herbs.

Practical planting

For purely practical purposes, it may not be necessary to have a herb garden at all, since many herbs will grow perfectly well in large pots, grouped within reach of the kitchen door. What is more, since the pots need not all stand together, sun and shade lovers can be kept apart, and those needing damp soil can stand in saucers frequently filled with water.

Other herbs make ideal edgings, particularly to rose beds, where the fresh green of parsley or the greyer green spears of chives not only set off the roses but also help to keep pests and diseases at bay. Thyme, lavender and rosemary are all at home on sunny gravel terraces and will often seed themselves while rosemary can also be trained up warm walls to act as a host for some light clematis such as *C. alpina*.

Even the flat dweller need not be entirely deprived of herbs, for small plants can be bought from markets or garden centres and grown for a while in internal or external window-boxes. It must be realized, however, that if these plants are constantly plucked they will not survive for very long. Another 'artificial' way of growing herbs is in the greenhouse, where, in winter, mint can be grown from plants lifted in autumn. In addition, parsley and other annual herbs sown in pots during the summer can be brought under cover before the first frosts.

KNOTS AND PARTERRES

One of the most persistent features to appear as a recurrent theme in gardens through the ages is the notion of flower-beds edged or patterned by some small-leafed evergreen shrub. Such beds were a major feature of Roman gardens, appeared in a simpler form in the medieval period, and became increasingly complex through the seventeenth and early eighteenth centuries, until they were swept away by Capability Brown and his followers whose idealized landscapes had no place for such conceits. The nineteenth century Italianate gardens, and those which sought to give an air of antiquity to 'Elizabethan' mansions of the newly-rich, revived the idea until it was lost again through rising labour costs. Now, with modern methods of weed control and hedge cutting, there is a new wave of enthusiasm for a form of gardening whose clean-cut lines contrast well with the super-abundance of flowers which make up the average English garden.

The pure knot

There are three main types to consider. The first and simplest has a straightforward clipped design set off against a plain background of gravel, crushed stone or brick. At its most basic—a pattern of green box in a panel of pale gravel—it has a sober elegance which can accord with any type of house, depending on the pattern chosen. But this is only a beginning, for there are many examples in gardening books of the seventeenth and eighteenth centuries in which the lines are made from

A seventeenth-century design reinterpreted in a modern garden to create an interesting green ring at the edge of a gravel terrace. The addition of the clipped golden hollies gives a vertical punctuation at the corners.

Opposite: Different dwarf evergreens, clipped neatly to shape, provide plenty of variation of colour and texture with which to emphasize the complexity of the design. The little tuft of dianthus, although rather touching, adds little to the general effect.

Stages in making a knot garden

How to set out your chosen pattern on the ground using pegs and string. From a small number of standard arcs many quite elaborate patterns can be achieved.

1. First work out the design on graph paper, working to a grid, then measure out the knot on the ground and peg out the corners.

2. Find the centre of the knot, if necessary by stretching string from corner to corner, marking the point where the strings cross with a peg. 'Trace' the pattern on the ground by tying string to the pegs. Then, using a stick tied to the other end of the string (which should be the length of the desired arc) mark out the pattern using the stick as a compass. Sprinkle sand or flour on the pattern to make it more obvious. Repeat round the square.

3. Place a peg halfway between the two corners and make another arc of the required radius. Repeat as necessary.

4. Join up any further points, marking out as before. When the pattern is complete plant with box or different herbs, or alternatively fill the spaces between with coloured gravel.

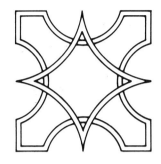

1.

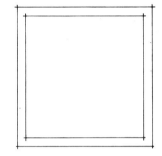

2.

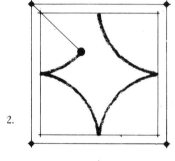

3.

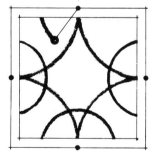

4.

materials of different colour or texture that twist and interweave like varied ribbons. Green and gold box, hyssop, dwarf lavender, santolina and variegated euonymus can all be used to differentiate one line from another. The enclosed compartments can then be filled with gravels of numerous shades, from cream through reddish and brownish hues to the plainer greys and green of limestone chippings.

Such schemes are surprisingly easy to construct, since once the ground has been levelled, weed-killed and prepared for planting, it can be covered by a layer of black plastic sheeting. On this the design can be painted in emulsion paint, the lines then being cut through with scissors before the plastic is firmly fixed down with strong wire shaped like old-fashioned hair pins. The young plants can then be planted through the appropriate slits and the whole covered by a good layer—at least 7.5cm (3in)—of the chosen hard material. Provided the ground has been well manured in advance, the young hedges will have a good start and can later be encouraged by spraying with foliar feed during the growing season, while weeds are totally inhibited by the hidden layer of plastic.

The closed knot

The next type uses the same technique of various plant ribbons to form the pattern, but replaces plastic and gravel with an infill of dwarf shrubby material, which is clipped level with the divisions to form a kind of raised carpet. Sometimes such schemes are sunk into paved areas so they appear as living rugs, but since the beds in which they grow must necessarily be sunk they might present a hazard to the short-sighted. Provided that, for the purposes of clipping, all parts can be reached from the edge, this variation is also fairly easy to maintain. It needs to be cut over—with perhaps a little vertical clipping to keep the ribbons distinct—only once each year and can have an organic fertilizer such as fish, blood and bone brushed in each spring to maintain consistent growth. The infill does not have to be entirely evergreen, and dwarf deciduous shrubs can give a pleasing seasonal variation to the effect. *Berberis thunbergii* 'Atropurpurea Nana', and 'Aurea' are particularly useful as contrast to the prevailing greys and greens, and they clip well.

The open knot
The third type really falls into categories, but a clipped pattern against a soil background is common to both. In one case permanent plants—for example, *Ajuga reptans* 'Atropurpurea', *Stachys lanata* and the rose 'Little White Pet'—are used to fill in the design. In the other, seasonal

bedding is used, changed two or three times each year. This last is the system favoured by Victorian gardeners and modern park keepers, while the first is less time consuming and has tended to replace it in private gardens. In both cases the plants are used as blocks of colour and texture, as a variation on the coloured gravels or clipped shrubs of the previous examples.

Early gardens showed another system, in which the strong pattern contained a collection of varied and, to judge by the illustrations, rather ill-assorted plants grown as individual specimens. Such a scheme might be suitable for the plant collector by giving a semblance of order to what is intrinsically a muddle, but it can seldom be visually satisfactory.

Opposite: A very simple, clear-cut pattern can absorb an infill of varied planting which might otherwise look messy. This is the type of knot work frequently seen in early garden pictures.

HERBACEOUS BORDERS

Double borders need to be planted in strong drifts which are repeated diagonally from one side to the other. Note the way in which the delphinium spikes, played off against the rounded shapes, repeat the grouping of trees and the church spire beyond the boundary.

The creation of good herbaceous borders, which traditionally are one of the glories of English gardens, is an extremely skilled and time-consuming task so careful consideration should be given to the nature of herbaceous planting. Too often the term is applied to any arrangement of perennial flowers, from a narrow strip of flowerbed to generous double herbaceous borders. The appearance of these beds will never be satisfactory if they are merely filled with clumps of brightly coloured hardy plants, placed with little relation to each other apart from their height. The superbly harmonious appearance of the best herbaceous borders results from an understanding of proportion and mass, colour and seasonal variation.

The first thing to realize is that, however extensive the border, it cannot be kept in full beauty for more than six weeks at most. Attempts to have 'something in flower all the year round' will simply result in little patches of unrelated colour springing up at various times, in a brown or green setting depending on the season. This is not visually effective, and a decision must be made as to the exact period when the border should be at its best. At other times during the growing season it will look well furnished and may have incidents of colour, but the major effort will be concentrated on a fairly short period.

The next thing to consider is that purely herbaceous planting dies down entirely in winter, leaving bare ground

Bold edging on both sides of the central path gives unity to these perfectly balanced borders.

which can look very dreary if seen at close quarters from the house. If the border is to be attractive in winter it will be necessary to include a good proportion of mainly low evergreen shrubs to reduce the visible extent of the soil. Planted in sweeping diagonal groups, some of which curl round and interlock, with a counterpoint of a few tall specimens to create promontories and islands to relieve the general flatness of the composition, these will largely solve the problems of the barren months, without reducing the impact of the summer display.

Many designs for herbaceous borders continue to perpetuate the basic error of planting in clumps but, as Gertrude Jekyll showed, this is the most ineffective way to use the available material. It is much better to plant in thin diagonal drifts, spreading the colour, when it is there, over the greatest area, and leaving only fine cracks, easily hidden by later flowering groups in front or behind, when it is over. In this way, plants like oriental poppies, which flower comparatively early and die off in an ungainly manner, can be set quite far back in the border to be lost behind the rising growths of later flowering subjects or covered over by the expanding but thin growth of something like gypsophila.

Miss Jekyll's system of having pots in the reserve garden, ready to drop into empty space to extend the flowering season, may not be practical today. It might well be tried, though, in the case of lilies, many of which seem to survive better in pots where they can be protected from many of the insect pests and diseases to be found in the open border. When in bloom they can be set out, the pots hidden by surrounding foliage and the stems supported by canes driven into the border behind, which will not only support the blooms but prevent the pots blowing over in a high wind.

Although this kind of 'mobile' planting may be difficult, the use of annuals and other bedding plants, such as nicotiana and pansies, is not. At the simplest they can be bought from the local market and garden centre, but ideally they should be sown directly on site or in boxes in a cold frame or greenhouse. If they are deadheaded frequently most will continue to flower until the frosts, or at least last much longer in bloom than the strictly herbaceous perennials with which they look much at home. The only problem is getting seeds in a range of suitable

Herbaceous plants can also be effectively displayed within the firm framework of a squared design, achieved with clipped box edges.

colours, rather than the rather bright ones which are more readily available. Although the use of half-hardy elements may seem to add to the labour of maintaining a border, they allow parts of the soil to be refreshed every year and reduce the amount of permanent material to be lifted, divided and replanted every third year or so.

Besides the plants to be put in afresh each year, there are those to be taken up, stored and replanted once the soil warms up again in the spring. Many people dislike dahlias, thinking only of the exhibition varieties with soup-plate flowers. In fact, many of the cactus, medium decorative and pom-pom types are graceful and bring a great deal of colour into the late summer and autumn borders, as do cannas which are treated similarly and have the added advantage of very handsome foliage. All can be started into growth early in a frost-free greenhouse, and can be grouped towards the back of borders at the beginning of June. Towards the front, giving the same kind of fleshy opulence on a smaller scale, go the tuberous begonias which require similar treatment.

For a successful border, good staking is essential and there is really no substitute for brushwood cut from hazel or other trees with firm, twiggy branchlets. This must be put in afresh each spring round the clumps of plants needing support, allowing the shoots to grow out in a natural way through the twigs, any visible parts of which can be cut away once the plants are fully grown. Most of the artificial supports obtainable from garden centres give the plants an unnatural, stiff outline or provide insufficient support. It is not advisable to stretch pig wire over the whole bed, held up by stout posts back and front. The support is too high for some of the lower plants, too low for many of the high ones and is clearly seen at all times along the outer edge of the border.

Of course, all these problems can be avoided by the use of plants which are too stout, or too low to be affected by wind and rain. In the same way, the chore of the three-yearly lifting, dividing and replanting routine can be avoided by using only those plants which can remain in the same place for a number of years, but in both cases the material available and the effects that can be achieved with it are severely limited.

Another excellent way of using many of the lower perennials is to create a simple pattern of formal beds, possibly edged with box and divided by paved paths for ease of maintenance. In these, asymmetric groups of herbaceous plants can be interplanted with drifts of tulips for spring display. This system of interplanting exploits one piece of ground to the maximum to provide either continuity of colour or display at different seasons. Many plants have handsome foliage even when not in bloom, and this can provide an excellent foil to bulbs, corms or lilies, most of which tend to have a rather thin habit of growth. For instance, in spring the Chinese paeonies show beautifully coloured shoots which look well with white, pink and ivory daffodils whose untidy dying foliage is hidden by the expanding leaves. Later the leaves shade the roots of lilies or help to support the ungainly growth of butterfly gladioli or *Hyacinthus candicans*. Finally, many of them turn to magnificent autumn colours to add to the late season effect.

It is best to provide a broad strip of paving to separate the border from the lawn. This allows groups of plants to lean forward, softening what might otherwise become too hard a line at the edge.

CONTAINER PLANTING

This simple grouping of plants and pots distracts the eye from the poor concrete finish of the steps. A saucer placed under each pot would retain water and prevent the clay and soil from drying out as quickly.

Container planting has become much more popular in recent years, partly due to a wider and improved range of containers, and partly because many people in towns, with only a small amount of outdoor space, want to grow plants for decoration, flavouring or food. Although containers are particularly useful in small gardens, or where there is little or no open soil available, they can also add interest and character to larger gardens. They may be grouped together to provide a striking focal point, at the base of steps or walls, or used to conceal unsightly objects such as downpipes or manhole covers. They can even be used to support uprights and crossbeams, enabling a whole area to be shaded without disturbing paving or walls, which may be an advantage in rented premises.

This generously planted urn acts as a striking focal point within the formal garden.

On constricted sites, containers, with a range of evergreen and herbaceous plants, may accommodate nearly all the planting. More short-term subjects—annuals and bulbs—will then provide a continuous and rewarding display of flowers. But even in larger and more permanent plantings, containers can be useful as a means of livening up an evergreen corner in midsummer or of introducing less hardy plants into a herbaceous border.

Types of container

There are many available materials, sizes and styles. Reconstituted stone or concrete is very heavy, especially when filled with soil; terracotta can be very decorative, but tends to absorb water and dry out quickly, cracking in frosty conditions; and timber containers must be painted or treated with preservative. If old beer barrels are used, the wood must never be allowed to shrink or dry out, because the metal hoops will then become loose and eventually fall off. More modern materials include plastic, which is very light, and fibreglass, which is also light and may have a more acceptable finish.

More unusual containers include lead water troughs, old clay chimney pots, hanging baskets, window-boxes and wall-mounted brackets. Although an antique lead urn may provide a memorable focal point, an inexpensive grouping of ordinary flower pots, varying in size and planting, can be equally striking.

Planting considerations

A great many plants, of all sizes and types, can be grown in containers, but the receptacle must be suitable for the size and root-spread of the particular plant. If a plant has a strong, well developed root system, it must be given plenty of space to grow. Large, heavy concrete or GRP containers are most suitable for trees and very big shrubs, as they give the plants space and stability at their roots. On the other hand, annuals, such as ageratum, petunias and polyan-

Top left: This stone trough is decorative enough for a simple planting of bulbs.

Top: A cheerful window-box display outside a town house of cream tulips and blue grape hyacinths.

Above: A sandstone basket-weave urn with an exuberant planting of 'Gartenmeister Bonstadt' fuchsias.

thus, with short, fibrous roots, can be accommodated in a shallow bowl. A little bit of ivy will set off the colour of the flowers and give solidity to the grouping.

Tulips and daffodils can be planted in two tiers and both will bloom at the same time. Wallflowers, geraniums and pelargoniums also do well in pots, but must be planted close together so that they appear to burst exuberantly out of the pot. Scented-leafed plants such as rosemary, sage and lavender will release their scent when brushed, and many other herbs can be grown for the kitchen. Even shade-lovers—bergenias, ferns and hostas—will thrive if they are kept out of the sun and moist. Lilies also do particularly well and are elegant and fragrant; they appreciate a lime-free soil, plenty of moisture and good drainage.

Care and maintenance

Many container-grown plants do not survive for long because insufficient thought is given to their requirements. Too often, plants of different species, accustomed to growing in a variety of habitats, are placed in the same container, the sun-lovers sharing the same site and conditions as the shade-seekers. It is better to group the plants as they would be in their natural habitat, and if the appropriate soil conditions are maintained—dry or damp, acid or alkaline—the plants should thrive.

Ample water and good drainage are necessary for all container-grown plants. There should be drainage holes at the bottom of the pot, and then a layer of crocks (broken pots) or stones. On top of this place a layer of dead leaves, turf

The planting in this old water trough stands out against the evergreen backcloth, and the outline shape echoes the form of the tree behind. The eye rests on the planter, instead of travelling through to the buildings beyond.

Weathered tree stumps can provide a sculptural element in a woodland garden, and are particularly effective when seen against the foliage behind. Succulents adapt well in this sheltered setting.

(grass side down) or even a piece of fibreglass blanket to prevent soil and moisture washing through the crocks.

Small containers of terracotta or wood, which tend to dry out quickly, can be lined with black polythene rubbish bags. The polythene, punctured at the bottom for drainage, should be laid over the crocks and brought up to the sides. When the container has been filled with soil, the polythene can be trimmed off just below the level of the container.

Commercial potting composts, such as John Innes or Levington, are available in various mixtures, adapted to the different growing requirements of the plants. Lime-hating plants such as azaleas or rhododendrons need an acid compost; they can be fed occasionally with a fertilizer such as Maxicrop. Lime-loving plants such as lavender appreciate the addition of limestone grit to the soil, which also helps drainage. Moisture-loving plants—bergenias, hostas and ferns—can be given a constant supply of water by standing the container in a shallow saucer or tray filled with stones or water. If the plants prefer dry conditions, the containers can be placed on bricks or tiles clear of the ground to allow the water to drain and air to circulate.

The plants will need occasional trimming, dead-heading or cutting back. They should also be repotted when their roots become congested in the original container. A regular programme of watering and feeding should be employed, for spasmodic bursts of treatment will lead to overwatering, followed by drying out.

LEGAL CONSIDERATIONS

Besides the physical factors of garden design there are the unseen but no less potent legal responsibilities in relation to the garden.

Until 1909, when Local Authorities were given power to adopt and administer planning schemes, a landowner could use his land in the way he wanted so long as he did not infringe the rights of other landowners. This led to some terrible scars upon the landscape. The Town and Country Planning Act 1932 extended the power of local authorities to control development on all land, urban or rural, to preserve buildings of special interest, to restore the land to its former condition if the owner had not been granted planning permission, and to protect trees or woodlands. Subsequently the legislation has been changed from time to time to regulate the way in which development may take place. The principal statutory framework is currently provided in the Town and Country Planning Act 1971 as amended. Normally no building operations can be begun or the use of land changed before a specific application to the local planning authority has been made and permission granted. There are, however, a number of instances in which deemed planning permission exists under the General Development Order 1977 (as amended) to allow the carrying out of certain minor developments. In these circumstances there is no need to apply for permission to the local planning authority. It is, though, important to read the order carefully to discover what is and is not allowed. Putting up fences and walls, for example, is permitted, but there are specific limits as to height.

The local planning authority usually employs an officer, who can enter property without permission and who in the case of unauthorized development may advise the authority to serve an 'enforcement' notice on the occupier and owner; continued disobedience may lead to prosecution and a heavy fine. Listed buildings are specially protected, and if any permission is sought to alter or extend or demolish such a building, the planning authorities will take into account how the work will affect any architectural or historic features and may ensure that these are preserved, or that original materials are used in the reconstruction. The provisions of the General Development Order are somewhat more restrictive in conservation areas. It is therefore more likely that an application for permission will be required in these areas for house extensions such as conservatories. It is obviously wiser and less costly to check up carefully on the position before commencing any development. In cases of real doubt, a procedure exists under section 53 of the 1971 Act for applying for a determination as to whether or not planning permission is required. Before determining any application for permission, the planning authority is required to seek the views of any party whom it considers may be particularly affected by the development. In Conservation areas, notice of the application must be displayed on the site. Objections from local residents will sometimes be an important factor in the authority's consideration of the application.

The existence of public or private rights of access to an adjoining property, may curb plans to alter or extend the garden so any conditions attached to the ownership and maintenance of the land should be checked.

Ownership of boundary property, such as hedges, walls or fences, is often a matter of dispute. The deeds, or the land certificate in the case of registered land, usually describe the boundaries of property in words as well as referring to a map for identification purposes. Sometimes it is necessary to find out who has paid for maintenance and repairs in the past, for they are presumed to be the owners; sometimes a boundary wall is the equal responsibility of the owners on each side; and sometimes boundary walls can each be the responsibility of different people, such as in terraced gardens in town. Often walls will need to be repaired or repointed before starting work on the garden, so it must be established who is responsible for the expense.

Problems involving neighbours are almost bound to occur from time to time, especially when changes are imminent. The most usual ones involve trees, weeds, the right to light, excessive noise and smells.

With trees it is an infringement of the rights of the owners to the unrestricted use of their land when branches and roots spread over or under neighbouring properties. The neighbours are then entitled to lop off any intruding part without notice, even if this act kills the tree. The fruit on an overhanging branch belongs to the owner of the tree, and the owner of the tree may also be responsible for damage caused directly or indirectly by the roots of the tree, such as walls cracking or subsiding or if they interfere with foundations.

Before carrying out work to any trees it is advisable to check whether the tree in question is the subject of a Tree Preservation Order or is in a Conservation Area. In both cases it is an offence to carry out tree works without following the correct procedure. If it is necessary to fell, lop, top or uproot trees in a Conservation Area, other than those already covered by a Tree Preservation order, six weeks notice must be given to the local planning authority, and consent obtained before commencing work. Exemptions from this requirement include trees not exceeding 75 mm in diameter at a height of 1.5 m. The penalty for unauthorized work or damage if a tree is cut down, uprooted or wilfully destroyed, or is wilfully damaged or topped, or lopped in a manner likely to destroy it may be a fine up to £1,000—or twice the sum which appears to the Court to be the value of the tree, whichever is the greater. For permission to proceed with tree work under these conditions, application should be made to the local planning officer and should include details of the tree sufficient to enable its identification, including species and position on site (specify front or back garden); details of the proposed works; and the reason for the works. The owner of a tree is also liable for injury caused to a neighbour by a falling tree or branch, only escaping liability if he did not know or could not have known that the tree was dangerous.

In the case of weeds, adjoining landowners cannot be liable for allowing weeds to grow and their seeds to be spread by the wind, but landowners have some protection through the Ministry of Agriculture, Fisheries and Food. The Weeds Act 1959 states that if injurious weeds such as dock, ragwort and thistles are growing on the land, the occupier of the land may be required to take action within a definite time to stop the weeds from spreading. If he fails to do so, he can be prosecuted and the work carried out by the Ministry or local authority at his expense.

A neighbour is not automatically entitled to light through his windows. There is, though, one important exception to this: if the landowner and those who preceded him have received daylight through their window for twenty years or more, they will have acquired a right to continue to have a reasonable amount of light while the house stands, so a neighbour is not allowed to put up a building which greatly interferes with the light. This is referred to in legal terms as the right to 'ancient lights' and can only prevent building. It is not applicable to gardens or, for instance, to the interference of light within a room by a tree or wall on neighbouring land. The general rule of thumb is that the angle of light restricted must be greater than 45°, but in reality, the quality of light must be reduced to make it insufficient for 'comfortable use and enjoyment'. A neighbour who has a fairly new house can be prevented from acquiring 'ancient lights' by the intending builder registering a notice with the local authority under the Rights of Light Act 1959.

The nuisance of noise is difficult to assess as there are no hard and fast rules, and people have different levels of tolerance—ringing church bells, barking dogs, adjacent factories or nightclubs all emit noise, but whether this can or must be tolerated is a different question. If the noise is made deliberately and unnecessarily in order to annoy a neighbour it is a deliberate nuisance and can result in prosecution under the Control of Pollution Act 1974. But usually the nuisance of noise is difficult to prove, involves witnesses and the granting of, or not granting, an injunction. Basically when normal rest and relaxation are seriously hampered and a neighbour or owner has to leave home for peace and quiet, a substantial nuisance has taken place. Similarly, objections to smells and smoke can only be taken to court if the landowner can prove that damage was caused directly by them, such as trees or crops burnt or destroyed. When the nuisance is caused by industrial operations prosecution can be originated under the Public Health Act 1936 or the Clean Air Act 1956.

To sum up, the law changes quickly and is so complex that expert and specialized advice should be sought and in most cases is vital. Many different authorities and regulations are involved, but it is almost always wiser to determine what is permitted by law before incurring the expense and inconvenience of embarking on something without necessary permission.

GLOSSARY

Acid Applied to soils (generally peaty or sandy) with a pH level below 7.0.

Aeration The breaking up of solidly-packed soil, usually by mechanical means, to allow air to reach the plant roots.

Aggregate The small stone content of a given mixture.

Alkaline Applies to soils, generally chalk, lime and clay, with a pH level above 7.0.

Annual A plant with a complete lifespan from seed to flowering, fruiting and death completed within one year or less.

Anti-desiccant spray A chemical which prevents loss of moisture.

Ashlar A facing of dressed stone-blocks on a backing wall of brick, rough stone or concrete block.

Ballast A mixture of sand and stone aggregate, usually associated with the mixture used for making concrete.

Batter The angle of a wall where it is made to lean inwards from the perpendicular.

Bedding plants Generally refers to half-hardy annuals which, having been raised elsewhere (usually in a greenhouse), are planted out in beds for summer display (summer bedding). Plants are now also planted in the autumn for spring flowering.

Biennial A plant that lives for two growing seasons (two years). In the first year, it grows vegetatively and in the second it flowers, fruits and dies.

Blinding A layer of sand laid to cover sharp edges of stone, such as in the case of a hardcore base or when paving a 'liner' for a pool.

Bond The way in which bricks, or stone, are laid to give structural strength.

Brick on edge A brick laid with the thin stretcher face uppermost.

Brushed aggregate The surface of concrete which has been brushed before setting (when 'green') to expose the selected stone aggregate to give a textured finish.

Conifer A plant, usually evergreen primitive trees and shrubs, that bears cones.

Contour line Used to indicate the relief and height of land from which the shape and form of hills and valleys, and the angles and directions of slopes can be obtained.

Cordon A method of training fruit trees by planting them at an angle. Plants are restricted to a single main stem by pruning.

Coursed Stone or brick laid in a particular pattern.

Coping The top course of a wall usually made of brick, stone or concrete, designed to prevent water from seeping down into the body of the wall.

Damp-proof course/waterproof course A course laid near the base of a wall to prevent moisture rising within the wall.

Deciduous A plant (generally a tree or shrub) which loses its leaves at the end of the growing season.

Dry-mix A mixture of sand and cement without any water added, sometimes used when laying brick or slab paving.

Espalier A method of training trees (usually fruit) flat with branches extended horizontally at equally spaced intervals.

Evergreen A plant that retains its leaves throughout the year.

Fall The slight slope created to carry water off hard surfaces to prevent flooding and puddling. The fall is directed towards open soil areas or especially drains or gulleys.

Fallow ground Where ground is cultivated and left (usually for one growing season) 'out of action' for a period of time. This could be either to eradicate traces of perennial weeds or to give the ground a rest.

Flocculation The process where small particles of a clay soil bind together forming larger aggregates, thus improving soil drainage and aeration. Flocculation is created by the addition of lime to a clay soil.

Frost pockets These are formed by cold air (which always flows downhill and on to low ground) being trapped by solid planting or buildings.

Green manure A quick-growing crop grown to be incorporated into the soil on which it grows. This increases the humus content of the soil which will then improve the soil water-holding capacity on a light soil and drainage on a heavy soil.

Ground cover Plants which, when grouped together, will form a weed-proof mat of ornamental foliage.

Ground water/water table The water travelling through the soil is referred to as the ground water. The water table is the level of that water at any given time. It varies according to soil conditions and the time of year.

Gulley A shallow channel to carry away surface water.

Hardcore A mixture of broken brick and/or stone used to create a firm base on which to lay concrete foundations or paving. It should not include any soil or traces of vegetation.

Herbaceous A perennial plant that does not form a persistent woody stem and is either deciduous—dying down to the ground annually or occasionally evergreen.

Hoggin A mixture of gravel and clay used as the binding agent in gravel paths and driveways.

Humus The dark brown residue formed by the break down of decaying organic matter in the soil.

Knot A flower bed divided into varying geometrical patterns by using clipped dwarf hedges.

Leaching Process by which nutrients are washed out of the soil, usually by rain.

Leader The uppermost, usually central, shoot of a woody perennial plant.

Liner A waterproof sheeting made of Butyl or P.V.C. used to create water features.

Microclimate The small variations within the overall climate of a given garden caused by surrounding factors.

Mortar A mixture of soft sand and cement used for walling and paving. Mortar is sometimes simply referred to as cement.

Mowing strip The placing of inert materials between lawn and border to prevent damage to the plants when mowing.

Mulching A layer of organic material laid on the soil surface that can suppress weeds, keep moisture in the soil, and provide nutrition. With alpines a gravel mulch will help cushion plants from rotting.

Neutral Applies to soils with a pH level of 7, in which the majority of plants will grow.

Organic Substances derived from the decay of living organisms, such as compost.

Parterre A flower bed laid out in a regular ornamental manner.

Pavier A thick brick especially manufactured for brick paving.

Perennial A plant that lives for more than two years. Perennials can be herbaceous or woody.

pH scale A measurement of alkalinity and acidity in soils. The scale runs from 0–14, 7 being neutral. Figures below neutral indicate acidity. The lower the figure, the higher the acidity. Figures above 7, indicate alkalinity. The higher the figure the higher the alkalinity.

Pruning The controlled removal of unwanted growth to encourage healthy vigorous new shoots.

Shelter belt The siting of trees and shrubs to deflect and filter prevailing winds.

Soil structure Describes the shape and size of the aggregates of soil particles. A good crumbly structure is the desirable product. Structure is produced by natural processes of wetting, drying, freezing and thawing and by the activity of roots and soil fauna.

Stretcher and header The different faces of a brick. The stretcher is the 'long' face, either when seen as the narrow side in walling or when laid on edge, or the 'wider' face when laid flat in paving. The header is the small end face of the brick.

Zone of visual influence The surrounding landscape which can be seen from within a garden site.

FURTHER READING

Balston, Michael, *The Well Furnished Garden*. London, Mitchell Beazley, 1986; New York, Simon & Schuster, 1987.

Beales, Peter. *Classic Roses*. London, Collins Harvill, 1986; New York, Henry Holt & Co.

Bean, W. G. *Trees and Shrubs Hardy in the British Isles*. London, John Murray, 1980, (8th edn.); New York, Scribners, 1974.

Beazeley, Elizabeth. *Design and Detail of the Space Between Buildings*. London, Architectural Press, 1962.

Bisgrove, R. *Your Problem Garden*. London, Mitchell Beazley, 1979.

Brookes, John. *The Garden Book*. London, Dorling Kindersley, 1984; New York, Crown, 1984.

Room Outside. London and New York, Thames & Hudson, 1985.

The Small Garden. London, Marshall Cavendish, 1984.

Caborn, J. M. *Shelter Belts and Windbreaks*. London, Faber & Faber, 1965.

Cane, Percy. *The Creative Art of Garden Design*. London, Country Life, 1966.

Chatto, Beth. *The Damp Garden*. London/New York, Dent, 1983. *The Dry Garden*. London and New York, Dent, 1983.

Chevreul, M. E. *The Principles of Harmony and Contrast of Colours and their Application to the Arts*. London, George Bell & Sons, 1890; New York, Van Nos Reinhold, 1967.

Church, Thomas D. *Gardens for People*. New York, McGraw-Hill, 1983.

Colvin, Brenda. *Trees for Town and Country*. London, Lund Humphries, 1965.

Cowell, F. R. *The Garden as Fine Art*. London, Weidenfeld & Nicolson, 1978.

Creasy, Rosalind. *The Complete Book of Edible Landscaping*. San Francisco, Sierra, 1982.

Crowe, Dame Sylvia. *Garden Design*. 2nd edn. London, Packard, 1981; New York, Hearthside Press, 1959.

Cox, Jeff & Cox, Marylin. *The Perennial Garden*. Emmaus, PA, Rodale Press, 1985.

Diekelman, John. *Natural Landscaping*. New York, McGraw-Hill, 1983.

Dirr, Michael. *Manual of Woody Landscaping Plants*. Champaign, II, Stripes, 1978.

Eckbo, Garrett. *The Art of Home Landscaping*. New York, McGraw-Hill, 1976.

Evison, Raymond J. *Making the Most of Clematis*. London, Floraprint.

Fairbroker, N. *New Lives, New Landscapes*. London, Architectural Press, 1970.

Ferguson, Nicola. *Right Plant, Right Place*, New York, Summit Books, 1984.

Fish, Margery. *Gardening in the Shade*. Newton Abbot, David & Charles, 1972; New York, Faber & Faber, 1984.

Fish, Margery. *Ground Cover Plants*. Newton Abbot, David & Charles, 1970; New York, Faber & Faber, 1980.

Foley, D. J. *Garden Ornaments, Complements and Accessories*. New York, Crown, 1972.

Gault, S. Miller. *Dictionary of Shrubs in Colour*. London, Michael Joseph, 1976; New York, Crown, 1976.

Hadfield, Miles. *Topiary and Ornamental Hedges*. London, A. & C. Black, 1971.

Henderson, Marge. *The House of Boughs*. New York, Viking, 1985.

Hessayon, D. G. *The Rose Expert*. London, PBI, 1981; *Be Your Own Rose Expert*. New York, Fell, 1977.

Hillier, H. G. *Hillier's Manual of Trees and Shrubs*. Newton Abbot, David & Charles, (5th edn.), 1981; North Pomfret, VT, David & Charles, 1981.

Hobhouse, Penelope. *Colour in Your Garden*. London, Collins, 1985; Boston, Little Brown, 1985.

Hoskins, W. G. *The Making of the English Landscape*. London, Penguin, 1955.

Hudak, Joseph. *Gardening with Perennials Month by Month*. Portland, OR, Timber, 1985.

Shrubs in the Landscape. New York, McGraw-Hill, 1984.

Trees for Every Purpose. New York, McGraw-Hill, 1985.

Hunt, Peter. *The Book of Garden Ornaments*. London, Dent, 1974.

Hunter, John M. *Land into Landscape*. London, George Godwin, 1975.

Hyams, E. *A History of Gardens and Gardening*. London, Dent, 1971.

Jekyll, Gertrude. *Colour in the Flower Garden*. London, Country Life, 1908.

Colour Schemes for the Flower Garden. Salem, NH, Ayers Co. Pubs., 1984.

Wood and Garden: Notes and thoughts, practical and critical of a working amateur. London, Longmans; Salem, Salem House, 1983.

Jekyll, G. and Mawley, F. *Roses for English Gardens*. London, Penguin Books; Salem, NH, Ayers Co Pubs., 1984.

Jellicoe, G. A. and S. *The Landscape of Man*. London, Thames and Hudson, 1975.

Jellicoe, Goode and Lancaster. *The Oxford Companion to Gardens*. Oxford, Oxford University Press, 1986.

Jellicoe, Susan and Allen, Marjory. *Town Gardens to Live In*. London, Penguin Books, 1977.

Johnson, Hugh. *The Principles of Gardening*. London, Mitchell Beazley, 1979; New York, Simon & Schuster, 1979.

Lane Fox, Robin. *Better Gardening*. Oxfordshire, R & L Beckley, 1982.

Larkom, Joy. *The Salad Garden*. London, Windward, 1984.

Laurie, Michael. *Introduction to Landscape Architecture*. New York, Elsevier, 1985.

Lloyd, Christopher. *The Adventurous Gardener*. London, Allen Lane; New York, Random House, 1985.

Lloyd, Christopher. *Foliage Plants*. London, Collins, 1973; New York, Random House, 1985.

The Well-Chosen Garden. London, Elm Tree Books, 1983; New York, Harper and Row, 1984.

Lovejoy, Derek and Partners. *Spon's Landscape Handbook*. London E. & E. N. Spon Ltd., 1978.

Page, Russell. *The Education of a Gardener*. London, Collins, 1983; New York, Random House, 1985.

Reader's Digest. *The Gardening Year*. London, Reader's Digest Association Ltd., 1974.

Reader's Digest. *Guide to Creative Gardening*. London, Reader's Digest Association Ltd.

Reader's Digest. *Reader's Digest Encyclopaedia of Garden Plants and Flowers*. London, Reader's Digest Association Ltd., 1984.

Reekie, R. Frazer. *Draughtsmanship*. London, Arnold, 1969.

Rose, Graham. *The Low Maintenance Garden*. London, Windward, 1983.

The Royal Horticultural Society, *RHS Concise Encyclopaedia of Gardening Techniques*. London, Mitchell Beazley, 1981.

Schenk, George. *The Complete Shade Gardener*. New York, HP Books, 1984.

Simonds, John. *Landscaping Architecture*. New York, McGraw-Hill, 1983.

Smyser, Carol. *Nature's Design*. Emmaus, PA, Rodale Press, 1982.

Stern, F. C. *A Chalk Garden*. London, Faber & Faber, 1960.

Swanson, Faith. *Herb Garden Design*. Hanover, NH, University Press of New England, 1984.

Taylor, Jasmine (ed.). *Conservatories and Garden Rooms*. London, Macdonald, 1985.

Tandy, Cliff. *Handbook of Urban Landscape*. London, Architectural Press, 1972.

Thacker, Christopher. *The History of Gardens*. London, Crown Helm, 1979; Berkeley, CA, University of California Press, 1979.

Thomas, Graham Stuart. *The Art of Planting*. London, Dent, 1984; New York, Godine, 1984.

Climbing Roses Old and New. London, Dent, 1965; Totowa, NJ, Biblio Dist., 1983.

Colour in the Winter Garden. London, Dent, 1984; Totowa, NJ, Biblio Dist., 1984.

Perennial Garden Plants. London, Dent, 1982; Totowa, NJ, Biblio Dist., 1982.

Plants for Ground-Cover. London, Dent, 1977; Totowa, NJ, Biblio Dist., 1982.

Tunnard, Christopher. *Garden in the Modern Landscape*. London, Architectural Press, 1938.

Verey, Rosemary. *Classic Garden Design*. London, Viking, 1984; New York, Congdon & Weed, 1984.

The Scented Garden. London, Mermaid, 1981.

Weddle, A. E. (ed.). *Techniques of Landscape Architecture*. London, Heinemann, 1981.

Whyte, W. S. *Basic Metric Surveying*. London and New York, Butterworth & Co., 1985.

Wilder, Louise B. *The Fragrant Garden*. New York, Dover, 1974.

Wood, Dennis. *Terrace and Courtyard Gardens*. Newton Abbot, David & Charles, 1970.

Wright, Michael. *The Complete Handbook of Garden Plants*. New York, Facts on File, 1984.

Wyman, Donald. *The Gardening Encyclopaedia*. New York, Macmillan, 1987.

Shrubs and Vines for American Gardens. New York, Macmillan, 1969.

Trees for American Gardens. New York, Macmillan, 1965.

PICTURE ACKNOWLEDGEMENTS

Page numbers in bold refer to colour illustrations

Rosemary Alexander: 8 (below), 21 (above), 24–5, 32, 33, **34**, 52 (above), **57** (below), **82**, 86, 88, 94 (above), 97 (below), 110, 112, 120, 134, 138, 176, 177 (both), **187** (above), 189, **210** (right), **211** (top left and top)

Heather Angel: 10, 19 (above), 20, 26 (both), 27, 35, **40** (both), 42 (below), 45, 50, 51, **52** (below), 59 (above), **61** (below), **62** (below), 64, **65** (above), 66, 67 (above), 70, 71 (both), 73 (both), 75 (above), 78 (below), 79, 89, **91** (both), 96, 129, 179, **182** (both), 184 (both), 185, 188, 193, **194** (above), **195** (all), 196 (below), 197, **199**, 202, 205, 206, 209, **211** (below), 213

Cement & Concrete Association: 125

Clive Corless: 115, 123, 132, **175**

Courtesy of the Trustees of the Chelsea Physic Garden: 6, 8 (above)

Marston and Langinger: 29, 180, 183

Tania Midgley: 78 (above), **173**

The National Trust: 68, 75 (Hidcote Manor), **43** (below, Cliveden, photo V. Collingwood)

Sydney Newberry: 23 (above)

Hugh Palmer: 2 (Bramdean House), 13, 18, 31 (Tresco Abbey), 39 (Saling Hall), 42 (above, Howick Hall), 44 (above, Barnsley House), 44 (below, Great Dixter), 59 (centre, The Gables), 59 (below, Ince Castle), 60 (Tintinhull House), 61 (above, Heale House), 63 (Holker Hall), 72 (Chidmere), 76 (The Priory), 77 (Levens Hall), 80 (Heale House), 87 (Essex House), 90 (High Beeches), 92 (Howick Hall), 93 (Heale House), 94 (below, Stone Cottage, Hambleton), 95 (Jenkyn Place), 97 (above, The Old Rectory, Farnborough), 170 (Levens Hall), 172, **175**, **178**, **186**, **187** (below), 198 (Tintinhull House), 200, **203** (Tudor Garden, Southampton), **207** (Bramdean House), 208 (Hatfield House), **210** (Holker Hall), 212 (Tintinhull House)

Anthony du Gard Pasley: 14 (both), **15**, 17 (both), 19 (below) 36, **43** (above), 47 (above), 53 (both), 54, 55 (both), **56**, 57 (above), 58, 62 (right), 67 (below), 81, 83, 85, 126, 201

Syndication International: 41

Hazel Le Rougetel: 192, **194** (below), 196 (above)

Harry Smith Horticultural Photographic Collection: 22, 38, 47 (below), 65 (below), 69, 140, 143, 148, 151 (both), 157, 159, 161, 165, 166, 167, **191**

Line drawings
Rick Blakeley: 141 (above)

Pat Gregory: 141 (below), 144, 158, 159, 160, 162

John Moreland: 12, 21, 23, 28, 30, 48, 49, 53, 106–7, 108–9, 113, 114–5, 118–9, 122, 123, 124, 125, 126, 127, 128, 129, 130, 131, 132, 133, 134, 135, 136, 137, 204

The charts on pages 164–5 are reproduced by kind permission of Granada Books (*Large Gardens and Parks*. Tom Wright).

219

INDEX

Page numbers in italics refer to captions to illustrations.

LIST OF SUPPLIERS

The following list of garden nurseries, suppliers and manufacturers is in no way comprehensive and is here to provide the reader with a few suggestions.

Conservatories, Greenhouses and Garden Buildings
Alexander Bartholemew
277 Putney Bridge Road
London SW15 2PT

L. F. Knight Ltd.
Reigate Heath
Reigate, Surrey
RH2 9RF

Machin Designs Ltd.
Ransome's Dock
Parkgate Road
London SW11 4NP

Marston and Langinger
20 Bristol Gardens
Little Venice
London W9 2JQ

Robinsons of Winchester Ltd.
Robinson House
Winnell Industrial Estate
Winchester
Hampshire SO23 8LH

C. H. Whitehouse Ltd.
Buckhurst Works
Bells Yew Green
Frant, Sussex

Fountains and Pool Equipment
Stapeley Water Gardens
922 London Road
Stapeley
Nantwich,
Cheshire CW5 7LH

Water Techniques
Unit 20,
Bookham Industrial Park
Church Road
Bookham, Leatherhead
Surrey KT23 3EU

Garden Furniture
Barlow-Tyrie
Springwood Industrial Estate
Rayne Road
Braintree, Essex

Charles Verey
Barnsley House Garden Furniture
Barnsley House
Cirencester

Chatsworth Carpenters
Estate Offices,
Derbyshire Estates
Edensor, Bakewell
Derbyshire DE4 1PJ

The Chelsea Gardener
Sydney Street
London SW3

Crace Designs, Andrew
Bourne Lane
Much Hadlam
Hertfordshire

London Architectural Salvage and Supply Co.
Market Street
London EC2A 4ER

Garden Ornaments
The Chelsea Gardener
Sydney Street
London SW3

Chilstone
Sprivers Estate
Horsmonden
Kent

Clifton, Little Venice
3 Warwick Place
London W9

Crowther of Syon Lodge Ltd.
Syon Lodge, Busch Corner
London Road
Isleworth
Middlesex

Haddonstone Ltd.
The Forge House,
East Haddon
Northampton NN6 8DB

Landscape Ornament Company
Voysey House,
Barley Mow Passage
Chiswick,
London W4 4PN

Mallett at Bourdon House Ltd.
2 Davies Street
London W1

Olive Tree Trading
Twickenham Trading Estate
Rugby Road
Twickenham, Middx.

Peschar, Hannah
Black and White Cottage
Ockley,
Surrey RH5 5QR

Bradstone Garden Products
Okus, Swindon
Wiltshire

Marshalls Mono Ltd.
Southowram
Halifax, West Yorkshire
HX3 9SY

Minsterstone (Wharf Lane) Ltd.
Station Road, Ilminster
Somerset TA19 9AS

Soil-Test Kits and pH Meters
Rapitest
London Road, Corwen
Clwyd, North Wales
LL21 0DR

Trelliswork
Traditional Trellis Ltd.
24 Holland Park Avenue
London W11 3QU

Trelliswork
West Mead Nursery
Clay Lane, Fishbourne,
Chichester, West Sussex
PO19 3JG

Turf
Rolawn Ltd.
Elvington
York YO4 5AR

General Nurseries
Clifton Nurseries
3 Warwick Place
Little Venice
London W9

Hillier Nurseries (Winchester) Ltd
Ampfield House
Ampfield, Romsey
Hampshire SO5 9PA

Nottcutts Nurseries Ltd.
Woodbridge, Suffolk
1P12 4AF

Perryhill Nurseries and Plant Centre
Hartfield
Sussex TN7 4JP

Scotts Nurseries (Merriott) Ltd.
Merriott, Somerset
TA16 5PL

Sherrards Garden Centre
Wantage Road
Donnington
Newbury, Berkshire
RG16 9BE

Specialist Nurseries
Alpine and Rock Plants
Edron Nurseries
Coldingham, Eyemouth
Borders

Fibrex Nurseries
Harvey Road, Evesham
Hereford & Worcestershire
WR11 5BQ

Jack Drake
Inshriach Nursery Aviemore
Scotland

Joe Elliot
Broadwel Alpines
Moreton-in-Marsh
Gloucestershire

Reginald Kaye
Waithman Nurseries,
Silverdale
Carnforth
Lancashire LA5 0TY

Azaleas and Rhododendrons
Exbury Gardens
Exbury, nr. Southampton
Hampshire SO4 1AZ

G. Reuth
Branch Nursery Crown Point
Ightam, nr. Sevenoaks
Kent

Bulbs
Avon Bulbs
Bathford, Bath
Avon BA1 8ED

R. Bowlby
P.O. Box 156
Kingston-upon-Thames
Surrey KT2 6AN

Broadleigh Gardens
Barr House
Bishops Hall
Taunton
Somerset TA4 1AE

Van Tubergen
Oldfield Lane
Wisbech
Cambridgeshire
PE13 2RJ

Michael Jefferson-Brown
Maylite Nartley
Worcester
Hereford & Worcester
WR6 6PQ

Camelias
Tregrehan Camellia Nurseries
Par, Cornwall
PL24 2SJ

Trehane Camellia Nursery
Staplehill Road
Hampreston
Wimborne, Dorset
BH21 7NE

Clematis
Fisks Clematis Nursery
Westleton,
nr. Saxmundham
Suffolk 1P17 3AJ

Great Dixter Nurseries
Great Dixter
Northam, Rey
East Sussex TN31 6PH

Treasures of Tenbury
Burford House
Worcestershire WR15 8HQ

Dianthus (pinks) and foliage-grey and silver plants
Ramparts Nursery
Bakers Lane
Colchester
Essex CO4 5BD

Foliage Plants and Unusual Plants
Barnsley House Gardens
Barnsley House
Barnsley, nr. Cirencester
Gloustershire G17 5EE

Beth Chatto Gardens
White Barn House
Elmstead Market
Colchester CO7 7DB

Hopleys Plants
Much Hadlam
Hertfordshire SG10 6BU

Fruit
Deacons Nursery
Godshill
Isle of Wight PO38 3HW

Laxton & Bunyard Nurseries Ltd.
Brampton
Huntingdon PE18 8NE

Herbaceous Plants
Bressingham Gardens
Diss
Norfolk 1P22 2AB

Kelways Nurseries
Langport
Somerset TA10 9SL

J. and E. Parker-Jervis
Martens Hall Farm
Longworth, nr. Abingdon
Oxfordshire OX13 5EP

Sweet Peas
W. D. & D. M. Marshman
Niton Nursery
Parkers Road
Cotton, Stowmarket
Suffolk 1P14 4QQ

Roses
David Austin
Bowling Green Lane
Albrighton
Wolverhampton WV7 3HB

Peter Beales
London Road
Attleborough
Norfolk NR17 1AY

E. B. Le Grice Ltd.
Norwich Road
North Walsham
Norfolk NR28 0DR

General Seeds
Thomas Butcher
60 Wickham Road
Shirley, Croydon
Surrey CR9 8AG

John Chambers
15 Westleigh Road
Barton, Seagrove
Kettering, Northants.
NN15 5AJ

Suttons Seeds Ltd.
Hele Road
Torquay, Devon
TQ2 7QJ

Thomas and Morgan
London Road
Ipswich 1P2 0BA

Herb Seeds
Hollington Herbs
Woolton Hill
Newbury, Berkshire
RG15 9XT

Suffolk Herbs
Sawyers Farm
Little Cornard,
Sudbury, Suffolk

Vegetable Seeds
Chiltern Seeds
Bortree Stile
Ulverston, Cumbria
LA12 7PB

J. W. Boyce
Soham, Ely
Cambridge CB7 5ED

W. Robinson & Sons Ltd.
Sunny Bank,
Forton, nr. Preston
Lancashire PR3 0BN